Just Care

Just Care

Ethical Anti-Racist Pastoral Care with Women with Mental Illness

Leah R. Thomas

LEXINGTON BOOKS/FORTRESS ACADEMIC
Lanham • Boulder • New York • London

Published by Lexington Books/Fortress Academic
Lexington Books is an imprint of The Rowman & Littlefield Publishing Group, Inc.
4501 Forbes Boulevard, Suite 200, Lanham, Maryland 20706
www.rowman.com

6 Tinworth Street, London SE11 5AL

British Library Cataloguing in Publication Information Available

Library of Congress Control Number: 2019915041

ISBN 978-1-9787-0177-9 (cloth)
ISBN 978-1-9787-0178-6 (electronic)

Contents

Acknowledgments

This book would not have been possible without the help of many people. First and foremost, I'd like to thank Dr. Traci C. West, Dr. Arthur Pressley, and Dr. Kate Ott. These three scholars encouraged me, both intellectually and personally, through their thought-provoking insights, feedback, and generative conversations. Particularly, I'd like to thank Traci C. West, whose generosity with her time and talents, coupled with her careful and incisive feedback, were invaluable not only to this project, but throughout the last nine (plus) years. I could not be more grateful for your mentorship, Traci.

This book would also not have been possible without the many chaplains who gave of their time and insights to allow me to interview them. My gratitude goes out to the eighteen chaplains in psychiatric chaplaincy who sat down with me and spoke openly and honestly about the challenge of chaplaincy with women with severe mental illness. Much gratitude, as well, to my own supervisor, the Rev. Dr. Emily Hall, whose flexibility and understanding allowed me the space to complete this project.

I wish to thank my friends and colleagues at Drew University who accompanied me throughout the process of writing this book, offering feedback, suggestions, and support along the way. I particularly want to thank Dr. Stephanie Day Powell and Susan Woolever, as well as the members of the Christian social ethics cohort and my summer writing group. Thanks for your belief in me!

Thanks to my parents, EJ and Pam Thomas, who offered material, emotional, and spiritual support throughout this entire process. Their encouragement (including reading a draft of a chapter) gave me the strength to move forward, especially in times when this was difficult. Thanks to my sister and brother-in-law, Holly and Bobby Orr, who graciously offered their time in the editing of this book, despite having two children under the age of four.

Thanks to my stepchildren, Chloe and Jonathan Wolma, who endured nights of me being locked in my study in order to finish this book. Thank you for your patience! And finally, thanks to my life partner, Stephen J. Wolma, whose steadfast presence, endless suggestions, careful editing, and challenging conversations continue to inspire me to be a more thorough and thoughtful writer. His generosity of time in keeping our household going during "crunch periods" allowed me the space to finish it. I am so grateful and lucky to have you in my life, Steve!

Last, but not least, I offer thanks to those women on E3 and D3 floors with whom I had the honor of ministering from 2010–2018. Their lives, their stories and their struggles both inspired this project and continue to invite me to be a better pastoral caregiver and person.

Introduction

Caring with Denise

I met Denise one of her first days on the unit, though her vacant stare and flat affect made it difficult to tell if she actually wanted to sit down with me or not. I soon learned that she had been in and out state psychiatric facilities for the last ten years. An African American woman, now age fifty, she had been hearing voices and having visual hallucinations since her twenties, most of which were religious in nature. Some of our first discussions explored these intense, tangible experiences of the Divine. Gradually, however, under the care of an interdisciplinary team, including an established psychiatrist, the voices began to diminish. The team was ecstatic. What a success story! Yet Denise confided in me that she felt deeply depressed, even suicidal. She had lost God. And she was willing to go to any length (even suicide) to hear his voice again. Sometimes the very medicine that takes away symptoms, also takes God. For a woman who may be homeless, a member of a racial or ethnic minority, and in an abusive relationship, the voice of God may be one of her few sources of support. How does a pastoral caregiver practice care in this situation, a care that both honors the religious, social, and cultural needs of the woman and simultaneously occludes the forces of power, patriarchy and white supremacy?

This book examines the way that the discipline of pastoral care within the Protestant Christian tradition has approached women who have been diagnosed with mental illness. Specifically, it seeks to investigate the responses of pastoral caregivers within the context of a psychiatric hospital. During the composition of this book, I myself was a chaplain at an in-patient facility in a northeastern state in the United States. It was my own years of fraught conversations with other chaplains about how "best" to care for the patients with whom we were ministering that led me to study the on-the-ground praxis of pastoral caregivers in this unique setting. It is important to begin with the recognition that pastoral care within Western society, particularly with the mentally ill, has existed in a dialectical relationship with Western psychology and psychiatry, both which are governed by a Western medical model.[1] This book argues that adherence to and influence of this Western medical model have constrained the ways that pastoral caregivers ministered with women, resulting in deleterious effects for women with mental illness.

Scholars within the fields of both psychiatry and pastoral care note that connections between a diagnosis of mental illness and concepts of race, gender, culture and socio-economic class have not been adequately addressed. Women are more frequently diagnosed with mental illness than men,[2] and women who are disadvantaged by poverty or who are of color are more likely than white women to experience mental disorder and less likely to seek treatment.[3] The predominance of the Western treatment model has influenced the ways in which pastoral caregivers have responded to women with mental illness. On one hand, some pastoral caregivers have heralded the Western medical model, and attempted to learn more about the intricacies of diagnosis, with the aim of engaging in a dialogue between ministry and psychiatry.[4] Yet, even those pastoral caregivers who have attempted to address this situation—both theoretically and empirically—have largely remained within the Western medical model; responses often include tendencies to bring theological resources to bear in ways that are dictated by the diagnosis and/or to refer the woman to secular professionals. Another group of pastoral caregivers has effectively sidelined the concept of diagnosis, harboring a sense of inadequacy about their ability to minister with people who have mental illness.[5] In some of these cases, there has been a resurgence in the importance of psychiatric diagnosis as it relates to ministry, many times as the result of a suicide of a prominent church member or leader.[6] In all of these approaches, the risk of operating within the Western medical model is that the pastoral caregiver can fall victim to a narrow, reductionistic understanding of the person, one which adversely affects the praxis and content of ministry.

This book investigates these issues through engagement with the voices of psychiatric chaplains, coupled with the scholarship of feminist and womanist Christian social ethics, and feminist, womanist, and intercultural pastoral care. Focusing on the relationship between a pastoral caregiver and a woman with mental illness, it explores the components of a justice-making relationship. In light of the constraints that a diagnosis of mental illness places on the relationship between a pastoral caregiver and a woman, how is mental illness defined, named, and approached by the pastoral caregiver? In what ways does this diagnosis determine the relationship and the assessment of the pastoral caregiver? How do pastoral caregivers attend to systemic factors—racism, sexism, socioeconomic, sociopolitical, and cultural—that may not have been incorporated in the diagnosis? What is at stake—physically, spiritually, and emotionally—in the relationship between a pastoral caregiver and a woman who has been diagnosed with mental illness? This book addresses these questions by constructing a feminist approach to ethical pastoral care as it pertains to women and mental illness. It argues that in order to engage in ethical pastoral care—a practice which supports the human dignity and worth of women with mental illness—the caregiver must see the "full humanity" of the woman in front of her. This is a practice which recognizes the woman as beyond the diagnosis, a participant in broader relationships and sociopolitical systems which surround and permeate the encounter. This "wider view" includes attention to the ways in which the systemic sociopolitical constraints have limited her freedom of self-expression, growth, sense of self, and access to material resources. Through an examination of, and attentiveness to, the ways that the voices of feminist and womanist scholars of Christian social ethics and pastoral care trouble approaches that focus solely on psychiatric diagnosis, the book offers a creative anti-racist-psychosocial-spiritual model of ethical pastoral care which is rooted in, and attentive to, a systemic analysis of power relationships.

Pastoral responses to women with mental illness have tended to follow trends within the disciplines of psychology and psychiatry, disciplines which have been rooted in a Cartesian-Newtonian model of human functioning.[7] Scholars from different disciplines sensitive to racial and systemic analysis, such as Collins Airhihenbuwa (public health), Emile Townes (Christian social ethics), and Suman Fernando (psychiatry), argue that mental illness is a cultural production, and as such is a construct which cannot be separated from social realities (namely race and class), biology, and the environment. The Western medical model has been dominated by the concept of diagnosis and a shift towards classifying mental illness as biological, marked by the classification of disorders. Suman Fernando, in *Mental Health, Race and Culture*, notes that the concept of diagnosis is represented as "objective," but in essence is deeply tied to notions of culture, including socially constructed notions of the human condition and normality versus abnormality.[8]

The specific nature of the psychiatric diagnosis, which relies on self-reported symptomology as opposed to supposedly objective analyses (i.e., CAT scans and X-rays), further problematizes the connection between diagnosis and culture.[9] The turn to the biological is also addressed by Gold and Gold, who note that the reconfiguring of mental illness in this direction has had both humanizing and dehumanizing implications. In their opinion, while it has lightened the "moral burden of madness," it has also solidified the boundary between persons who are diagnosed and persons who are not. Before the twentieth century, mental illness could be a result of unrequited love or a penalty for violating God's law. While the depiction of the person with mental illness as a "moral lesson" for the remainder of society was problematic, the current turn to the biological has its own set of issues: "When science began telling us that madness was etched into our genes and our brains, what had been a flexible boundary became a closed border—with the mentally ill on the wrong side, as distant from us as ever."[10] Gold and Gold argue that the current focus on diagnosis of disorders has only heightened the already present stigma towards those with mental illness. Robert H. Albers, in *Ministry with Persons with Mental Illness* agrees, using terms like "unclean" and "set apart" to refer to the feelings of those with mental illness. He maintains that those who are diagnosed with mental illness "are frequently pejoratively labeled with inhuman epithets, thus spawning inhumane treatment. Even though their malady is neither infectious nor contagious, they are often treated as though coming into even remote contact with them will somehow contaminate or sully the character of other people."[11] Various studies on stigma against those with mental illness confirm that the turn to the biological and the use of diagnosis and classification of disorders, has not resulted in a decrease of stigmatizing attitudes toward those who have been diagnosed with mental illness. In fact, numerous studies confirm that a majority of people in the United States and in many countries in Western Europe continue to harbor stigmatizing attitudes about those who have been diagnosed with mental illness.[12] In a 2002 study, Corrigan and Watson found that a diagnosis of mental disorder was linked to attitudes of fear, public avoidance, and a sense that those who were ill were somehow responsible for their illness. This has resulted in behavioral impacts such as withholding of treatment, social avoidance, and advocacy for mandatory treatment in institutions.[13]

The discipline of pastoral care has not been immune to the influence of the Western medical model, as is evidenced by both historical and contemporary research and publications. It has, however, existed in both conversation and tension with these movements within psychology and psychiatry. According to Fernando, before the onset of the Western medical model, dialogue around the mental and spiritual states of a human being mostly existed within the realms of philosophy and religion.[14] This remains the case today within many Eastern and African philosophical and religious traditions. It is also notable that the stigma against mental illness seems less apparent in some Asian and African societies.[15] As Western psychology and psychiatry split off from religion and philosophy to become the dominant scientific medical model in the West, Christian theologians who were engaged in pastoral care were forced to respond to this shift. As noted by Glenn H. Asquith (1946–2017), a prominent author in the field of pastoral care who taught at Moravian Theological Seminary, on one hand, the psychological sciences fostered a new engagement with the field of pastoral care. On the other, it symbolized the "diminution of theological understandings of human life and offered alternative, if not competitive, conceptions of human distress and its alleviation."[16]

The responses by those considered the "fathers" of the field of pastoral care mirrored this dichotomy, ranging from outright disdain for the disciplines of psychiatry and psychology to acceptance and engagement. The latter is evident in the work and life of Anton Boisen and Seward Hiltner,[17] and later, in such figures as Paul Pruyser,[18] Wayne Oates[19] and Donald Capps.[20] The vast majority of the figures within this group, "acknowledged the legitimate role of psychiatry as an interpretive perspective on human behavior"[21] as well as supporting "neurological and biological conditioning of all human action."[22] In the last decade, scholarship about persons with mental illness within the field of pastoral care has continued an approach of acceptance and engagement with psychiatry. Much of the literature surrounding the intersection of mental illness with pastoral care follows a treatment model, elucidated in such literature as *Mental Illness and Psychiatric Treatment, A Guide for Pastoral Counselors*[23] and *Ministry to Persons with Mental Illness and their Families*.[24] In these books, each chapter focuses on a form of diagnosable mental illness. The chapters usually lead with an informative piece drawn from psychiatric sources, if not directly written by a psychiatrist. They provide information about the history of the disorder, the diagnostic criteria, and common treatments. The latter portion of the chapter, or response, is usually written by a pastoral caregiver who focuses on the theological issues and ministerial opportunities raised by the first part of the chapter. While a few of the pastoral theologians in these current works admittedly recognize that the person is larger than his/her diagnosis, the very format of these books highlights their adherence to the Western treatment model.

Additionally, feminist, womanist, liberationist and intercultural pastoral theologians have recognized that the discipline of pastoral care has historically been dominated by an androcentric approach which has been defined by whiteness, patriarchy, privilege, and U.S. and Western European cultural values. Scholars of feminist, womanist, and intercultural pastoral care such as (without limitation) Pamela Cooper-White, Bonnie Miller-McLemore, Carrie Doehring, Christie Cozad Neuger, Emmanuel Lartey, Caroll Watkins Ali, Phillis Isabella Sheppard, Teresa E. Snorton, and Beverly R. Wallace have advanced approaches that have addressed these limitations, by taking into account the field of feminist and womanist theology (with its emphasis on the historic dynamics of power and oppression of women, other marginalized people, and the environment), as well as scholarship around liberation theology[25] and interculturality.[26] A number of these (and other) authors in feminist, womanist, liberationist, and intercultural pastoral care have noted how models of pastoral care have been inattentive to broader social systems and to the needs of women and other marginalized groups.[27] Yet while these scholars have done much to advance pastoral care beyond the dominant cultural worldview, few of them focus specifically on the issue of mental illness, especially as it relates to the rise of the Western treatment model. For example, while many feminist scholars of pastoral care have written about the particular issues that should be considered when counseling women, the topic of women with severe mental illness is often limited to a chapter in a larger work. Scholars of intercultural pastoral care often note the ways that dynamics such as racism, classism, and sexism can become embodied in an encounter, omitting an explicit focus on the presence of mental illness and how this might interact with these systemic dynamics.[28] Womanist scholars of pastoral care frequently emphasize an intersectional approach to pastoral care with women of color, and some, notably Sheppard, recognize that the trauma that women experience must be central in their theories.[29] Others (Wallace and Snorton) note that differences between the history, culture, and experiences of women of color (as compared to those of white women) translate into dissimilarities between the two groups in their experiences of grief and in the ways in which they express (or do not express!) certain emotions, such as anger. Yet even within these contextual analyses of pastoral care, the presence of severe mental illness (beyond trauma) is frequently not a focus. With the possible exception of Stephen Pattison, who places the mentally ill as the central case study within his argument that pastoral care needs to be more attentive to systemic factors, a diagnosis of severe mental illness is sidelined by most other feminist, womanist, liberationist, and intercultural scholars of pastoral care. While the scholarship of these authors will be a conversation partner—particularly Pattison's *Liberation Theology and Pastoral Care* (1994), Lartey's *In Living Color* (2003), Sheppard's *Self, Culture and Others* (2011), Doehring's *The Practice of Pastoral Care* (2014), and Cozad Neuger's *Counseling Women, A Narrative Pastoral Approach* (2001)—I will expand the focus to include the issue of mental illness and its relationship to the Western medical model.

The combination of adherence to a Western treatment model, with its emphasis on diagnosis, and the historic biases of pastoral care have limited the ways in which pastoral caregivers have ministered to and with women with mental illness. The concept of diagnosis, represented as objective, has had the tendency to reduce the woman to a certain set of traits as presented by the *Diagnostic and Statistical Manual for Mental Disorders* (hereafter referred to as the *DSM*). The *DSM*, the most recent version being the *DSM-5*,[30] contains a description of every known mental illness and is often referred to as the "Bible of Psychiatry."[31] Pastoral care, in offering responses to this reductionistic model, has also largely positioned itself under similar limitations. Feminist and womanist pastoral care have offered an answer to the historic biases of pastoral care, but have for the most part sidelined the issue of mental illness. This book argues that the disciplines of feminist, womanist and liberationist Christian social ethics and pastoral care are necessary to propose an ethical way of doing pastoral care with women who have been diagnosed with mental illness. It asserts that the position of the pastoral caregiver, when informed by these two disciplines, allows her to see the woman as a holistic person who is at the same time both influenced by, and greater than her diagnosis. The confluence of these disciplines allows the pastoral caregiver to hold in tension the contributions of the fields of psychology and psychiatry, while maintaining attentiveness to the larger systems and socioeconomic factors which influence and constrain the life of the woman, and to respond accordingly. It posits that this is a way of approaching pastoral care with women with mental illness which allows the pastoral caregiver to reimagine and reframe pastoral care with the woman as a mutual relationship of justice, that is, Just Care.

Feminist, womanist and liberationist Christian social ethics and pastoral care are essential tools for engaging and challenging both the limitations of the Western medical model and its impact on the worldview of pastoral care, especially as the two relate to the holistic health of women with mental illness. These two interdisciplinary conversation partners allow the relationship between the pastoral caregiver and the woman to be viewed both individually and systemically. From this perspective, the relationship between the individual pastoral caregiver and woman avoids reductionism through an awareness that this relationship exists as a strand in the web[32] of larger relationships, systemic factors and constraints. The addition of feminist and womanist Christian social ethics to conversations about the pastoral care of women with mental illness provides a necessary and corrective lens through which to view this pastoral relationship. The emphases of Christian social ethics—the "structures, institutions, processes, systems, and the ways in which individuals and groups both respond and shape them"[33] are crucial to an analysis of pastoral care with women with mental illness. Many feminist and womanist scholars of pastoral care have, in the last twenty-five years, advanced an approach that privileges some of the emphases of Christian social ethics, particularly the "structures, institutions, processes and systems" that surround and permeate the pastoral care encounter.[34] Some womanist scholars, in particular, explore how these structures, institutions and processes—particularly those of systemic racism and sexism—shape and mis-shape the psyche of African American women.[35] Yet, how does this broader systemic analysis apply to women with mental illness, particularly those caught in psychiatric institutions which are governed by the Western medical model? What specific ethical issues arise when an analysis of power, gender, race and oppression are brought to bear on this situation? Finally, in the words of Christian social ethicist Emilie Townes, given that a womanist ethic "is never content to merely react to the situation: it seeks to change the situation,"[36] how does this influence and change the response of the caregiver and the surrounding community?

This book will build upon the work of womanist and femininst Christian social ethicists, specifically Emilie Townes and Aana Vigen, to inform this endeavor. In Townes' work, *Breaking the Fine Rain of Death* (1998), she uses a womanist methodology to highlight the cultural production of personal and public health, particularly of African American women. While her method attends to gender, it is part of a "more rigorous theo-ethical analysis that seeks a realism about the social order that then moves into a consideration of the steps needed for transformation."[37] In Vigen's work, most notably her book *Women, Ethics, and Inequality in U.S. Healthcare "To Count Among the Living"* (2006), she highlights the racism and classism of the American medical system. Using interviews from Latina and Black women seeking health care, she places their stories alongside healthcare statistics, theology and social ethics. In conversation with these (and other) scholars of Christian social ethics, this book examines the role of sociopolitical, economic, racial, gendered, and cultural dynamics of the pastoral relationship between a pastoral caregiver and a woman with mental illness. Yet, while Christian social ethics is attentive to a systemic analysis of health and healthcare, including the ways in which this system disadvantages women, very little in the discourse around health in social ethics addresses mental illness. This book expands the systemic analysis of health and healthcare to include the realm of mental illness by placing the voices of psychiatric caregivers at the center of its moral discourse. It argues that this move allows for the emergence of alternative norms of pastoral caregiving, particularly that of care which has at its center insights gleaned from an intersectional analysis alongside insights from critical race theory. This is ultimately a practice of care which has both individual and communal components, and holds a commitment to justice at its center.

A trialogue between the voices of psychiatric caregivers, and feminist, womanist and liberationist pastoral care and Christian social ethics is needed in order to break open the understanding of the care and treatment of women with mental illness. This will create the space to propose a more expansive model of caregiving which is attentive to ethical issues raised by a systemic, intersectional analysis. Particularly when care is approached through the lens of Christian social ethics, Just Care asserts that care with women with mental illness—particularly those women in psychiatric institutions—exist at the intersection of multiple dehumanizing systems. As has been noted by Christie Cozad Neuger in *Counseling Women* (2001), the onset of mental illness itself can be linked to social forces, particularly those stressors that tend to be more common among women, such as intimate violence and generational poverty. Yet Christian social ethics also prompts the practitioner to examine the surrounding culture of the psychiatric hospital itself, one governed by the western medical model, with its relative silence around questions of culture, race and ethnicity. This wider analysis reveals a situation of grave injustice, which disproportionately affects women of color who are plagued by individual and communal stressors. It necessitates a care which *must* have justice at its center, holding in tension the particularity of each encounter with the systemic factors which surround and permeate this encounter in order to provide ethical pastoral care. Just Care has certain essential components, including care that both begins with the woman and embodies an awareness of the chaplain's own social location and embedded and lived theologies. It is both communal and individual, and is attentive to the intersection of culture, gender, race and class. Finally, Just Care is rooted in the power of encounter, has an expansive view of health, and puts spirituality at the center of its care. Ultimately, Just Care incorporates attention to both the individual and to broader systemic realities in its aim towards liberation from injustice.

This book aims to impact the training, praxis, and method of pastoral caregivers as each pertains to women with mental illness. It will address the ways in which the field conceptualizes ministry with and for those with mental illness, proposing concrete, ethical action for pastoral caregivers based on the components of Just Care.

METHOD

When defining the method of this book, Sandra Harding's distinction between the terms method and methodology will be helpful. According to Harding, methods are "techniques for gathering evidence"[38] and are specific to the discipline, while methodologies are "theories and analyses of how research should proceed and how evidence should be gathered."[39] This book will pursue an interdisciplinary, feminist method. It will embody a particular type of interdisciplinarity, in that it will privilege the fields of pastoral care and Christian social ethics, as it employs both theoretical and empirical sources. The theoretical sources will include an investigation of the history of Western psychiatry and pastoral care, as well as attention to the social, cultural and political norms and policies that govern conversations of illness, diagnosis and treatment. This book notes that to label a method "feminist," does not presuppose that there is an agreed upon definition of feminism, nor that its methodological assumptions will be defined solely by content nor by its objects of study. How then, will this feminist method be defined? This book will privilege Alison Jaggar's definition of feminist research, as "distinguished by its commitment to producing knowledge useful in opposing the many varieties of gender injustice. . . . a tradition of inquiry that seeks knowledge for emancipation."[40] The method of this book will therefore explore the interplay between systemic realities and liberation from injustice, while, at the same time, recognizing that assumptions which support gender inequality have frequently been used to justify further oppression and inequality.

In placing a relationship between a pastoral caregiver and woman at the center of this book, I privilege the role of experience as a source of knowledge in my method. This is in line with tenets of feminist Christian social ethics and pastoral care, which recognizes the importance of experience—particularly those experiences which have been excluded from dominant dialogues—alongside other theoretical and empirical data. At the same time, however, it is not my intention to have the experience of one pastoral caregiver stand for all. I instead want to explore the numerous factors that frame this encounter, as well as the layered aspect of the encounter itself. Again, in the words of Jaggar, "One challenge for feminist methodology in the humanities is to consider how to construct salient categories between the individual and the universal, and how to recognize systematic forms of domination while finding humanity in diversity."[41] This challenge will frame my analysis of both the theoretical sources and the experiences of pastoral caregivers.

In order to engage the experience of a pastoral caregiver in a situation of ministry with those with mental illness, I have employed a qualitative research method. I conducted semi-structured interviews with eighteen pastoral caregivers at three psychiatric hospitals in a northeastern state in the United States. I recruited these pastoral caregivers through informal contacts, and then subsequently, through the "snow ball" method, where I asked those I had interviewed to recommend and/or refer others. These caregivers were of different races, ethnicities and ages. I chose pastoral caregivers at psychiatric hospitals because they have the greatest frequency of pastoral contact with those with mental illness, without being psychologically trained as a pastoral counselor. They also frequently bring their work with psychiatric patients back to their ministry in their home churches, and therefore offer a model that can be transferred to a parish or pastoral setting.

The conversations that I undertook with these caregivers included questions regarding their interactions with women with mental illness, including how they spoke about pastoral care and how they began an interaction. I also asked which issues they prioritized in the interaction and the method(s) they used to make these types of decisions. I inquired as to whether they were cognizant of and attentive to systemic factors—notably race, culture and class—in their interactions. Finally, I asked about the influences on their model of chaplaincy. This research could be considered a form of grounded theory,[42] in that I attempted to "be as faithful to the data as possible"[43] by listening to my participants and reading (and re-reading) transcripts to become aware of themes and patterns in the interviews. In this way, the theoretical frames I constructed were "grounded" in my interviews. Yet, I also recognize that "Every research interaction and the stories they generate are co-constructed by the researcher and the researched."[44] My scholarly training in the fields of feminist and womanist pastoral care and Christian social ethics, my own social and cultural positionality as a white educated woman, and my overarching project, contributed to the ways I heard these interviews, what I found interesting and noteworthy, and which themes emerged.

My position as a chaplain in an in-patient psychiatric institution at the time of this book also informed this study, and grants me insider status in this field, which can be both beneficial and limiting. I chose to study women at psychiatric institutions because I worked with them daily, and was privileged to hear their stories, pains, struggles and joys. My long-term relationship with women in psychiatric institutions led me to reflect on the pastoral care that was being offered to them, not only by me, but by all who do ministry within this setting. While ministry as a chaplain within a psychiatric hospital can take many forms, within the state in which I ministered, it included ongoing one-on-one meetings with patients, leading spirituality groups and services, and being a member of the larger team (composed of a psychiatrist, psychologist, social worker, and nurses) for patient consultations. As an insider, this offered me access to information and contacts I may not have been able to obtain otherwise. I had a relationship with my supervisor, who recommended chaplains that I could interview at other institutions. It also allowed me to better hear and more likely understand the stories of the chaplains with whom I was speaking. Yet, I also recognize that insider status could limit my own objectivity, and/or have caused me to overlook what was being taken for granted. The fact that I worked with some of the interviewees could also have limited what participants were willing to share with me, as they knew we would still be working together after the interview, and did not want to impinge on our mutual respect and/or professionalism. On the other hand, it could have caused some participants to share more deeply with me than they would have with another interviewer, because they knew and trusted me.

This feminist qualitative study is both exploratory and explanatory. As exploratory, it seeks to identify and discover important categories of meaning, especially as they relate to concepts of care and diagnosis with women with mental illness. It also seeks to identify larger systems that inform the world of the caregiver and the woman receiving care. As explanatory, it seeks to identify the beliefs, attitudes and policies which shape this care, as well as the ways in which caregivers speak about these dynamics, and to propose plausible relationships shaping this phenomenon.[45] It will ultimately build upon these case studies, and the beliefs, attitudes and policies therein, to propose a theory of ethical pastoral care with women.

It is of note to recognize that feminists have leveled critiques of the methods by which social science research, particularly qualitative research, has been carried out. Among these critiques are the frameworks of logical dichotomy and abstract individualism, as well as the so-called objectivity of the researcher. I will explore these critiques in order to propose the ways in which I will address them in this book.

According to Joey Sprague, a professor of sociology at the University of Kansas, in *Feminist Methodologies*, logical dichotomy is the framework that has drawn the most criticism from feminist scholars. Logical dichotomy "makes sense of a phenomenon by opposing it another in a construction that is represented as mutually exclusive and exhaustive."[46] This includes concepts of mind/body, nature/nurture, and public/private. Feminists have noted that these so-called "dichotomies" are more often either continuums along a spectrum, and/or much more complex than these dualisms suggest. For example, asking whether a human trait (or illness) is due to "nature" or "nurture" obscures the many ways that biology and social circumstances interact. Consider nutrition. Eating nutritiously contributes to good health, yet eating fresh fruits and vegetables is dependent on access to healthy food, which is directly connected to racial and social dynamics of the community in which someone was raised, and whether this community had access to healthy foods, as well as the material wealth to purchase them. Feminists therefore speak against dichotomies in social science that are used without reflection, arguing that these can "hide social relations that allow members of one social category to benefit at the expense of those in another."[47]

Abstract individualism, or "talking of the individual in isolation from and unconnected with its interpersonal, historical and physical context"[48] enables social scientists to speak of concepts like gender, race and class in isolation from one another. To separate these concepts is to deny that race is organized in gendered ways, and experienced differently by women and men. It also does not recognize that class presents itself in racially and gender-specific ways. Sprague recognizes that when researchers ascribe to approaches such as abstract individuation and logical dichotomy, "it becomes easy to objectify those whom we study . . . or the tendency to talk of and treat people as though they were objects, devoid of subjectivity, the opposite of agents who are developing analyses of their situations and working to cope with them."[49]

Feminists have also offered criticisms of the so-called "objective" researcher. Feminist and womanist scholars such as Nancy Hartstock, Donna Harraway, Dorothy Smith, and Patricia Hill Collins have advanced "feminist standpoint theory" to illustrate the limitedness and constructedness of every viewpoint, including (or especially) that of the researcher. While these scholars differ in their particularities as they relate to standpoint theory, in general feminist standpoint epistemology privileges the experiences and standpoint of women, who are themselves diverse as they relate to systems of race, ethnicity, class, and sexual orientation. It recognizes that "all knowledge is constructed in a specific matrix of physical location, history, culture, and interests, and that these matrices change in configuration from one location to another."[50] Knowing is not relative, it is "partial, local and historically specific."[51]

Along these lines, feminists have critiqued any research that hides the researcher, as well as research which participates in the objectification of research subjects. Sprague notes that the experience of the researcher is frequently relegated to introductions, appendices, memoirs and reflections. She further recognizes that, "both the field and the way the researcher enters into and participates in that field are organized by gender, class and race."[52] Gender can both create certain opportunities and also provide obstacles. Race functions similarly. Regarding researchers and subjects who are white, she suggests that, "Whites studying other whites are typically unaware of the racial/ethnic character of the situation they are observing."[53]

As a feminist researcher, I attempted to foster awareness of these critiques in my research and analysis. The interdisciplinary nature of this study, the format of the interviews themselves and the questions asked therein, and the attempt at multi-layer analysis which is attentive to intersectionality, offers alternative frameworks to logical dichotomy and abstract individualism. For example, I asked the chaplains open ended questions about the ways that they began a pastoral interaction, how they made an assessment, and whether dynamics of race/ethnicity and class have made themselves apparent in their encounters with women. Other than that, I invited the chaplains to simply talk, while communicating to them via active listening that I was attentive to their stories. I attempted to guard against both logical dichotomy and abstract individualism with my attentiveness to the overlapping ways that gender, race and class manifest themselves—both in the lives of the women in the psychiatric hospitals as well as in the lives of the caregivers with whom I was speaking.

In order to address and confront the notion of myself as an "objective" researcher, I recognize that engaging in these interviews and analysis involves the necessary step of examining my social location as a white woman who has had training and experiences both in the classroom and in the field of chaplaincy, specifically with women with mental illness. My own whiteness is a crucial part of all of my interactions. I am aware that my whiteness can blind me to certain racial dynamics, particularly when interviewing others about concepts of race. My whiteness could have played into the notion of the "invisibility" of race in my encounters with other whites. On the other hand, in interviews with chaplains of color, my whiteness and all that is attached to that, including the history of white supremacy in this country and the current ways that this is manifested in psychic and material inequalities between white people and people of color, was "in the room," a (named or unnamed) factor in the conversation. This dynamic may have altered their responses not only to questions about race, but also about other issues as well.

My racial identity is also a factor in the racial composition of the network of people I knew and who agreed to be interviewed. I recruited the pastoral caregivers through informal contacts. Further recruitment was through the snowball method. Though I attempted to include chaplains of different races, ethnicities and ages in my sample, I ended up with an overwhelming majority of white women. On one hand, this is a reflection of the racial composition of chaplaincy departments in psychiatric institutions in this state, which employs more white people as chaplains than people of color. I am not, however, unaware of the role my own embodiment may have had in this dynamic. Did white women feel "safe" speaking with me because I was also a white woman? Were they quicker to recommend their friends (who also happened to be white women) because the interaction was "easy"? I recognize I also need to reflect on the role of my gender in these interactions, especially as the interviews centered around ministry with women. How did my embodiment as a cisgender woman affect my interactions with both women and men around this topic? Did my embodiment allow other women to feel as though they were "insiders," meaning that our embodiment and self-identity gave us a certain standpoint/understanding when it came to the needs of other women? If so, how did my embodiment as white women both inform and limit the ways I reflected on the needs of women of color? On the other hand, how did it affect my interactions with men?

I will also attempt to decenter my own perspective in my analysis by employing some of the strategies recommended by feminist researchers. One of these is listening for alternative standpoints. Feminist researchers have noted that qualitative interviewers have traditionally dismissed people's hesitations, stumbling over words, or comments about searching for the right words as indications of inarticulateness. Yet, feminists recognize that what can be perceived as inarticulateness can also point to "a lack of fit between one's knowledge of daily practices and struggles and the hegemonic worldview."[54] This book will attempt to listen for these "gaps" and hesitations within the conversations to point to areas where this struggle may present itself. As will become evident in chapter two, these hesitations and/or stumbling over words became especially noticeable in conversations around the topic of race.

A further step in decentering my perspective is to find alternative formats for reporting findings. Feminists have experimented with approaches which not only highlight the limitations of the researcher, but also allow the subjects the space to truly express themselves. This occurs in a variety of formats, one of which focuses on a narrative approach, while another emphasizes giving the research subjects a voice. Kathy Charmaz and Richard Mitchell (1997) suggest that researchers present their observations in a narrative format, offering the reader a sense of the research process and allowing the reader to relive the experience as the researcher did.[55] Other feminist qualitative researchers emphasize giving their research subjects "voice" in their texts. This involves using more of the actual words of research subjects, including somewhat larger swatches of interview transcripts in order to convey the thinking of the research subject.[56] This book will attempt to give the research subjects voice by including their own words whenever possible, while recognizing that the researcher's voice and decisions ultimately drive the text.

STRUCTURE OF BOOK

The structure of this book will be as follows. The first chapter will explore the rise of the Western medical model, with particular attention to those developments that have impacted the relationship between psychiatry, psychology and pastoral care. It will begin with an examination of foundational debate around the origin and nature of mental illness within the Christian tradition and the fields of psychiatry. It will then examine three trends in the development of psychiatric diagnosis that have influenced the field of of pastoral care: the rise of psychological sciences, heralded by rise of psychoanalytic movement, the production and publishing of the *DSM III* in 1980 (and subsequent shift from categories of psychoanalysis to categories of symptomology), and the "turn to the biological" within the field of psychiatry. It will close with an examination of the contributions of feminist, womanist and liberationist scholars of pastoral care and ethics in such areas as a systemic critique of medical model, and the presence of racism, sexism and classism within the medical model and practice of diagnosis.

The second chapter will be an exploration of experiential sources, particularly the voices of psychiatric caregivers, to highlight what we know, and what we need to know, in order to develop ethical, anti-racist pastoral care. It will begin with a description of the research sites, the three state psychiatric hospitals in a northeastern state, as well as my first impressions of these facilities. It will then describe the demographics of the interviewed chaplains. It will continue with an exploration of several important themes that emerged from the interviews with the chaplains, including the assertion of their call to see the "full humanity" or the "wholeness" of the person in front of them in a system (or on a team) which frequently engaged in a reductionist understanding of the person. Many times, this resulted in relationships with the larger treatment team that were characterized by numerous dynamics, from misunderstanding to contention. This dynamic will be put into dialogue with John Swinton's characterization of spirituality in the Western world, as well as Ann Bedford Ulanov's insights about the importance of spirituality in treatment and healing. The chaplains' assertions of the importance of seeing the "full humanity" of each person also coexisted alongside encounters where dynamics of race and/or class were difficult to address and/or invisible, particularly for white chaplains. Given this reality, this chapter will explore a variety of cultural and political understandings that may inform the worldview of these chaplains, as well as potential explanations for white chaplains' inability to engage the topic of race. This will take place in conversation with Christian social ethicists Traci West and Jen Harvey, as well as psychologists Eduardo Bonilla-Silva and Derald Wing Sue.

The third chapter will examine the processes by which chaplains make assessments of the "problem" or "issue at hand" in the encounter with a woman with mental illness. This chapter recognizes that assessment is the process by which caregivers themselves make their own "diagnosis." It will inquire as to the role of their training and the tools at their disposal, and will explore the relationship between their assessment and their stated view of the importance psychiatric diagnosis. It will also probe for similarities with scholars and practitioners of pastoral care, highlighting the unnamed presence of scholars of pastoral care in their models of assessment. Finally, it will draw parallels between their positions and the relationship between science and theology, noting that while most chaplains seem to favor a "dialogical" view, an "integrationist" view may expand possibilities for the incorporation of further issues of justice.

The final chapter will bring these voices and viewpoints together in its construction of an anti-racist-psychosocial-spiritual model of ethical pastoral care: Just Care. It will challenge the current norms of pastoral caregiving, enumerating the ways that the contributions of feminist and womanist Christian social ethics and feminist, womanist, and liberation pastoral care propose theoretical foundations which hinge on the centrality of justice and the importance of culture. In light of these contributions, it will propose a model of pastoral caregiving that is attentive to both the interpersonal dynamics and sociopolitical systems in the interaction between the pastoral caregiver and the woman. Just Care will speak to the field of pastoral care, especially its relationship to the current Western medical model, suggesting that pastoral caregivers occupy a particular space which allows them to interact with this model in such a way as to embody care which begins with the woman, but does not end there. Just Care, as a way of approaching pastoral care with women with mental illness, allows the pastoral caregiver to reimagine and reframe pastoral care with the woman as one that is both individual and communal, and one which allows for advocacy to coexist with the intimacy of encounter. Just Care ultimately challenges chaplains to embody a commitment to justice for women with mental illness through their training, educational opportunities, self-reflection and advocacy.

Just Care offers a care that enables the caregiver to ask larger questions about the encounter with Denise, questions that place justice at its center. This model of care explores how her race, gender, culture, and sexuality influence and interpenetrate the encounter between herself and the caregiver. It also asks how these same factors might shed light on the distinct and important place of spirituality in her life. It is a practice of care which engages in an expansive analysis of the larger culture of the psychiatric hospital, and the ways that her named diagnosis and the values of the Western medical model may have influenced and limited her perception of herself. Just Care is a model of care in which the caregiver is also asking questions about the ways that her own embodiment, particularly her race and gender, might be impacting the encounter. It is a care in which advocacy necessarily coexists with the intimacy of this encounter; a care in which the chaplain is encouraged to engage in larger efforts to create more responsive churches for Denise when she is discharged, and a more welcoming society for women diagnosed with mental illness. Finally, Just Care does not overlook the culpability of the larger society for the systemic harm that can create situations where women, particularly women of color like Denise, are caught in the intersection of dehumanizing systems. It offers instead a more authentic, ethical, anti-racist, psychosocial-spiritual model for pastoral care between the pastoral caregiver and a woman like Denise.

NOTES

1. Suman Fernando, *Mental Health, Race and Culture: Third Edition* (New York: Palgrave Macmillon, 2010), 29–32.

2. This phenomenon has most recently been explored in Daniel Freeman and Jason Freeman, *The Stressed Sex: Uncovering the Truth about Men, Women, and Mental Health* (Oxford, 2013), in which the researchers analyzed twelve large-scale surveys from the UK, United States, Europe, Australia, New Zealand, South Africa, and Chile. With results fairly consistent across race and culture, their findings show that women appear to experience psychological disorder 20 to 40 percent more frequently than men.

3. See Nancy Grote et al., "Engaging Women who are Depressed and Economically Disadvantaged in Mental Health Treatment," *Social Work* Oct 52.4 (2007): 295–308; Ronald C. Kessler et al., "A New Perspective on the Relationships among Race, Social Class, and Psychological Distress," *Journal of Health and Social Behavior* 27 (1986): 107–15; Stevan E. Hobfoll et al., "Depression Prevalence and Incidence among inner-city pregnant and postpartum Women" *Journal of Consulting and Clinical Psychology* 63 (1995): 445–53.

4. See Robert H. Albers et al., eds. *Ministry with Persons with Mental Illness and Their Families* (Minneapolis, MN: Fortress, 2012); Gregory Collins and Thomas Culbertson, *Mental Illness and Psychiatric Treatment, A Guide for Pastoral Counselors* (New York: Routledge, 2003); Donald Capps, *Understanding Psychosis: Issues and Challenges for Sufferers, Families, and Friends* (Lanham, MD: Rowman & Littlefield, 2010).

5. See Gerard Leavy, Kate Loewenthal, and Michael King, "Challenges to sanctuary: The clergy as a resource for mental health care in the community," *Social Science and Medicine* 65.3 (2007): 548–59; Andrew J Weaver, "Has there been a Failure to Prepare and Support Parish-Based Clergy in their Role as Frontline Community Mental Health Workers: A Review," *Journal of Pastoral Care and Counseling* 49.2 (1995): 129–47.

6. A prime example of this would be the suicide of twenty-seven-year-old Matthew Warren, son of Rick and Kay Warren, pastors of Saddleback Church. This event prompted the church to engage in conversation within American Evangelical churches as to practices of supporting those with mental illness. In the case of Saddleback, it resulted in a 2015 two-day

conference, "Gathering on Mental Health and the Church," which brought together clergy and mental health professionals with the aim of "providing practical support and training to Christians around the area of mental illness." ABC's website "Religion and Ethics," accessed February 2017, http://www.abc.net.au/religion/articles/2015/10/09/4328908.htm.

7. Fernando, *Mental Health, Race and Culture*, 29–30.

8. Ibid., 33.

9. Jeffrey Lieberman, *Shrinks the Untold Story of Psychiatry* (London: Weidenfeld & Nicolson, 2015). Lieberman reveals that while psychiatrists offer "hypotheses" about the specific etiology of certain disorders, these remain at the level of hypothesis, as neurological research has not reached the point where they can be confirmed.

10. Joel Gold and Ian Gold, *Suspicious Minds: How Culture Shapes Madness* (New York: Free Press, 2014), 13.

11. Albers et al., *Ministry with Persons with Mental Illness*, 3.

12. See Bruce C. Link, "Understanding Labeling Effects in the Area of Mental Disorders: An Assessment of the Effects of Expectations of Rejection." *American Sociological Review* 52 (1987): 96–112; Jo C. Phelan et al., "Public Conceptions of Mental Illness in 1950 and 1996: What is Mental Illness and Is It To Be Feared?" *Journal of Health Social Behavior*. 41 (2000): 188–207; P.M. Roman and H.H. Floyd, "Social Acceptance of Psychiatric Illness and Psychiatric Treatment," *Social Psychiatry* 16 (1981):16–21.

13. Patrick W. Corrigan and Amy C. Watson, "Understanding the Impact of Stigma on People with Mental Illness," *World Psychiatry* Feb 1.1 (2002): 16–20.

14. Fernando, *Mental Health, Race and Culture,* 28.

15. Horatio Fabrega Jr., "Psychiatric Stigma in Non-Western Societies," *Comprehensive Psychiatry* 32.6 (1991): 534–51. Fabrega recognizes that the lack of stigma in these societies could be due to a variety of cultural factors, not limited to a dearth of research in these areas of the world. His hypothesis is that the lack of sharp demarcation between psychiatric and non-psychiatric illnesses in these cultures renders stigma less severe than in Western countries.

16. Glenn Asquith, *The Concise Dictionary of Pastoral Care and Counseling* (Nashville: Abingdon, 2010), 68.

17. Boisen (1876–1965) is widely considered the chief founder of the Clinical Pastoral Education model, a program of professional training for chaplains through long-term supervised relationships, usually in a group setting. We will explore Boisen and CPE further in chapters 2 and 3. Hiltner (1909–1984) was a professor at both the Divinity School of Chicago and Princeton Theological Seminary. He is noted as an influential American theologian who worked to overcome theological positivism. Pastoral care scholar Don Browning reveals that while mainline Protestants, including such figures as Anton Boisen and Seward Hiltner were on the whole favorable towards psychoanalytically-oriented psychiatry, their responses were qualified by "working to limit the role of psychiatry" while advocating for the importance of religious and ethical dimensions of life. See Don Browning, *Religious and Ethical Factors in Psychiatric Practice* (Chicago: Nelson-Hall, 1990), 20.

18. Pruyser (1916–1987) was a clinical psychologist at the Menninger Clinic who contributed much to psychological theories of religion. He is perhaps best known for his seminal book, *The Minister as Diagnostician*. We will examine Pruyser more in chapter 3.

19. Oates (1917–1999) was a pastoral theologian, clinical educator, and prolific author. He served as professor of psychiatry and behavioral sciences at the School of Medicine, University of Louisville and taught pastoral theology at Southern Baptist Theological Seminary. We will explore Oates more in chapter 3.

20. Capps (1939–2015) was a professor of pastoral theology at Princeton Theological Seminary. He wrote prolifically about pastoral care, and also focused specifically on certain topics within mental illness, including psychosis and narcissism.

21. Browning, *Religious and Ethical Factors*, 21.

22. Ibid. It should be noted, however, particularly in the case of Boisen and Hiltner, that they offered critiques of those forms of psychiatry that advanced medical reductionism. For more on this, see Browning, *Religious and Ethical Factors*, 22–30.

23. Gregory Collins and Thomas Culbertson, *Mental Illness and Psychiatric Treatment, A Guide for Pastoral Counselors* (New York: Routledge, 2003).

24. Albers et al., eds. *Ministry with Persons with Mental Illness*. There are, however, exceptions to this trend, including Don Browning, who argues that since psychiatry is a social practice as well as a science, it is in need of a public philosophy of psychiatry. He defines this as a philosophy that would "clarify the moral foundations of its practice, identify the kind of practice psychiatry is, and relate this practice to a variety of other practices that make up the larger context of social action." See Browning, *Religious and Ethical Factors in Psychiatric Practice*, 20.

25. A contextual theology rooted in the actions of the Latin American Catholic Church when they began questioning the poverty, oppression and totalitarianism of the social order in the late 1960s. Known for its "preferential option" for the liberation of the oppressed, and its praxis-oriented inductive model, it utilizes Marxist ideology in its understanding of the social order. For more see Stephen Pattison, *Liberation Theology and Pastoral Care* (Cambridge: Cambridge University Press, 1994), particularly 19–58.

26. Emmanuel Lartey defines interculturality as it relates to pastoral care in his seminal work, *In Living Color: An Introduction to Intercultural Pastoral Care* (London and Philadelphia: Jessica Kingsley, 2003) as that term, "in preference to cross-cultural or transcultural, [that] is used to attempt to capture the complex nature of the interaction between people who have been influenced by different cultures, social contexts and origins, and who themselves are often enigmatic composites of various strands of ethnicity, race, geography, culture, and socio-economic setting," 13.

27. See Pattison, *Liberation Theology and Pastoral Care*; Jeanne Stevenson Moessner, *In Her Own Time: Women and Developmental Issues in Pastoral Care* (Minneapolis, MN: Augsburg Fortress, 2000); Christie Cozad Neuger, *Counseling Women, a Narrative, Pastoral Approach* (Minneapolis, MN: Augsburg Fortress, 2001); Sheryl Kujawa-Holbrook, ed. *Injustice and the Care of Sounds: Taking Oppression Seriously in Pastoral Care*. (Minneapolis, MN: Augsburg Fortress) 2009; Joretta Marshall and Duane Bidwell eds., *The Formation of Pastoral Counselors: Challenges and Opportunities* (New York: Haworth, 2006); Emmauel Lartey, *In Living Color: An Intercultural Approach to Pastoral Care and Counseling*, 2nd edition (New York: Jessica Kingsley Publishers Ltd., 2003); Carrie Doehring, *The Practice of Pastoral Care: A Postmodern Approach,* Expanded and Revised Edition (Louisville, KY: John Knox Press, 2014); Caroll Watkins Ali, *Survival and Liberation: Pastoral Theology in African American Context* (1999); Phillis Isabella Sheppard, *Fleshing the Theory: A Critical Analysis of Select Theories of the Body in Light of African American Women's Experience* (Dissertation, Chicago Theological Seminary, 1997) and *Self, Culture and Others in Womanist Practical Theology* (New York: Palgrave MacMillan, 2011)

28. While Doehring does address the presence of PTSD in her book, this is not her focus, nor does she expand her analyses to include other instances of mental illness. See Doehring, *The Practice of Pastoral Care*, "Stepping into a Vietnam Veteran's Story," 25–34.

29. See Sheppard, *Self Culture and Others*, particularly chapter 7.

30. The *DSM-5* was published in 2013. We will discuss more about the publication of this manual in chapter one.

31. Lieberman, *Shrinks the Untold Story of Psychiatry,* 87. He continues that the DSM is known as the bible of psychiatry "for good reason—each and every hallowed diagnosis of psychiatry is inscribed within its pages. . . . The *DSM* might just be the most influential book written in the past century."

32. This image was first proposed by Bonnie McLemore in "The Living Human Web," in *Images of Pastoral Care* (St. Louis: Chalice, 2005), 40–47.

33. Emilie Townes, *Breaking the Fine Rain of Death : African American Health Issues and a Womanist Ethic of Care* (New York: Continuum, 1998), 2.

34. Jeanne Stevenson Moessner, *In Her Own Time: Women and Developmental Issues in Pastoral Care* (Minneapolis, MN: Augsburg Fortress, 2000); Christie Cozad Neuger, *Counseling Women, a Narrative, Pastoral Approach* (Minneapolis, MN: Augsburg Fortress, 2001); Sheryl Kujawa-Holbrook, ed. *Injustice and the Care of Sounds: Taking Oppression Seriously in Pastoral Care*. (Minneapolis, MN: Augsburg Fortress) 2009; Joretta Marshall and Duane Bidwell eds., *The Formation of Pastoral Counselors: Challenges and Opportunities* (New York: Haworth, 2006); Emmauel Lartey, *In Living Color: An Intercultural Approach to Pasto-*

ral Care and Counseling, 2nd Edition (New York: Jessica Kingsley Publishers Ltd., 2003); Carrie Doehring, *The Practice of Pastoral Care: A Postmodern Approach,* Expanded and Revised Edition (Louisville, KY: John Knox Press, 2014); Caroll Watkins Ali, *Survival and Liberation: Pastoral Theology in African American Context* (Duluth, MN: Chalice, 1999), Phillis Isabella Sheppard, *Fleshing the Theory: A Critical Analysis of Select Theories of the Body in Light of African American Women's Experience* (Dissertation, Chicago Theological Seminary, 1997) and *Self, Culture and Others in Womanist Practical Theology* (New York: Palgrave MacMillan, 2011); Beverly R. Wallace, "A Womanist Legacy of Trauma, Grief and Loss: Reframing the Notion of the Strong Black Woman Icon" in *Women out of Order* (Minneapolis, MN: Fortress, 2010), Teresa E. Snorton, "What about All Those Angry Black Women?" in *Women Out of Order* (Minneapolis, MN: Fortress, 2010).

35. Ali, *Survival and Liberation*; Carolyn McCrary "Interdependence as a Normative Value in Pastoral Counseling with African Americans," *Journal of Interdenominational Theological Center* 18, 1–2 (Fall–Spring 1990–1991); P. Rosenblatt and Beverly R. Wallace, *African American Grief* (New York: Brunner Routledge, 2005); Elizabeth Johnson Walker, "Counseling Grace: A Pastoral Theology," in *Women out of Order*, 243–54.

36. Emilie M. Townes, "Living in the New Jerusalem: The Rhetoric and Movement of Liberation in the House of Evil," in *A Troubling in My Soul: Womanist Perspectives on Evil and Suffering*, ed. Emilie M. Townes (New York: Orbis, 2001), 84.

37. Townes, *Breaking the Fine Rain of Death*, 1.

38. Sandra Harding, *Feminism and Methodology* (Bloomington: Indiana University Press, 1987), 2.

39. Ibid., 3.

40. Alison M. Jaggar, ed., *Just Methods, An Interdisciplinary Feminist Reader* (Boulder, CO: Paradigm, 2008), ix.

41. Ibid., 6.

42. See Joey Sprague, *Feminist Methodologies for Critical Researchers* (Lanham, MD: Rowman & Littlefield, 2005), 130.

43. Ibid.

44. Ibid., 131.

45. See Catherine Marshall and Gretchen B. Rossman, *Designing Qualitative Research* (Thousand Oaks, CA: Sage, 1999), 33.

46. Sprague, *Feminist Methodologies*, 13.

47. Ibid., 15.

48. Ibid., 16.

49. Ibid., 18.

50. Ibid., 41.

51. Ibid.

52. Ibid., 121.

53. Ibid., 122.

54. Ibid., 152.

55. Kathy Charmaz and Richard G. Mitchell, "The Myth of Silent Authorship: Self, Substance and Style of Ethnographic Writing," in *Reflexivity and Voice* ed. Rosanna Hertz. (Thousand Oaks, CA: Sage, 1997), 193–215.

56. See Paget, "Experience and Knowledge," Human Studies 6: 67–90, 1983; Catherine K. Riessman, *Narrative Analysis* (Thousand Oaks, CA: Sage, 1993).

Chapter One

Psychiatric Diagnosis and Pastoral Care

An Overlapping and Interrelated History

Any effort to examine pastoral caregiving in a psychiatric hospital must be attentive to the powerful ethos that exists within this environment and the ways that those forces shape this sphere. Religious caregivers who minister within the confines of a psychiatric hospital necessarily have an awareness of the non-religious, medical ways that the patient is defined in that institutional setting. Their own perception of the woman's mental and spiritual well-being develops within this environment and, as such, is heavily influenced by the field of psychiatry and the ways that this field names its patients. Perhaps this is most evident in the concept of psychiatric diagnosis. Psychiatric diagnosis itself is usually defined as the identification and labeling of a mental disorder based on observable signs and symptoms.[1] Yet, psychiatric diagnosis within a psychiatric hospital also functions to name and categorize the patients themselves, bringing with it certain named and unnamed underlying moral values.

This chapter will focus on the evolution of the concept of psychiatric diagnosis within the rise of the Western medical model. I argue that the concept of psychiatric diagnosis is the principle framework that organizes and defines the environment in which the religious caregiver operates.[2] This chapter will explore this concept in light of its relationship to pastoral care. It will attend to the ways that this concept has influenced, and continues to define, how the pastoral caregiver approaches a woman with mental illness. This investigation will be undertaken with attentiveness to inherent racism and sexism that can be seen within the rise of psychiatric diagnosis, as well as to the ways that the evolution of this concept has been accompanied by underlying moral values and assumptions.

Most scholars of the history of psychiatry consider the modern concept of psychiatric diagnosis emblematic of the rise of the modern Western medical model.[3] The definition of psychiatric diagnosis offers a glimpse into a larger debate in both psychiatry and in pastoral care, namely, the debate around the origin and nature of mental illness. Discussions regarding the origin and nature of mental illness have been central in both fields since their inception and any examination of the relationship between modern psychiatric diagnosis and pastoral care must be attentive to this deeper question. This chapter will explore the foundations of this debate and point to its manifestation as exhibited in the rise of the asylum. This example is important as pastoral caregivers in a psychiatric hospital today carry out their ministry within this institutional setting, which is the modern heir of the asylum. It also illuminates the ways in which the construction of the nature of mental illness directly relates to options for treatment and healing.

This chapter will then highlight three events that both illustrate this debate and point to major trends in the development of psychiatric diagnosis that have influenced the evolution of the field of pastoral care. The first is the rise of the psychological sciences, heralded by the advent of the psychoanalytic movement and the prominence of the ideas of Sigmund Freud in the United States; the second is the production and publishing of the third edition of the *Diagnostic and Statistical Manual of Mental Disorders* (hereafter the *DSM III*) in 1980; and the final is the current "turn to the biological"[4] within the field of psychiatry.

These three events are important for an analysis of the relationship between Western psychiatric diagnosis and pastoral care with women with mental illness. First, scholars within the field of psychiatry consider the onset of psychoanalysis as a tremendous, influential shift in the field.[5] The prominence of Freud's thought in the early twentieth century caused psychoanalysis to take root at most major programs of psychiatry offered at universities in the United States, eventually becoming a litmus test for a degree in psychiatry. Similarly, in the field of pastoral care, Asquith, notes that, "beyond question the single most important influence of the twentieth century on pastoral care was the emergence and prominence of the psychological sciences."[6] This explosion of psychological sciences can be traced to the figure of Freud; the work of Freud, William James,[7] and their successors influenced pastoral theologians to incorporate insights from the psychological sciences into their understanding of the necessary professional care that should be offered by pastors and chaplains, and seminaries were prompted to create courses in "practical" theology alongside classical theology. It also inspired such pastoral theologians to birth the clinical pastoral education movement.[8]

The second factor, the production and publishing of the *DSM III*,[9] is a concrete manifestation of the debates over psychiatric diagnosis. The *DSM III* foregrounded such questions as whether psychiatric diagnosis should be informed by psychoanalysis or by scientific research, as well as the role of psychiatry within the psychological sciences. Published in 1980, the *DSM III* was the moment when the definition of psychiatric diagnosis shifted from the categories of psychoanalysis toward those of symptomology. These debates also spilled over into the discourse on pastoral care in the United States. Informed by the rise of the psychological sciences, the pastoral care debates included a push toward a clinical paradigm of pastoral care. The concept of "pastoral diagnosis"[10] was an example of this clinical approach. Pastoral care scholarship as it relates to mental illness has manifested this wider debate, with scholars falling along a spectrum in terms of their relationship to a clinical model of pastoral care and pastoral diagnosis. While many scholars herald a clinical model of pastoral care, they differ as to which psychological model they would privilege in their ministry.[11] The shift toward symptomology in psychiatry, with the consequential movement toward a more clinical model of pastoral care among scholars and practitioners of pastoral care, has had tremendous implications for religious caregivers.

The increasing emphasis on diagnosis—pastoral or otherwise—raises questions for pastoral caregivers within a psychiatric facility. Do pastoral caregivers in a psychiatric facility need to have an awareness of the psychiatric diagnosis to properly accompany the patient? Should pastoral caregivers formulate their own "pastoral diagnosis" in order to discern which steps they should take in the interaction? How does attention to dynamics of culture, race and gender on the part of the religious caregiver ultimately influence the care offered by religious caregivers within this environment? How do these separate but sometimes overlapping notions of diagnosis expand or limit the ways in which the interaction between a religious caregiver and a woman diagnosed with mental illness might proceed?

Finally, a "turn to the biological"[12] within psychiatry has been characterized by an increased role of scientific, particularly neurological, research. It has also been accompanied by a "therapeutic confidence" in psychiatric diagnosis, which tends to consider psychiatric diagnosis "objective," and the field of psychiatry simply another branch of medicine. Yet, in the same vein, psychiatrists also recognize the gap between hoped-for biological explanations for mental illness and actual findings of research in the fields of genetics and neuroscience.[13] The "turn to the biological" has also influenced pastoral care, particularly as it relates to mental illness. In a number of books on psychiatric pastoral care, the first part of the resource focuses on a form of diagnosable mental illness, while the latter portion of the work elucidates theological and ministerial issues.[14] Scholars within this literature admit that they recognize that the diagnostic process itself is a "precarious undertaking,"[15] while also advancing a format that embraces these very diagnoses with a certain confidence that echoes the therapeutic confidence of psychiatry. While a few of the pastoral theologians in these current works admittedly recognize that the person's needs are more complex than her or his diagnosis, the very format of their books highlights their adherence to the Western diagnostic scheme.

Feminist, womanist and liberationist scholars of pastoral care and ethics offer critiques of the Western medical model, including its diagnostic process. While their focus is frequently on larger issues of health and health care (as opposed to mental illness),[16] these voices offer important contributions to these conversations, as they offer a way forward in terms of their content and method. For example, feminist and womanist scholars of pastoral care have advocated for a shift in the definition of "care" from being understood as counseling toward care as part of a "wider communal, cultural and social context."[17] This includes a recognition of the need to account for a systemic analysis their approaches. Feminist and womanist Christian social ethicists echo the need for systemic analysis, particularly as this pertains to questions of justice around issues of health and healthcare. These two approaches have much to say about approaches to diagnosis within the Western medical model. For example, Townes' emphasis on health as a cultural production suggests that conversations about psychiatric diagnosis must always exist alongside analyses of cultural, socio-economic and socio-political factors that surround and shape it.

For example, scholars such as Christian social ethicist Aana Vigen notes that environmental stress brought on by being a woman of color a racist society cannot be overlooked in the etiology of mental illness. Racist attitudes also taint providers evaluations of the presence of mental illness, revealing the existence of "provider bias." This can translate into women of color receiving pharmacological (as opposed to counseling) treatment options and higher involuntary institutionalization rates. Other scholars of both feminist and womanist Christian social ethics and pastoral care assert that connections between the etiology and diagnosis of mental illness and systemic racism and sexism cannot be overlooked. The racial and gender bias within the sphere of mental health mirrors the social, political, cultural, and economic systems within society that disadvantage women, particularly women of color. Issues of psychiatric diagnosis and treatment are directly connected to other issues that women experience, such as violence, poverty, homelessness and the disparity in mental health research, most notably in research around pharmaceutical interventions. These insights from these feminist, womanist and intercultural scholars must be given prominence, particularly in light of the presence and pervasiveness of psychiatric diagnosis in the psychiatric facility.

The concept of psychiatric diagnosis cannot be analyzed without attention to cultural, socio-economic and socio-political factors that shape and impact it. Also of note is the reality that, within the psychiatric milieu, these factors are frequently unnamed and/or hidden. Religious caregivers, therefore, may often encounter these dynamics without an awareness of them, which impacts their ability to incorporate them in their responses to the women with whom they minister.

THE RISE OF THE WESTERN MEDICAL MODEL AND THE FOUNDATIONAL DEBATE: THE ORIGIN AND NATURE OF MENTAL ILLNESS

Jeffrey A. Lieberman, chairman of the psychiatry department at Columbia University, chief psychiatrist at the Columbia University Medical Center located in the New York Presbyterian Hospital, and past president of the American Psychiatric Association and co-author Ogi Ogas, a research fellow at the Laboratory for the Science of Individuality at the Harvard Graduate School for Education, published a book entitled *Shrinks: The Untold Story of Psychiatry* (2015). Their stated reason? Lieberman notes that "the profession to which I have dedicated my life remains the most distrusted, feared, and denigrated of all medical specialties."[18] He himself reveals that in his current and past positions, he receives haranguing emails that make threats against him personally and deride his profession. He asserts that from its moment of conception, [Western] psychiatry has been "a strange and wayward offspring: a stepchild of medicine,"[19] and that it has, as a field, "trumpeted more illegitimate treatments than any other field of medicine, in large part because—until quite recently—psychiatrists could never agree on what actually constituted a mental disorder, much less how best to treat it."[20] Lieberman's statement is important for this project for a couple of reasons. First, it names the foundational debate which has plagued both psychiatry and pastoral care—the definition of mental illness and the most effective ways to treat it. His statement, however, also points to the certainty with which a notable figure within the field of psychiatry views the current practice of diagnosis and treatment. The implication of this quote is that current praxis and scholarship within the field of psychiatry has answered the decades-old question of what constitutes a mental disorder and how to treat it and, at long last, put this problem to rest.

The foundational debate to which Lieberman refers has a deep and complex history, which is intertwined with the concept of psychiatric diagnosis. An understanding of the concept of diagnosis must investigate the ways that this debate has been an undercurrent in both the fields of psychiatry and in the Christian tradition. Yet a look at this debate within these two fields reveals an overlapping, interrelated history. Historians in both psychiatry and religion note that a hard distinction between the fields of modern medicine and religion is a relatively new phenomenon, becoming most noticeable in the last two hundred years with the rise of the Western medical model.[21] Some historians would suggest that the history of mental illness before the rise of the Western medical model point was one dimensional, intertwined with concepts of religiosity that linked mental illness to sinfulness and moral failure.[22] While this was a significant component of this history, it should be noted that the history has also been fraught with tensions over the origin and nature of its maladies. Other historians problematize this distinction as too simplistic, suggesting that the entirety of the history of psychiatry included consternation over the origin and treatment of mental illness, as well as over the role of religion within the field.[23] Even within the last two hundred years, Heather H. Vacek, Dean of Faculty and Associate Professor of Church History at Pittsburgh Theological Seminary, argues in *Madness: American Protestant Responses to Mental Illness* (2015) that in the United States, mental illness was defined from a variety of perspectives, such as practical, spiritual and medical. Throughout each era, descriptions were directly tied to "presuppositions about the causes of illness and the professional groups that claimed authority to define and treat mental illness."[24]

While disagreements over the origin and nature of mental illness within the fields of psychiatry and Christianity have been complex in nature, it must also be noted that the link between mental illness and transcendent, religious forces has plagued the history of mental illness, its roots stretching back to antiquity. Theodore Millon (1928-2014), Professor Emeritus at Harvard Medical School and the inaugural president of the International Society for the Study of Personality Disorders, recognizes that in ancient civilizations, mental processes were "an expression of transcendent magical action caused by external forces,"[25] with mental illness linked to the "destructive" or "evil" forces.[26]

Roy Porter (1946–2002), a preeminent British medical historian and former director of Wellcome Institute for the History of Medicine, chronicles in *Madness: A Brief History* (2002) the ways that madness was linked to supernatural forces as both a "fate and a punishment" throughout many ancient communities, including the Israelites, Greeks, Hindus, Babylonians, and Mesopotamians.[27] The Hebrew Scriptures, for example, reveal a communal understanding of both insanity and evil as linked to curses visited upon the Israelites who failed to obey the Lord. Figures such as King Saul and King Nebuchadnezzar exhibit the ways in which mental derangement was one of many punishments for sinfulness among the ancient Israelites.[28]

Turning to the Christian tradition, Porter looks to Constantine's triumph over "barbarians," to argue that this event "gave the official sanction in centuries to come for supernatural thinking about insanity."[29] He, along with other scholars, note that a brief examination of Christian scripture and teaching reveal that "madness" can usually be traced either to sinfulness, witchcraft, or a battle between the Holy Ghost and the Devil for the soul of the madman.[30] While, at times, mystics and those deemed "holy" could be possessed by a "good madness," evidenced in their visions and/or writings, more commonly, "the madman's loss of reason was thought to render him [sic] less like his rational God and was usually taken to be a sign of devilry or possession."[31] So called unclean spirits required a spiritual antidote. Within the Catholic tradition, this took the form of exorcisms, masses and pilgrimages to certain shrines.[32] Turning to the American Protestant tradition, Vacek argues that both shifting professionalization and stigma against mental illness inhibited American Protestants' ability to live out their mission to "care for the entire person." This stigma was partly due to the "persistence of theological notions which linked mental maladies with sin."[33] Vacek reveals that this stigma linked mental disorder with weakness, deviance and responsibility for one's own illness.

Yet, as elucidated earlier, explanations of the origin and nature of mental illness were not limited to simply religious, transcendent forces. Even in the earliest periods of Greek civilization, when the origin of insanity was commonly viewed as divine in nature, a number of Greek scholars were also the first to conceive of mental illness as a disease.[34] Greek medicine also endorsed both physiological and psychological remedies as antidotes to madness.[35] The disposition toward seeing insanity as somatic continued throughout the writings of some Medieval medicine traditions and the medical writings of the Renaissance. It was expounded upon by seventeenth century philosophers, particularly Rene Descartes, Thomas Hobbes, and John Locke.[36] The tension, therefore, around the origin and nature of mental illness in ancient Greek civilization continued throughout the complex history of mental illness in society, with figures in every era questioning the religious roots of mental illness and offering alternative explanations. The origin and treatment of mental illness continues to be the foundational dispute beneath many of the current debates around psychiatric diagnosis, as the ways in which one defines and names mental illness directly relates to the ways that one endeavors to treat it.

In the United States, debates about the origin and treatment of mental illness cannot be separated from the social and cultural realities of a nation that relied on the labor of persons reduced to enslaved black bodies. Debates about mental illness as it pertained to enslaved blacks frequently served a political and economic function. Pro-slavery doctors construed mental illness as any mental state or behavior that included resistance to slavery, creating such "diagnoses" as drapetomania and dystehsia aethiopica. Drapetomania was coined by pro-slavery doctors to speak of "flight and insanity," while dystehsia aethiopica was a behavioral malady whose primary symptom was characterized as the desire to destroy the property of white slave owners.[37]

Despite these diagnoses, however, the overriding view of mental illness by white society as it related to enslaved blacks was that they were immune to emotional pain and mental illness. This view had both moral and political implications in that it "released physicians and owners from the responsibility of shielding black slaves from painful medical procedures and justified torture such as branding, whipping, hobbling and maiming."[38]

As the emancipation of black slaves became a legal reality, the 1840 United States census revealed that free blacks suffered far more with ill health, especially in terms of mental illness, than did enslaved blacks. This census asserted that enslaved blacks "enjoyed low rates of disease and suffered almost no mental illness."[39] The argument advanced in this census was that blacks "sank into insanity" when having to provide for themselves and undergo pressures of daily life.[40] This further boosted assertions that slavery was essential to preserve the health of blacks, while enslavement and segregation was necessary to protect whites" from the contagion of freed blacks.[41]

This brief survey of the history of the foundational debate around the origin and nature of mental illness reveals social, cultural, political, and religious components. An awareness of this history is important for a number of reasons. As the caregiver and care seeker navigate their relationship in the context of the psychiatric institution, these components are present, named or unnamed. The particular role of religion and spirituality in this history reveals that religion was not morally neutral in the construction of mental illness. Maladies of the mind were frequently blamed on the immoral behavior of the one who was struggling. As such, it should not be surprising that this had social and political repercussions, one of them being the creation of the asylum.

The Creation of the Asylum

The prominence of the social, cultural, political and religious factors in the construction of mental illness in western societies is perhaps best seen in the creation of the asylum. It is significant for this study that the asylum is frequently linked to eras in history when the explanations for the origin of mental illness leaned towards the religious. While those eras that advanced more scientific explanations were not spared the endorsement of treatments that would be considered barbaric by modern standards, those periods when religious explanations held the day frequently meant the exclusion and mistreatment of those with mental illness. For example, many scholars note that Hippocratic beliefs were for the large part sidelined during the Middle Ages in favor of superstition, demonology, and exorcism.[42] It was this emphasis on supernatural—particularly on demonic forces—as the origin of mental illness, that in part led to the creation of the asylum.[43]

Insane (or Lunatic) asylums—large communities intentionally geographically set apart from society in order to separate those considered "undesirable" and "abnormal" from the remainder of society—were the structural, institutional antidote to those deemed "homeless, psychotic or demented." Though the first asylums began to emerge near the end of the Middle Ages, the first psychiatric institution in the United States can be dated to 1773 in Williamsburg, Virginia. Its stated purpose was "to make provision for the Support and Maintenance of Idiots, Lunatics, and other Persons of unsound Minds."[44] By 1860, twenty-eight of the thirty-three states had "public institutions for the insane."[45]

The creation of the asylum in European history additionally can be traced to a particular interpretation of the origin of mental illness as linked to immorality. Popular belief was that the roots of mental illness were linked to the open and fluid quality of society, therefore an institution that could administer a disciplined, moral routine would compensate for the deficiencies in society and therefore "cure" mental illness.[46] Rothman relates that it was the institution itself, as separate from "mainstream" society, that would result in treatment: "Incarceration in a specifically designed setting, not the medicines that might be administered or the surgery that might be performed there, would restore health."[47] This separation also had an overtly religious dimension, as it was also portrayed as a way to "protect" God-fearing souls from "contracting" mental illness. The religious impulse was so much a part of these institutions that, in some nations, denominational differences led to separate religious asylums.[48] Later theories on the invention of asylums as places separate from the remainder of society have also proposed that fear of the moral disintegration of society (as well as of the incarcerated individuals themselves) was as much a factor in their invention as any other named morality.[49]

The "great confinement,"[50] as the historical penning of people with mental illness into asylums is sometimes called, sparked social and cultural analysis of this phenomenon. Michel Foucault famously argued that the asylum functioned as a tool of social control, where mental illness was connected to culturally-constructed societal values. Though "mental illness" appears to have its roots in medicine, in reality, it is illness, "only insofar as it is a form of behavior that is not integrated by that culture."[51] The forced separation of the "mad" from society not only resulted in a physical barrier, but also robbed madness of its ability to critique and transform society, such as the ability of the "mad" to exercise their freedom of speech to mock their superiors. Other scholars, such as Millon, note that the treatment of people in asylums was justified by the notion that those who were mentally ill were also seen as "possessed" and were therefore undeserving of being treated with dignity; as such every measure must be employed to rid them of their "demons."[52] Practices such as straightjackets, bloodletting, purges and shock treatments were the norm.

Historians of psychiatry also note, however, that moral reformers of the late Enlightenment leveled heavy critiques of the inhumane conditions in asylums, advocating instead for "moral therapy."[53] Adherents of moral therapy believed that healing occurred through the treatment of the insane person as a human being. Reformers such as Philippe Pinel (1745–1826) and William Tuke (1732–1822) opened asylums modeled on the ideals of bourgeois family life. Patients lived, worked and dined together and abandoned "medical" therapies for "moral" ones: "kindness, mildness, reason and humanity, all within a family atmosphere."[54] If madness was a breakdown of the "internal, rational discipline" of the sufferer, the asylum must "reanimate reason or conscience."[55] Work therapy and staff vigilance was advanced instead of restraints. Asylums were planted in the countryside and soon became self-sufficient entities.

Yet, in the last third of the nineteenth century the optimism of moral therapy gave way to a propensity toward security and sedation. Numbers of people who were committed to asylums skyrocketed as those who exercised behaviors traditionally classified as vice, sin, and/or crime were increasingly committed, as well as "the senile, the demented, epileptics, paralytics, sufferers from tertiary syphilis and other degenerative neurological disorders."[56] The inability of moral therapy to rehabilitate the insane suggested that mental illness was chronic, ingrained, and perhaps hereditary. Given this new awareness, psychiatrists deemed that little could be done except shutting such people away in a place where they would be separate from society and prevented from "breeding future generations of recidivists and imbeciles."[57] Treatment shifted from moral therapy toward habitual use of sedating drugs and a decline in personal therapy. In the words of Porter, the asylum idea reflected the "long-term cultural shift from religion to scientific secularism":

> In traditional Christendom, it was the distinction between believers and heretics, saints and sinners which had been crucial. . . . This changed, however, and the great divide since the age of reason became that between the rational and the rest, demarcated and enforced at the bottom by asylum walls.[58]

The asylum was also connected to construction of gender and race. Many historians have argued that in the nineteenth century (and beyond), the social construction of sex and gender—including the emotional traits aligned with women as well as the presence of female reproductive organs—resulted in women being more likely to be committed to mental institutions.[59] For example, Anne Digby, a feminist historian, examines the roots of the linkage between the fields of gynecology and psychiatric illness. Through an exploration of the evolution of the field of gynecology in the eighteenth and nine teenth century, she argues that women's reproductive functions defined her "character position and value" in society,[60] while at the same time both "influencing and being influenced by an array of nervous disorders."[61] It was assumptions such as these which undergirded the attitudes of the medical establishment toward women, often justifying commitment in an asylum. Other scholars note that Victorian women who rebelled against constructions of domesticity risked being classified as "insane" and sent to the asylum.[62]

In terms of race, James McCune Smith, an African American physician, revealed that the asylum was also tied up with constructions of race. He asserted that in the southern part of the United States, "there was almost no accommodation for the diagnosis and mental health treatment. Blacks were typically barred from mental hospitals, and those too deranged to work were dumped into almhouses and jails."[63] Any investigation of the "mental health" of southern blacks also needed to reflect the reality that emotional health was frequently akin to "being fit to work."[64]

As blacks were typically barred from asylums, some states allotted funds for "negro" asylums for the insane or had separate facilities on the grounds of the white asylums.[65] It is significant that it is the labor of the black "insane" patient that often built and maintained these institutions. As was the case with many (if not all) segregated institutions, these negro insane asylums frequently had substandard facilities and treatment options. In fact, as late as 1955, black patients at Rusk State Penitentiary-turned-negro-insane-asylum staged a rebellion to advocate for improved therapeutic options, cessation of prisoner beatings, and freedom of movement and quality food for all patients, regardless of color.[66]

The debate over the origin and treatment of mental illness has therefore been interrelated with the ways that such topics as health, mental illness, religiosity, gender, and race have been constructed and enforced by society. The history of the asylum has functioned as a tangible manifestation of some of these dynamics, exhibiting how shifts in beliefs around the origin and nature of mental illness can manifest in drastically different treatment alternatives. While the presence of the asylum remained a constant over hundreds of years, the approach to the treatment of those within the asylum varied as differing constructions of mental illness gained prominence within society.

The Rise of the Psychological Sciences

The rise of the modern Western medical model, including modern concepts of psychiatric diagnosis, is yet another manifestation of this central debate around the origin and nature of mental illness. The roots of the Western medical model are frequently traced to the early 1800s. Many factors, both religious and cultural, came together to influence the rise of this model.

Millon points to such factors such as the waning of supernaturalism, the beginnings of modernism, the influence of liberating thought of the Renaissance, and a reawakened interest in the classical writings of the Greeks, including the work of Hippocrates.[67] In the words of Shorter:

> Psychiatry has always been torn between two visions of mental illness. One vision stresses the neurosciences, with interest in brain chemistry, brain anatomy and medication, seeing the origin of psychic distress in biology of the cerebral cortex. The other vision stresses the psychosocial side of the patients' lives, attributing their symptoms to social problems or past personal stresses to which people may adjust imperfectly.[68]

The beginnings of the bio-psychiatric movement are traced to physicians such as Franz Mesmer (1734–1815) who attempted to bridge the gap between research on the brain and psychiatric disorders. Though none of them were able to link psychiatric disorders to physiological evidence, the work of these physicians gave rise to the distinction between neurologists and psychiatrists. While the former (neurologists) focused on disorders with an "observable neural stamp," the latter (psychiatrists) dealt with "invisible disorders of the mind."[69] It was the absence of these biological markers that created a void in psychiatry into which psychoanalysis could step with confidence.

Sigmund Freud (1886–1939) and the subsequent rise of psychoanalysis around the time of the Second World War precipitated major shifts in the field of psychiatry. This shift included both the role of the psychiatrist and the ways that illness and diagnosis were classified. The entry of psychoanalysis into U.S. psychiatry was responsible for a shift in the United States from the psychiatrist as alienist to the psychiatrist as psychoanalyst. Psychoanalysis also influenced the theory and categories which undergirded a diagnosis of mental illness.[70]

Prior to the rise of psychoanalysis, the psychiatrist was literally alienated from his colleagues both physically and intellectually. I use the term "he" purposefully here, as women were denied access to positions such as these during this time period. He lived in the asylums where he practiced, and was therefore geographically isolated from his colleagues. He was also intellectually isolated due to internal conflicts over the nature and treatment of mental illness. The diagnosis and treatment of mental illness only heightened his distance from his colleagues in the medical field. Diagnosis was linked to whatever theory was "in vogue" at the time, and treatment, in a large sense, was defined in a custodial manner. Psychiatrists were the custodians of institutions, and ensured that patients diagnosed as mentally ill were separated from the broader society, and did the least amount of harm to themselves and others. While this frequently took the form of treatments considered "barbaric" by current standards, Lieberman suggests that psychiatrists were doing their best with the sparse tools at their disposal.[71]

The entry of Freud into the conversation around mentl illness resulted in a "radical redefinition"[72] of the field. While psychoanalysis never fully dominated European psychiatry, in the United States a combination of factors resulted in psychoanalysis taking root at major university programs of psychiatry, eventually becoming a litmus test for a degree in psychiatry. Before Freud, mental illness was linked to institutionalization; the dividing line existed between those who needed to be separated from society and those who did not. With the onset of psychoanalysis, "Freud blurred the boundary between mental illness and mental health, since psychoanalytic theory suggested that almost everyone had some kind of neurotic conflict."[73] Many psychiatrists went from those existing on the edge of medicine and society, where they worked with those who were socioeconomically disadvantaged and considered "outsiders," to establishing office-based practices, with white, wealthy, educated and influential patients.[74] Psychiatrists became figures who were consulted by governmental agencies and Congress and were featured in high-profile magazines. In Lieberman's words, "being 'shrunk' had become the ne plus ultra of upper-middle class American life."[75]

The focus on office-based practices meant a shift away from the seriously mentally ill patient of the asylum. And in the asylum itself, the marriage of psychoanalysis and psychiatry enabled Freud's concepts to be applied to those with severe mental illness.[76] This resulted in the reality that "little was or could be done to alleviate the symptoms and suffering of people living with the day-to-day chaos of severe mental illness."[77] Freudian theories of psychoanalysis also became the bedrock for diagnosis and, as such, diagnosis became a subjective practice, linked to the individual psychoanalyst's interpretation of the underlying neuroses in his patient.

The entry of psychoanalysis into psychiatry resulted in shifts that affect religious caregivers to this day. The first is the training and worldview of the psychiatrist and the interplay between these factors and diagnosis. As set forth in chapter four, an analysis by Christian social ethics reveals that these factors cannot be viewed apart from issues of power. The entrance of the categories of psychoanalysis have also had an immense effect on the pastoral caregiver, as the rise of psychoanalysis was a defining moment not only for psychiatry, but also for the field of pastoral care.

Pastoral Care and the Rise of the Psychological Sciences

As noted by Asquith, a scholar of pastoral care who taught at Moravian Theological Seminary, many scholars consider the emergence and prominence of the psychological sciences to be the single most influential development for twentieth century pastoral care.[78] On one hand, pastors and theological educators were quick to discern the influence of the rise of psychological sciences and incorporate them into their own ministry. Leaders such as Anton Boisen, Richard Cabot, and Helen Flanders Dunbar, considered the co-founders of the Clinical Pastoral Education model, were at the forefront of this effort. On the other hand, the rise of psychology also "symbolized the diminution of theological understandings of human life and offered alternative, and at times competitive, conceptions of human distress and its alleviation."[79]

Any attempt, however, to chronicle the responses of pastoral care scholars and practitioners to the psychological sciences must also recognize that the definition of pastoral care has undergone considerable evolution over time. Scholars note that as one surveys this history, the diverse understandings of the endeavor"[80] become apparent. As illustrated by Asquith, what constitutes pastoral care is rooted in "the basic religious conviction of the community. But it is also rooted in the historical, political and social fabric of a given time and place."[81] E. Brooks Holifield, a professor of American Church History at Emory University,[82] echoes this sentiment, arguing, in *A History of Pastoral Care in America* (1983), that "to trace the changing styles of pastoral care in America is to tell a story of transformations in theology, psychology and society."[83] Theological constructs (such as Christology, soteriology and ecclesiology) therefore play a role in the definition of pastoral care, as pastoral care frequently reflects the teachings of the Christian tradition in which it is embedded. Yet, the political climate, economic factors, and various forms of secular knowledge also contribute to one's description and praxis of pastoral care.[84]

The rise of the psychological sciences challenged pastoral care to interpret ministry in light of current psychological theories. It also prompted pastoral theologians to utilize these theories to reinforce the distinctiveness of ministry from other professions. Scholars who study this phenomenon frame the interplay between pastoral care and the psychological disciplines in different ways. Holifield proposes that the shift in "clerical consciousness" enabled a transition from the notion of salvation to a cultural ideal self-fulfillment. This shift reveals some of the factors which enabled the "triumph of the therapeutic" in society.[85] Asquith counters that this shift proposed by Holifield may be "too easy" as scholars of pastoral care struggled without a resolution to the issue of theological understanding in relationship to the rise of the psychological disciplines.[86] Other scholars point to the importance of one strand of psychological theory (such as Rogerian or object relations) and chronicle the ways that this strand has manifested itself in pastoral care.[87] The fact that the relationship between the psychological sciences and the field of pastoral care is characterized in divergent ways by several scholars is significant; it points to the fact that historians and pastoral theologians who study pastoral care recognize the influence of the psychological sciences and offer a variety of ways to account for the resulting shifts in the field. It could also be argued that pastoral care followed the shifts in psychology more than those in psychiatry, and was therefore receptive to the figures and theories of psychology in a more direct way than to the shifts in psychiatry. Yet Browning, in chronicling the relationship between psychiatry and religion, counters this argument, asserting that "from the moment modern psychiatry emerged as a distinct profession, psychiatry and religion have overlapped and at times overtly competed. The reason for this is clear: both seek to heal forms of brokenness that stand on the ambiguous borderline between body and what is variously referred to as 'psyche' or 'spirit.'"[88] Browning reveals that the three fields are inextricably linked, as chaplaincy in a psychiatric hospital exhibits. The ministry of psychiatric chaplaincy, in particular, necessitated an attentiveness and deference to the field of psychiatry, as exhibited by scholars within pastoral care who have written specifically on mental illness.[89]

Among those figures who were the first to embrace the rise of the psychological sciences, especially as related to pastoral care with mental illness, were the founders of Clinical Pastoral Education for ministers and theological students, namely Boisen, Cabot and Dunbar. Boisen and his colleagues are of particular importance for a study of chaplaincy with the mentally ill for a variety of reasons. First, Boisen's model for clinical pastoral training continues to be of importance in the field of chaplaincy and is a requirement for those who want to consider the field a profession. This model (currently referred to as Clinical Pastoral Education or CPE) now grounds the profession and was developed in dialogue with and response to those who were mentally ill. Boisen's scholastic work was also influenced by his own struggles with mental illness, chronicled in his autobiography *Out of the Depths* (1960),[90] and commented on by many scholars of pastoral care, including Donald Capps and James Dittes.[91]

Together with Cabot, an American physicist and ethicist who taught at Harvard Medical School, Boisen established the first clinical pastoral education group at Worcester State Hospital in 1925. Boisen's basic insights came from his ministry with patients at mental hospitals. He considered these patients "living human documents . . . whose pain and healing could illuminate the nature of religious experience."[92] In *Exploration of the Inner World* (1936), he argued that emotional and mental collapse is actually an "encounter with God that could lead either to a new integration of the personality or fall into total inner disarray."[93] Also in 1936, Cabot and Russell Dicks published the groundbreaking book *The Art of Ministering to the Sick* (1936), which posited a method that continues to ground the Clinical Pastoral Education movement.[94] In response to the ideas of Boisen and his colleagues, it took only two decades for most major seminaries to appoint full-time faculty versed in the burgeoning field to teach pastoral care and for substantial literature to begin to appear.

Due to Boisen's influence in Protestant theological education, Clinical Pastoral Education gradually evolved to become a paradigm that continues to ground much of the training for chaplains in general hospitals. The incorporation of the psychological sciences into pastoral theology also helped to prompt seminaries to offer courses in "practical" theology alongside classical theology, and contributed to the rise of a "clinical" paradigm of pastoral care.[95] These movements, as well as the evolution of the pastoral counseling movement, became the primary places where the psychological sciences were in dialogue with ministry. Yet, while these forums were tangible examples of the intersection of pastoral care and the psychological sciences, they also reveal a lack of attention to ministry with the mentally ill. In the words of Donald Capps, though there is evidence that serious mental illness has been increasing over the past two hundred years, this has not been reflected in pastoral care journals, nor in major publications.[96] As the field of pastoral care continued to evolve in light of the psychological sciences, some took up the mantle of ministry that focused on those with mental illness. Among those figures who focused on those with mental illness were Paul Pruyser, Wayne Oates, and Donald Capps. These figures will be further investigated in the remainder of this book. As feminist and womanist scholars of pastoral care brought attention to communal contextual and intercultural models of pastoral care, this did raise attention of issues of trauma and the unique manifestation(s) of depression, anger and grief in women of different races, classes, and ethnicities.[97] Yet, even in these resources, the topic of severe mental illness was frequently not center stage, and the ways that these new paradigms might speak to ministry with women with mental illness have not been fully explored.

The entry of the psychological sciences into the field of pastoral care was a defining moment for the field, resulting in models of training and education for pastoral caregivers that persist to this day. Yet, it is important to recognize that the theory and praxis of pastoral care has become increasingly silent as it relates to severe mental illness. The fact that care and assessment of those with mental illness continues to be dominated by training that is based on a psychodynamic model[98] must also be seen in light of Freud's own contention that his theories were less useful in situations of those with severe mental illness. As the field of psychiatry evolved away from diagnoses based on categories of psychoanalysis (evidenced by the publishing of the *DSM III* and subsequent versions of the *DSM*), this has also affected the ways that pastoral caregivers relate to their colleagues in psychiatric institutions. The voices of psychiatric caregivers will highlight some of these realities in chapter two.

Publishing of the DSM III

Unlike the history of the discipline of pastoral care, charting the history of the current concept of psychiatric diagnosis reveals a shift towards those of symptomology and (ultimately) biology. It is perhaps easiest to chronicle the rise of the concept of "diagnosis" through examining the creation of the *Diagnostic and Statistical Manual of Mental Disorders* (*DSM*). Lieberman and Ogas argue it may be one of the most influential books written in the past century, as it not only affects the institutionalization or incarceration of thousands of people, but also "dictates the payment of hundreds of billions of dollars to hospitals, physicians, pharmacies, and laboratories by Medicare, Medicaid, and private insurance companies."[99]

When tracing the origins of the *DSM*, it is interesting that scholars look to the 1840 United States Census. It was this infamous census that listed disabilities for the first time, defining them as "deafness and blindness."[100] Ten years later, the category "mental illness" was added to the section on disability in the Census, ascribing to those who were mentally ill the adjectives "insane and idiotic."[101] As has been indicated earlier, this census was used to justify slavery, purporting that rates of insanity were higher among freed slaves than among enslaved blacks. Yet, Lieberman notes that the construction of the very term "mental illness" was also directly connected to race, as "[w]ithout any clear guidance, each marshal ended up with his own idiosyncratic notion of what constituted a mental disability—notions that were often influenced by outright racism."[102] According to the American Statistical Association in 1843, "[i]n many towns, all of the colored population are stated to be insane; in very many others, two-thirds, one-third, one-fourth or one-tenth of this ill-starred race are reported to be thus afflicted."[103] Edward Jarvis, trained in mental illness and statistics, also revealed that the 1840 census reflected a "mysterious appearance of the imaginary black insane"[104] among the northern data. For instance, the town of Worcester, Mass was purported to have "133 colored lunatics and idiots" but this was actually the number of white patients in the Worcester State Hospital for the insane.[105]

By the twentieth century, the census turned its attention to gathering information on mental illness from those in mental health institutions, yet soon realized this was an extremely challenging endeavor, as each institution had its own method of diagnosis. Thus, in 1917, the American-Medico-Psychological Association[106] charged its committee on statistics with establishing a uniform system of diagnosis, entitled *The Statistical Manual for the Use of Institutions for the Insane,* or the *Standard.*[107] Despite the existence of the Standard, however, there was little consensus on the basic categories of mental illness, as each university, hospital and geographical region defined a diagnosis of mental illness in accordance with its own understanding of psychoanalysis, philosophy, and local needs.

The *DSM I* and *DSM II* followed the tradition of the Standard, linking diagnosis to tenets within psychoanalysis, which included attention to the etiology of the illness. Scholars who study psychiatry consider the controversial shift from categories based on psychoanalysis (*DSM I* and *II*) toward the classification of mental disorders based on symptomology (*DSM III*) to be one of the most influential movements in the history of psychiatry.[108] It is notable that the genesis of this movement was a suggestion from the *DSM III* task force. They proposed "dropping the one criterion that psychoanalysts had long considered essential when diagnosing a patient's illness: the cause of the illness, or what physicians termed etiology."[109] Rather than focusing on the source of mental illness, the new manual sought to determine the presence and longevity of specific symptoms in the patient and then compare these symptoms to an established set of criteria for each disorder. In the words of Lieberman, "The *DSM III* represented a revolutionary approach to mental illness, neither psychodynamic nor biological, but able to incorporate new research from any theoretical camp."[110]

Of course, the *DSM III* was not authored without significant consternation and debate. Psychoanalysis had been in a position of prominence in the field of psychiatry for nearly four decades; psychoanalysts controlled academic departments, hospitals, private practices and the American Psychiatric Association. At the heart of the psychoanalytic diagnostic system was the Freudian concept of neurosis.[111] The *DSM III* sought to remove the category of neurosis from the diagnostic manual, and to ban psychoanalytic theory from psychiatric diagnosis, in favor of a symptomatic approach. After much debate and political maneuvering, the *DSM III* Task Force managed to do just this.[112]

This important development represented a shift from focusing on the causes of mental illness, which included the investigation of philosophical, theological, and scientific discourses, toward a comparison of perceived symptoms and signs (themselves evaluations) against "values implicit in the discipline of psychiatry."[113] Fernando argues that these "implicit" values are analogous to the values of Western society, with its focus on the separation of the mind, body and individualism, as well as gendered and racist assumptions.[114] These cultural values will become increasingly evident in the final movement within Western psychiatry, the "turn to the biological." Yet, the debates that culminated in this seismic shift within psychiatry were also evident in pastoral care, specifically in the rise of the practice of pastoral diagnosis.

The Push for Pastoral Diagnosis

Following the rise of the psychological sciences and the push toward symptomology based on scientific findings, pastoral care debates included a push toward a clinical paradigm of pastoral care, promoting such values such as personal autonomy, individual freedom, a belief in progress, and a non-moralistic view of religion.[115] As a response to the emphasis on diagnosis within psychiatry, the practice of pastoral diagnosis also arose during this time. The pastoral care scholarship of Wayne Oates, Paul Pruyser, and Nancy J. Ramsay offer examples of the heralding of the clinical model, and were instrumental in creating categories and/or practices by which pastors could make a "pastoral diagnosis."[116] Other scholars of pastoral care, such as Loren Townsend, have offered a critique of pastoral diagnosis.

In order to chronicle the rise of the clinical-pastoral movement, and in particular the concept of pastoral diagnosis, I will rely on the work of Loren Townsend, a preeminent scholar in pastoral care.[117] Townsend's scholarship traces the developments in the clinical-pastoral movement where he outlines the development of the concept of pastoral diagnosis in the twentieth century.[118]

Townsend notes that figures such as Charles Holman (1932) and Charles Kemp (1947) were some of the first scholars to advocate for paradigms of pastoral/religious care that took into account the diagnostic movements that had occurred in the medical realm. Wayne Oates was primary among these scholars, authoring over fifty books in half a century.[119] Oates' books address a variety of topics on the intersection of religion and psychiatry, including (but not limited to) the overlap of psychiatry and certain religious teachings, the religious care of depressed and schizophrenic patients, religious symbology, and religious diagnosis. While Oates did not produce a system for pastoral diagnosis, he incorporated religious and theological components into psychiatric diagnosis.[120] His approach to pastoral diagnosis can ultimately be seen in his praxis, in which he "paid careful attention to religious dimensions of personality and how religiosity, religious symbol and religious content interacted with psychiatric diagnosis and psychopathology."[121] As his scholarship progressed throughout his career, Townsend argues that Oates "is much more diagnostically sophisticated and comes close to anticipating a clinical theology."[122]

While Oates is a prime example of the effect of the increasing importance of psychiatric diagnosis on the field of pastoral care, Townsend argues that the origin of the term "pastoral diagnosis" should be credited to psychiatrist Edgar Draper (1965).[123] While writing about the importance of psychiatric diagnosis, Draper offered a definition of pastoral diagnosis as "an orderly, structured approach to pastoral problems which taps all the resources of the minister, including his compassion (heart) and objectivity (head). It eventuates in a tentative conclusion as to what the trouble is, opening the way for appropriate action."[124] Draper maintained that pastoral diagnosis was focused on "moral life" as opposed to "mental health," likening pastoral diagnosis to "a spirit of inquiry" about the former. Avoiding a strict classification system, he advocated against the pastoral caregiver meddling in psychiatric diagnosis. In contrast, the life and work of British psychoanalyst Frank Lake encouraged the pastoral caregiver to embrace psychiatric diagnosis, with the purpose of evaluating the religious components therein. Suggesting that competent psychiatric diagnosis was a medium for the Holy Spirit, Lake explored psychoanalytic categories with an eye towards theological analysis. He also rejected the term "clinical theology" in the United States, particularly for the reason that it drew a boundary between the fields of psychiatry and theology.[125]

If Draper and Lake introduced the concept of pastoral diagnosis, Townsend asserts that Paul Pruyser brought it into the mainstream.[126] Pruyser's book *The Minister as Diagnostician* (1976) urged pastoral caregivers to embrace their ability to formulate a pastoral diagnosis, which he considered to be separate from psychiatric diagnosis. Pruyser recognized that people seek aid from their pastors due to their desire to view themselves and their problem from a theological perspective. Pastors, in their attempt to alleviate pain and suffering, should therefore provide a diagnosis based on theological categories. While acknowledging that there are understandings of diagnosis that are inappropriate to the pastoral encounter, Pruyser defined his concept of diagnosis as "the exploratory process in which the troubled person is given an opportunity to assess and evaluate himself in a defined perspective, in which certain observations are made and specific data come to light, guided by conceptual and operational tools in a personal relationship with a resource person."[127] Throughout the book, Pruyser provides seven guidelines for pastoral diagnosis; these include the Awareness of the Holy, Providence, Faith, Grace, Repentance, Communion and Sense of vocation. Pruyser continued to build upon his notion of pastoral diagnosis in his subsequent works on the intersection of pastoral care and mental illness. *Religion in the Psychodynamic Perspective* (1991) includes such essays as "The Seamy Side of Religious Beliefs," and "Assessment of Religious Attitudes" which explore the relationship between religious acts, ideas and psychological coping mechanisms. According to Townsend, the influence of Pruyser brought pastoral diagnosis to the "institutional foreground": "Pastoral counselors were now expected to do pastoral diagnosis, though concrete standards for this practice were far from universal and generally left to the individual counselor's or training program's creative imagination."[128] While the extent of the pervasiveness of the praxis of pastoral diagnosis among pastoral caregivers during this period can be debated, what is apparent is that there was a plethora of scholarship around pastoral diagnosis among scholars of pastoral care (including feminist scholars) during this time. It is significant that this was also the period when the *DSM III* (1980), *DSM-III-R* (1987), and *DSM IV* (1994) were published, which advocated for increasingly detailed schemes of symptom analysis in the practice of psychiatric diagnosis.

In its clearest iteration, Townsend suggests that pastoral diagnosis relied on a "religious diagnostic schema that juxtaposed religious and psychotherapeutic language and produced seamless dual diagnoses and clinical strategies."[129] Yet, he also notes that there was much diversity among those who continued to write on pastoral diagnosis, exhibited by the numerous theories and methods in the scholarship. In his opinion, notable conversation partners within the dialogue around pastoral diagnosis in the last twenty years are such figures as Carroll Wise, Valerie Demarinis, Larry Kent Graham, and Nancy Ramsay. This book will highlight the work of Nancy Ramsay as emblematic of feminist scholars of pastoral care who offered both a critique and a constructive proposal for conceptualizing pastoral diagnosis. It should also be noted, however, that dialogues around pastoral diagnosis were paralleled by the presence of other scholars who avoided the concept in favor of a focus on the role of theological reflection.[130]

Ramsay begins *Pastoral Diagnosis: A Resource for Ministries of Care and Counseling* (1998) by reiterating that the process of diagnosis is "not a neutral process; it has both interpretive and constructive functions."[131] She demonstrates that all forms of diagnosis rely on three interdependent criteria: anthropological assumptions, communally shared guiding values, and a mutually understood dynamic of authority in the helping relationship.[132] Diagnosis both reiterates the assumptions of the practitioner and validates the usefulness of those assumptions for naming reality.[133] She uses these criteria to both analyze therapeutic paradigms and also to highlight underlying assumptions in ecclesial paradigms.

Ramsay advocates for pastoral diagnosis, arguing that it must be attentive to the "explicit theological contexts" in which the former assumptions are rooted. She locates her own definition of pastoral diagnosis in the tradition of Oates and Draper, specifically in her attention to the "breadth of human experience, which includes religious experience."[134] Yet she also suggests that pastoral diagnosis is a "hermeneutical process" that necessitates an attentiveness to one's own pastoral identity, including factors such as social location and embodiment. Her own methodology for pastoral diagnosis begins with experience and "draws upon theological and other disciplines in order to mediate more effectively the transformative, redemptive love of God so as to empower for discipleship."[135] She notes that this frequently requires critical reflection on the part of the pastor, including the ability of pastors to articulate the guiding assumptions and ethical values of their own therapeutic and theological approaches, as well as the ability to attend to one's ever-evolving pastoral identity.

Ramsay's application of her criteria of diagnosis to that of pastoral diagnosis allows her to address constructions of authentic power within the pastoral relationship, including the structural and symbolic dimensions of such power, and to probe anthropological assumptions of the pastor, particularly concepts of human freedom, fulfillment and the human predicament. She also examines ethical values that inform the practice of pastoral diagnosis, offering a revisionist ethic that she terms "freedom for love" or "a relational ethic to enhance various features of the human being necessary for individual and communal flourishing."[136] With this framing, Ramsay both offers critique of the concept of pastoral diagnosis, while simultaneously proposing a way forward based on feminist theological principles. It is notable, however, that while there is attention to intersectional realities within the body of her larger work, she could have gone a bit further with this particular analysis. Giving voice to the realities of race and class in this volume would have only strengthened the anthropological and communal assumptions she stresses.

Though there are other feminist and liberationist scholars who attempt to reframe and reclaim the concept of pastoral diagnosis, arguing that it can be based on feminist theological principles,[137] many scholars in pastoral care also critique the concepts of diagnosis and pastoral diagnosis. Townsend is emblematic of such scholars, incorporating the theory of Michel Foucault and literature from psychiatrists to offer his critique. His central thesis—that the practice of pastoral diagnosis raises many of the same problems as the practice of psychiatric diagnosis—is extremely relevant to our investigation of caregivers in psychiatric institutions. Townsend begins by drawing parallels between pastoral diagnosis and medical diagnosis:

> Though the diagnostic systems proposed in this second trajectory are diverse, they all produce the same tensions. All are hierarchical. That is, the client does not have access to psychological and theological knowledge possessed by the professional pastoral counselor. Like medical diagnosis, pastoral diagnosis is a professional activity that rarely invites the client into full participation. This can objectify clients, participate in diagnostic reductionism, support medical and psychological assumptions that oppress clients, and disconnect theological reflection from the broader life of faith communities.[138]

The contention that the practice of pastoral diagnosis is both hierarchical and disconnected from those to whom it is attempting to minister recognizes that a practice such as this can inadvertently result in reductionism and oppression. Townsend also notes that the growing chasm between professional pastoral counseling and congregational leadership have led to a shift in the use of pastoral diagnosis. As professional pastoral counselors have advocated for parity with mental health professionals, this has prompted an evolution within the profession away from pastoral diagnosis and toward medical-psychological diagnosis using the *DSM*. This, however, only promotes a larger reliance on the concept of diagnosis as advanced by the *DSM*, as the legitimacy of pastoral counselors becomes linked to their knowledge and application of the current version of the *DSM*.

Townsend maintains that while the *DSM* itself—particularly the *DSM-5*—incorporates attention to issues of spirituality and spiritual diagnosis, "pastoral counselors have had little, if any, influence in this medical-psychological process."[139] Rather, the fields of psychiatry and psychology are both defining the norms for spirituality, as well as granting it professional legitimacy.[140] Townsend uses both the theory of Michel Foucault and the current controversies around the *DSM-5* to critique the concept of psychiatric diagnosis. Both of these sources "illustrate how diagnosis is a practice that constructs social meaning and is tied to particular anthropological assumptions, political mechanisms of power, and distinct cultural histories."[141]

Townsend argues that Foucault's work is important for several reasons: first, it reveals how diagnosis has been used as an instrument of social control. Secondly, it poses challenges to modern anthropological assumptions. Finally, it is foundational for postmodern theologies and approaches to psychotherapy. In Foucault's analysis, the construction of mental illness occurs in response to "culturally specific and questionable social and ethical commitments,"[142] which render mental illness as outside of acceptable cultural norms. Diagnosis, in particular, often functions as a tool of control and a way to enact social discipline or to correct deviance, as it builds barriers between those who are deemed normal and those who are not. This "normalization" allows mental health professionals to "create and exert knowledge/power" by drawing lines between healthy and pathological individuals and systems.[143] Power is expressed as medical knowledge, "the norms that create psychopathology are based in deviation from administrative regularity, family obligations and social standards rather than organic pathology."[144] Foucault notes that any type of resistance or disorder in society can now be pathologized, and psychiatry has accomplished this largely through the process of linking madness and illness and pathologizing this conduct, and then "providing a system of classification (diagnosis)" as well as standards for correction. Diagnosis remains the central player in psychiatric power:

> It assumes (1) control of normalizing knowledge, (2) the ability to objectify clients and know them better than they know themselves; (3) the ability to "subjectify" or attribute character to individuals who think, feel and act in particular ways; (4) the knowledge to predict and explain individual differences; and (5) possession of knowledge to correct deviations from "normal."[145]

Townsend uses Foucault, along with a critique of *DSM-5*, to argue that the practice of pastoral diagnosis should be retired. First, he argues that pastoral counselors have abandoned it in favor of psychiatric diagnosis and show little interest in investing the time and energy into creating a separate diagnostic schema. Secondly, pastoral diagnosis "would always be a system of fallible social constructs lacking any direct relationship to treatment methods"[146] and would be subject to similar ethical and practical problems that plague contemporary psychiatry. Instead of pastoral diagnosis, Townsend argues for the creation of "pastoral engagement with interdisciplinary diagnostic practices."[147]

A Critique of Diagnosis

While Townsend's critique of diagnosis arises in his analysis of pastoral diagnosis, he is joined in his critique of psychiatric diagnosis by feminist, womanist and liberationist scholars. Many of these scholars root their arguments in the broader discussions of systemic injustice. They point to the reality that health itself is a cultural production, and symptoms, by their very nature, are self-reported and also cannot be separated from social realities, such as race, class and larger cultural, economic and political factors. These include feminist and anti-racist scholars such as Castellano Turner, Bernard M. Kramer, Elaine Carmen, and Elizabeth Pleck, who analyze the concept of diagnosis with an eye toward racism and sexism. Feminist and womanist Christian social ethicists have also joined the conversation; Aana Vigen and Emilie Townes offer their critique by highlighting the links between diagnosis, health and healthcare in general.

Castellano Turner and Bernard M. Kramer, both scholars of clinical psychology, highlight the link between the categories of "abnormal behavior" and racism, noting that racist ideas can permeate certain theoretical assumptions in the field of psychiatry. This assumption leads to "theories of mental illness based on the genetic inferiority of an entire population."[148] That is, racism can promote links between abnormal behavior and genetic inferiority. They argue that it is important to recognize cross cultural variations in mental illness as variations in specific symptoms, rather than essential differences between racial groups. Racist perspectives also tend to root mental health problems in the individual and nuclear family rather than in social-cultural systems, while downplaying the connections between environmental stress and the onset of mental illness. They highlight that the sustained existential stress that many African Americans experience as members of a racist society—including but not limited to discrimination in education and occupation, lack of access to health care, segregation in isolated communities, and attacks on self-esteem—cannot be overlooked as factors in the etiology of mental illness. They also point to the role of class in the mental health equation, recognizing that class is not a separate variable from race, but rather "relative poverty is the primary effect of racism."[149] If race is a source of stress, then the dual oppression of racial discrimination and poverty in the lives of many African Americans and other groups of non-white racial and ethnic identities may result in higher rates of both stress and mental health problems. While most of this book focuses primarily on the African American population in relationship to psychiatric diagnosis, Turner and Kramer's insight is an important one, given the shift towards biological theories as explanations for the etiology of mental illness.

Turner and Kramer also highlight that the issue of psychological assessment and diagnosis has been "a particular concern in the African American community for many decades."[150] They point to the abuse of psychological testing in schools that has culminated in limitations on educational opportunities for African Americans, as well as the use of culturally-based diagnostic criteria in mental health testing that fails to take into account major cultural, social, class and power differentials between African Americans and whites. In terms of the diagnoses that are meted out, ethnic minorities in the United States are more likely to receive diagnoses of "serious and long-standing psychopathology," while being less likely to receive psychotherapeutic services.[151] A study by Loving and Powell (1988) found that Black male patients were more likely than any subset of the population to receive a diagnosis of "paranoid schizophrenic," a diagnosis which contains elements of "suspiciousness, dangerousness and violence."[152] This has been confirmed by later such studies. Aana Marie Vigen notes that a 2005 *Washington Post* study of one of the largest psychiatric databases in the United States found that Blacks and Latinos are "significantly more likely" to be diagnosed with schizophrenia than whites. As noted in this study, "[a]lthough schizophrenia has been shown to affect all racial groups at the same rate, [John Zeber] found that blacks in the United States were more than four times as likely to be diagnosed with the disorder than whites. Hispanics were more than three times as likely to be diagnosed as whites."[153] Over and above this, John Townsend notes that there is a tendency to treat African Americans who have been diagnosed with severe mental illness with pharmacology as opposed to psychotherapy.[154]

Racism is also a factor in institutionalization. Several scholars have noted that state hospitals serve as a haven for those with "few options" in society: "Poor, uneducated persons who lack family and community supports still predominate in state and county hospitals."[155] Blacks are overrepresented in these custodial institutions and disproportionately represented among involuntary commitments.[156] A 1990 report from the National Institute of Mental Health also revealed that African Americans and Latinos had briefer stays in psychiatric inpatient facilities, coupled with a higher recidivism rate.[157]

Vigen links these trends with provider bias. She notes that "subjective impressions of doctors largely influence whether a patient is deemed mentally ill or not."[158] Though providers tend to regard themselves as "unbiased," "rational," and "objective," their individual racial assumptions and stereotypes, reflective of biases and assumptions present in larger society, color their interpretation of symptoms. Yet, while provider bias is a factor in diagnosis, Vigen also notes that the wider socio-economic system is frequently overlooked in this analysis. As such, she reveals a chasm between a "national tolerance for socio-economic equality as a factor in disparities" and the prejudice on the part of an individual actor.[159] Socio-economic inequality is treated as "less troublesome" and is therefore more acceptable than discrimination on the part of an individual.

The connection between the etiology and diagnosis of mental illness and sexism also cannot be overlooked. The gender bias within mental health again mirrors the social, political, cultural, and economic systems within society that disadvantage women based on their embodiment and/or self-identification. The link between sexism and psychiatric diagnosis is directly connected to other major public health issues that women experience, such as violence against women, poverty, homelessness, and the disparity in mental health research, most notably in research around pharmaceutical interventions.

Violence against women can be considered "the single greatest health risk for women."[160] Scholars such as feminist historian Elizabeth Pleck examine the importance of the recognition of the role of Freudian theory in the relationship between psychiatric diagnosis and intimate violence. In her opinion, Freud's renunciation of the seduction theory actually functioned in a *harmful* capacity for both women and children,[161] because it led to the assumption that children or women who brought charges of rape or violence could not be believed. Pleck chronicles how therapists who were trained in the Freudian method were taught not to inquire about past abuse, and, if abuse was uncovered, to doubt its validity, instead pointing to unconscious desires as the root of the supposed fantasy of abuse. Freud's view of masochism, likewise, was also harmful to women who were undergoing family violence. For example, Helene Deutsch, one of Freud's disciples, applied Freud's theory of masochism to the concept of women who had been raped. Deutsch's theory suggested that the reason that abused women remained with their assailants was that "they secretly enjoyed the pain that was inflicted on them."[162] In fact, some women were "diagnosed" as "so masochistic" that they sought out men who would mistreat them.[163] Pleck suggests that Freudian thought encouraged a system of classification and diagnosis that held women responsible for their abuse, positioning the origin of this action as the woman's own "unconscious desire" or "masochism." This system of classification or diagnosis, nestled within a larger sexist society, offered credence to the notion that women who had experienced violence could not be trusted, which kept psychoanalysts from inquiring about patterns of abuse in the life of the woman. On a societal level, Pleck relates that it also promoted a system of morality "in which perpetrators of family violence were not held responsible for committing illegal and immoral acts."[164] While scholars such as Pleck offer helpful insights about the relationship between Freudian theories of diagnosis and abuse, there is a relative silence around possible spiritual and pastoral aspects of these issues. It is important to recognize the approach of research such as that of Pleck when inquiring about approaches of both religious caregivers and church communities in regard to connections between mental illness and abuse.

More current research about violence against women recognizes violence as a "one of the most destructive consequences of the sexual inequality in existing social institutions."[165] It underlines both the pervasiveness of this violence, as well as the fact that it "occurs in every social class and every racial, cultural, ethnic, religious and educational group."[166] This research has culminated in an extensive reformulation of the psychological theories of women's lives, notably, as it relates to links between intimate violence and severe mental illness. It is not incidental, for example, that 72 percent of female psychiatric inpatients have histories of physical or sexual abuse (or both) or that studies of outpatient programs reveal that over 50 percent of women were sexually abused in childhood.[167] Though not all victims of intimate violence develop mental health issues, victims of intimate violence are "faced with a complex array of social, emotional and cognitive tasks to make sense of experiences that threaten body integrity and life itself."[168] The inevitability of a destructive impact on cognitive and affective processes that accompany the trauma of abuse, including the recurrence of involuntary thoughts, feelings, and nightmares that alternate with periods of denial or distance through psychic numbing or outright dissociation, are well documented in literature on the psychological effects of abuse.

Given these statistics, it is disconcerting that the literature on recovery and treatment from intimate violence "has had little to say about the treatment of chronic mentally ill populations."[169] Physical, sexual and emotional abuse is the norm for most women in inpatient facilities. It occurs in their histories and sometimes also on an ongoing basis within the facilities in which they are housed. Carmen recognizes, however, that much of the literature on trauma assumes the absence of other forms of mental illness.[170] She notes that situations of abuse in the lives of women may be particularly challenging for clinicians or caregivers, as severe mental illness may cause women to isolate or compartmentalize the effects and experiences that would otherwise overwhelm them through defenses such as repression, dissociation or altered states of consciousness.[171] In this way women decontextualize the experience for themselves, that is, the experience is repressed or disconnected from the context in which it occurred. Decontextualization may also allow these women to present the experience to others in a bizarre or unidentifiable way. In a similar vein, Carmen suggests that mental health professionals themselves also "remain generally unaware of the social and psychological consequences of abuse" and exhibit "considerable confusion" about the conceptualization, relevance and meaning of intimate abuse in the treatment of psychiatric disorders.[172] Carmen's insights have grave implications for the relationship between sexism and psychiatric diagnosis, especially as it relates to chronically mentally ill women. The fact that trauma literature assumes an absence of other forms of mental illness, while mental health professionals tend to lack general knowledge about the social, cultural and personal implications of abuse as it relates to psychiatric disorders, renders women with mental illness in a space where their diagnosis and treatment may frequently be based on an incomplete and inaccurate portrait of their lives. It is likely that both incorrect medication and/or therapeutic techniques could be the result of this disconnect. Religious caregivers within this environment will almost certainly be influenced by this situation, perhaps responding with an inaccurate assessment of women's pastoral needs, particularly when abuse is concerned.

The provider bias noted by Vigen is also operative in regards to gender dynamics. To this day, studies reveal that women are more likely to be diagnosed with a mental illness than men and that male psychiatrists "tend to endorse the stereotype of women having emotional problems."[173] As mentioned in the previous section, this is intensified when the patient is a woman of color and can reinforce multiple levels of victimization and discrimination. Womanist ethicist Emilie Townes, as part of her womanist methodology in *Breaking the Fine Rain of Death*, seeks to analyze health and health care in African American communities through a lens that takes into account race, gender, and class as "necessary tools" for both analysis and a constructive effort. While mental health is not her focus, in her chapter on sexism, she illustrates how sexist ideology has informed medical opinion, practice and prescription. She explores the lack of access and participation of women in clinical trials, which is integrally connected to issues of diagnosis and treatment. Townes relates that science has historically been in service of rendering women the "weaker sex," whether through mid-1800s practices of measuring the size of women's skulls or physicians' understandings of the "delicacy of womanhood."[174] She demonstrates that this has continued to this day. A 1985 report commissioned by the Public Health Service found that "there was gender bias in health-care research and delivery."[175] This had resulted in gaps in knowledge about women's illness and health. Yet, while this report caused the National Institute of Health to urge the inclusion of women in NIH-funded research, women continued to be excluded until a revised set of guidelines was issued in 1990.

Townes notes that in relationship to women's health, the primary concern of advocates has been on reproductive health and how women were treated in the examining room, rather than "how women are treated in the laboratory and in the highly politicized arena of funding research."[176] Why has this been the case? She reveals that researchers assert that women's monthly hormone fluctuations complicate research while increasing costs. Yet, these same researchers then conclude that women are "just like men anyway" and therefore can develop pharmacological interventions based on male-only studies. In an example taken from the realm of mental health, Townes notes that it is perhaps for this reason that anti-depressants are more effective in men than in women, though women suffer from depression twice as frequently as men.[177]

Townes notes that when we turn our attention to the dual oppression affecting racial-ethnic women, this has resulted in few clinical trials that have focused on racial-ethnic women, including a significant dearth in research as to the ways that genetics, environment and medication combine to produce decreased mortality rates in these women. This is intensified by the fact that when racial-ethnic women are part of clinical trials, they are reduced to the phrase "women of color," which glosses over the significant differences between and among these women: "In fact women of color may well differ from each other more than they do from White women."[178] When "women of color" are the focus of clinical trials for pharmaceutical drugs, it is frequently because the issue is considered a "social problem" or because the drug is high-risk and the side effects unknown. For example, money has been allotted to study Black teenage pregnancy, as racist stereotypes have deemed this a "societal issue." These studies have continued even as the frequency of pregnancy among African American teenagers has declined. The first birth control pill, on the other hand, was tested on 132 Puerto Rican women, as it was unclear how the high levels of estrogen would affect women. This same pill was never marketed in the mainland United States. While Townes does not separate out psychiatric drugs from other drugs in her analysis, the trends she uncovers are reflections of how wider racist and sexist dynamics in society may be coupled with the interests of large corporations, culminating in a detrimental impact on women of color who need access to the medical interventions controlled by these corporations. It is therefore not a huge leap to assume that the trends noted by Townes exist in the sphere of psychotropic drugs as well. These trends demonstrate hidden social values in which the lives of women, and particularly women of color, are not the "standard" around which treatment options are developed, even those therapeutic options that are supposedly created specifically for them! This tangible praxis reveals that the lives of women, specifically of women of color, are deemed inferior in the eyes of white U.S. culture and more likely to receive improper medical interventions. Values such as these undergird the psychiatric milieu of which religious caregivers are a part.

The structural economic inequality that women experience is also a factor in their relationship with mental illness and health. Compared with men, women are more likely to be in poverty and remain in poverty. They continue to face discrimination in the workforce, are still paid less than men, and are more likely to be the head of single-parent families. Families headed by women also tend to be the poorest in society. Race only intensifies this inequality. According to psychologist Deborah Belle, "Black women heading families face a risk of poverty that is more than 10 times that of White men heading families, and Puerto Rican female family heads face a poverty rate that is almost 15 times that found among White male family heads."[179] These factors converge with other systemic constraints to render Black and Hispanic women more likely to be homeless than men and to have higher rates of being uninsured than White women.

Many studies have been conducted on the relationship between poverty and mental illness, specifically the fact that poverty is a risk factor in the development of mental illness.[180] While the theories around causality vary, most believe that poverty increases vulnerability to a variety of factors, physically, psychologically and sociologically. The extreme stress brought on by poverty has a negative impact on emotional wellbeing. This, coupled with links between poverty and the quality of the environment, the lack of access to healthcare, and the decreased quality of received care creates conditions in which the rates of mental illness are greater among those who are in poverty. This can frequently take the form of a lack of funds available for early intervention and outpatient care, care that could prevent future inpatient hospitalization. Many patients with severe mental illness who lack medical insurance frequently, "do not receive ongoing medical care, but rather receive sporadic care, mostly at the late stages of the disease,"[181] and therefore lack access to preventative care. Factors like unemployment and job loss, which both cause a plunge in socio-economic status and are more frequently experienced by those who already lack financial resources, also render those who experience them more prone to the development of mental illness.

Warner's study (1994), which focused specifically on inpatient psychiatric facilities, found that people with lower economic status not only spent more time in the hospital, but also were re-admitted more often than those of higher economic status.[182] Bye and Partridge (2003) also conducted a state-level analysis on the influence of economic and demographic factors on the rate of care in inpatient psychiatric hospitals. They found that an increase in a state's poverty rate is directly correlated with an increase in that state's hospitalization rate for mental illness.[183]

Townes notes that health is a "cultural production" in which we all participate: "As such, we must recognize the biological, social, environmental, and economic conditions that surround us and have profound impacts on our health."[184] Given this, the concept of psychiatric diagnosis cannot be analyzed without attention to cultural, socio-economic and socio-political factors that shape and impact it. These factors are frequently hidden in the psychiatric milieu, therefore religious caregivers may often encounter these dynamics without an awareness of them, or how to incorporate them in their responses to the women with whom they minister.

The Turn to the Biological

The preceding section has demonstrated that scholars from a variety of disciplines have emphasized the reality that health itself is a cultural production, and symptoms cannot be separated from social realities, such as race and class, and larger cultural, economic and political factors. This section will build upon these insights to highlight that these factors are all but invisible within the modern Western medical model. The third movement in psychiatry that has influenced pastoral care is the "turn to the biological" or an approach to psychiatry as scientific, objective and verifiable. In the words of Lieberman, modern psychiatry has undergone a "brain revolution." Brain imaging techniques of the late 1970s and 1980s allowed psychiatrists to observe the very first physical abnormality in the brain to be associated with mental illness.[185] This has been coupled with an increase in the number of psychiatric neuroscientists, as well as investigations into the genetic origin of mental illness. According to Lieberman, these three movements have created a "new kind of psychiatry," an "enlightened and effective medicine of mental health."[186] It has also resulted in a "therapeutic confidence" that had previously dodged the field: "We have entered a period of scientific advances that will produce a stream of innovations more dazzling than any that have come before."[187]

Scholars also admit, however, that the advances in the field of psychiatry have not resulted in the clarity for which they had hoped. While brain imaging techniques have revealed much about the neurobiology of major psychiatric disorders, it is also "without any pathognomonic findings that could be incorporated into the *DSM 5*."[188] Psychiatric neuroscience is a fledgling field in its infancy. Though many looked to the findings of genetic research with great anticipation, including the overlap of certain genes associated with multiple psychiatric disorders, the implications of these findings are at best unclear.[189] In sum, there does not exist undisputed biological evidence for the majority of diagnosable mental illnesses. Lieberman expresses it thusly: "The only undisputed biological explanations of the origins of mental illness are for General Paraesis of the Insane (caused by syphilis bacteria), pellagra (a form of dementia), and more recently Alzheimer and other forms of dementia and drug-induced psychosis."[190] When it comes to the major forms of mental illness, modern psychiatry can offer little more than hypotheses.

It was around the concept of psychiatric diagnosis, yet again, where these tensions played themselves out. The publishing of the *DSM-5* in May 2013 became the catalyst for psychiatrists and wider society to weigh in on the "dazzling" (to borrow from Lieberman) new brand of psychiatry, alongside the gap in biological evidence for mental illness. The process of the creation of the *DSM-5* took place behind closed doors with the chair of the *DSM III*, Robert Spitzer, and the chair of the *DSM IV*, Allen Frances, excluded from the conversation.[191] The *DSM-5* was published amidst much controversy; voices from within the field and without—including anti-psychiatry activists and stakeholder groups[192]—voiced discontent about both the process and content. The former chairs of *DSM III* and *IV*, both distinguished professors at prominent universities, also weighed in, often in quite public ways.[193] In the words of Nemeroff and Weinberger, when the planning for the *DSM-5* began ten years prior, there was little inkling "that the process and final product would engender such a remarkable level of criticism, rhetoric, and passion as we have now witnessed."[194]

Why the controversy? Partly, psychiatrists admit,[195] scientific research around mental illness was not able to keep pace with the goal of the *DSM-5*: the hope that psychiatric diagnoses would include, in addition to signs and symptoms, "various biomarkers of the major disorders including schizophrenia, bipolar disorder, and major depression, with reasonable measures of sensitivity and specificity."[196] In reality, this promise was not able to be realized, partly due to the tools at psychiatry's disposal. As to whether the *DSM-5*, as a classification system, was more clinically valuable and more biologically valid than its predecessors (the *DSM IV* being the most recent)—scholars were divided, with notable professors of psychiatry weighing in on both sides.[197] Critics critiqued a variety of factors, including (but not limited to) the lack of scientific evidence to support some of the revisions, the broadening of some of the definitions of mental illness, the use of a consistent methodology for altering diagnoses, as well as the influence of the pharmaceutical drug industry on the content of the manual.

As has been noted, one of the most outspoken critics of the *DSM-5* was Allen Frances, the former chair of the *DSM IV*. Frances not only took issue with the process by which the *DSM-5* was created, but was (and is) also largely critical about its result. In *Saving Normal* (2014), Frances cautions that the *DSM-5* has been recklessly expanded from the earlier versions of the *DSM*, to the point where almost anything can be considered pathological.[198] He contends that biases of committee members have combined with the corporate interests of "Big Pharma" to create a system of "diagnostic inflation." According to Frances, this "diagnostic inflation" risks the misallocation of medical resources, in the form of needless doctor's visits and unnecessary and excessive treatment.[199] Frances argues that the *DSM-5* will ultimately have a mental, social and economic impact. He also asserts that the lowered thresholds for psychiatric illnesses could exacerbate an over-diagnosis problem, while also encouraging the "wholesale imperial medicalization of normality." When normal variation in mood is pathologized, this could result in increased profits for pharmaceutical companies, paid for by those who should not have been diagnosed with mental illness. He also believes it could shift responsibility for healing away from the individual, who has the capacity for resilience and self-healing, and into the hands of "Big Pharma" which will inevitably benefit with profits of millions.[200]

The lowered thresholds for a diagnosis of mental illness can also have the unintended result of false epidemics. Frances recognizes that he himself, as chair of the *DSM IV*, could be implicated in the false epidemics around Autism and ADD, where false positives were the result of a seemingly innocuous change in wording in the *DSM IV*.[201] The addition of Bipolar II also "coalesced with the interest of pharmaceutical companies and became an 'enormously popular diagnosis.'"[202] This meant that the prescription rates for these drugs saw a sharp increase, even though they caused serious side effects to those to whom they were prescribed.

How has this "turn to the biological" affected the realm of pastoral care? As pastoral care is not a singular entity, it is difficult to posit "one" response to the turn to the biological. Responses generally seem to fall along two major lines. On the one hand, some pastoral theologians have accepted and embraced the system of classification proposed by the *DSM IV* and *DSM-5*, and have created resources to help the pastoral caregiver to better understand the intricacies of these diagnoses, as well as their application to pastoral care.[203] The second group of scholars of pastoral care offer an expansive critique of the larger systemic realities that frame concepts of diagnosis and treatment, even if they do not directly address the issue of psychiatric diagnosis. Many of these scholars would consider themselves feminist, womanist or liberationist scholars of religion, such as Christie Cozad Neuger, Beverly Wallace, and Teresa Snorton. These scholars offer a way forward that, if applied to the concept of diagnosis, would challenge the "turn to the biological" in a variety of ways.

In the last decade, the "turn to the biological" within psychiatry has caused scholars of pastoral care who study Christian ministries that serve mentally ill people to embrace a functional approach. *Ministry with Persons with Mental Illness* (Albers) is emblematic of this, an approach that is also shared by such resources as *Mental Illness and Psychiatric Treatment* (Collins) and *A Minister's Handbook of Mental Disorders* (Ciarrocchi). In these books, each of the chapters focuses on a form of diagnosable mental illness or illnesses, such as depression, anxiety disorders, psychotic disorders, personality disorders. The resources lead with an informative piece, usually written by a psychiatrist, or drawn from psychiatric resources. They frequently provide information about the theory and history of the disorder, the diagnostic criteria, and common treatments. The latter portion of the resource, or response, offers theological reflection and ministerial opportunities in relationship to these diagnoses. As such these books claim to be providing a "holistic approach" to the topic.

It would be inaccurate to say that all of these books advocate for a simple acceptance of the diagnostic classification of the *DSM*. In their introduction, for example, Albers et al note that the diagnostic process itself is a "precarious undertaking," and that the *DSM IV* "makes amply clear that acceptable behavior is predicated on what is considered as appropriate given the cultural context in which the person lives."[204] They also recognize that ministry exists within a variety of different cultural contexts and that the minister should do her part to familiarize herself with these cultures. Yet, the overarching goal of the book is education *about* psychiatric diagnosis, rather than an examination of the frameworks and premises that inform and guide this practice. As such, racial and gendered assumptions that have the potential to alter the process of diagnosis remain hidden. Given this, one could argue that the very format of the book highlights their adherence to the Western treatment model and the therapeutic confidence that accompanies the "turn to the biological."

Other scholars in this camp have built on the work of Boisen (1876–1965), Pruyser (1916–1987), and Oates (1917–1999) and tend to approach mental illness topically, focusing on one illness at a time, rather than adopting a survey approach. Donald Capps is an example of these scholars, particularly in his topical engagement with a variety of types of mental illness. Throughout his career, he has written extensively on the intersection of mental illness with pastoral care, authoring *The Depleted Self: Sin in a Narcissistic Age* (1993), *Social Phobia: Alleviating Anxiety in an Age of Self Promotion* (1998), and *Fragile Connections: Memoirs of Mental Illness for Pastoral Care Professionals* (2005). Capps, along with co-author Nathan Carlin, have also analyzed the presence of articles in mental illness in journals of pastoral care from 1950–2003.[205] They found that as a group, the journals reflected "the enduring significance of mental illness for pastoral care professionals."[206] They also note, however, that articles tended to approach mental illness topically, and that the three topics of depression and suicide, alcoholism, and intellectual disability accounted for 25 percent of the articles of mental illness published over the fifty year span. While there were a significant number of articles on narcissistic personality disorder, schizophrenia, and dementia, other disorders were relatively underrepresented.[207]

The second group of scholars of pastoral care tend to question larger systemic frameworks that ground concepts such as that of diagnosis. Feminist, womanist, intercultural, and liberationist pastoral theologians have recognized that the discipline of pastoral care has historically been dominated by an androcentric approach which has been defined by whiteness, privilege, and U.S. and Western European cultural values. In response, as has been noted, they have advanced an approach that has attempted to address these limitations, by taking into account the fields of feminist and womanist theory and theology—with its emphasis on the historic dynamics of power and oppression of women and other marginalized people—as well as studies in interculturality. A number of authors in feminist, womanist, intercultural, and liberationist pastoral care have noted how models of pastoral care have been inattentive to broader systems and to the needs of women and other marginalized groups.[208] Feminist pastoral care has also re-envisioned the notion of care "from care understood as counseling to care understood within a wider social, religious and political context."[209]

While feminist and womanist scholars of pastoral care have done much to advance pastoral care beyond the dominant cultural worldview, few of them focus specifically on the issue of mental illness, especially as it relates to the rise of the Western treatment model.[210] There are, of course, exceptions. Pattison, in *Liberation Theology and Pastoral Care* (1994), places the mentally ill as the central case study in his argument for pastoral care which is attentive to systemic factors. Feminist scholars of pastoral counseling also address counseling with those with mental illness, though this is rarely the focus of their work.[211] Yet, while few feminist and womanist scholars of pastoral care focus explicitly on the concept of psychiatric diagnosis within mental illness, the topics they do address, as well as their methods, provide ways for addressing and challenging the current "turn to the biological."

The first topic of note is the shift from "care as counseling" toward care as "part of a wider communal, cultural and social context."[212] Greider, Johnson, and Leslie highlight that the entry of feminist pastoral care into the realm of pastoral care in the last twenty-five years has been foundational for this shift. They argue that the writings of feminist scholars of pastoral care have advocated "for the survival and thriving of ourselves and other women, of collective human life—children, women and men together—and of the creation as a whole."[213] These writings have exhibited seven main foci that have influenced this monumental shift within pastoral care: Ekklesia and its ministry, marginalized people and taboo topics, female experience, theological education, soulfulness, violence, and systems of care. Greider et al. argue that while none of these themes alone characterizes the communal context of pastoral care, seen together they contribute (along with writings from other non-feminist authors) to the emergence of a communal contextual paradigm that now is operative in pastoral care.[214] This communal contextual paradigm, if applied to issues of psychiatric diagnosis, would have much to say about the process of formulating this diagnosis, and the content of said diagnosis, particularly in light of the "turn to the biological."[215]

Feminist and womanist scholars of pastoral care and Christian social ethics have also tackled issues of violence and trauma within women's lives. As has been previously noted, the relationship between violence against women and trauma and psychiatric diagnosis is significant and in need of greater attention. The latest "turn to the biological" within psychiatry has included research on the physiological response to violence and trauma, and the newest version of the *DSM-5* has reflected this with an increased focus on trauma-related and stressor-related disorders.[216] The writings of feminist and womanist scholars of pastoral care on violence against women and trauma are important to this conversation. Cozad Neuger, for example, has explored the cultural and religious narratives of harm that have formed society and the church, offering a pastoral care paradigm of resistance that works against these core narratives. In "Narratives of Harm: Setting the Developmental

Context for Intimate Violence," she challenges the "medical model of sickness and a behavioral model of problems" that has been foundational to the discipline of pastoral care.[217] She charges that women who have experienced trauma have historically been pathologized, rather than given the opportunity to process and integrate their traumatic history. They have also not been given the opportunity to analyze those skills that previously helped them survive in a life-or-death situation. Beverly Wallace, in "A Womanist Legacy of Trauma, Grief and Loss," explores differences in the grief and trauma experiences of African American and Euro-American women, due to disparate historical and cultural narratives within U.S. society. She explores how "more often than not, racism is implicated"[218] in African American women's experiences of loss and trauma, as well as in the ways they cope with these experiences. Growing up as a woman of color in the midst of systemic racism, black women are taught that they should be strong and responsible, even to the point of denying the expression of their own emotions. She notes how pastoral caregivers who are inattentive to issues of systemic racism might inadvertently be harmful to African American women.

Traci West, a Christian social ethicist, also speaks to the relationship between Black survivors of intimate abuse and psychiatric diagnosis in her work *Wounds of the Spirit* (1999). While psychiatric diagnosis is not her focus, she reveals that certain psychiatric characterizations of those who have been battered (for instance, as "masochistic" or suffering from borderline personality disorder) "implies an emotionally sick collusion in their own abuse."[219] She also recognizes that some mental health clinics rely on diagnostic categories, as opposed to naming the emotional trauma that has surfaced in the face of violence. West asserts that when anguish becomes collapsed with psychotic behavior, it becomes "a scientifically validated method of community dismissal."[220]

Feminist scholars themselves also recognize the racism that has been part of pastoral care discourse. Sheryl Kujawa-Holbrook asserts that the failure of pastoral care to bring about authentic healing and reconciliation is largely a result of "the overall dominant culture within American society [which] often does not recognize or strive to correct the deep power imbalances experienced by all marginalized people."[221] She and co-contributors to the volume *Injustice and the Care of Souls*, advocate for the importance of anti-racist pastoral care, which, she asserts, depends on an approach that requires multiple strategies.

Kujawa-Holbrook embraces the wider notion of care, pushing for a definition of care that goes beyond the individual in favor of care as "integral to the vocation and mission of the whole people of God."[222] This pastoral care must, as a central component, take into account white privilege, by examining the impact of racism in pastoral care situations, as well as the ways in which faith communities can address racism. It must recognize that racism is a "profoundly spiritual concern," one that morally restricts and damages whites, and also is manifested in the internalized oppression of the pastoral caregiver. Anti-racist pastoral care involves "reinvisioning our communities through the eyes of God."[223], and involves a commitment to developing cultural competence in order to reshape pastoral care. This allows pastoral caregivers to: (1) know the difference between race, ethnicity and culture and be able to apply this within pastoral settings; (2) get in touch with issues of prejudice and stereotypes; (3) recognize how racial identity informs power relationships; (4) understand the ways that categories of race, ethnicity, gender, economic class, and sexual identity are organizing principles; (5) recognize that there are multiple centers of truth whose legitimacy is often determined by the amount of power given to a particular perspective; and (6) develop a rich symbolic life and cultivate spiritual stamina.

As the fields of psychiatry and pastoral care shift towards a "turn to the biological," anti-racist pastoral care would also need to recognize the presence of biological theories of race within U.S. society. Joseph L. Graves Jr., a scholar of biological studies, reveals that the majority of geneticists, evolutionary biologists, and anthropologists agree that biological races do not exist within the human species. He notes that "none of the physical features which have historically defined races—including skin color, hair type, body stature, blood groups *and disease prevalence* [emphasis mine]—unambiguously corresponds to the racial groups that we have constructed."[224] He maintains that while race is a social construction, resulting from the unique political and cultural history of the West (in general) and the United States (in particular), the fallacy of biological theories of race continue to dominate the cultural ethos of the United States. While he recognizes that human biodiversity does exist, he asserts that Western attempts to describe this biodiversity "have been motivated by racist social agendas and infused with racist ideologies."[225] The work of scholars who explore biological theories of race is important to this book as it troubles thinking that blindly links certain "disorders" (particularly mental disorders) with particular racial groups. Graves highlights that any theory that purports to link the two without a social and cultural analysis of race in the United States may fall victim to ascribing racial categories with a power to explain human characteristics that "they simply do not have."[226]

The "turn to the biological" has also raised larger questions that pertain to pastoral care, but have yet to be addressed. While Gold and Gold are psychiatrists rather than pastoral theologians, their book *Suspicious Minds* reflects on the human dimension of the turn to the biological. Gold and Gold assert that the reconfiguring of mental illness in this direction has had both humanizing and dehumanizing implications. While previous depictions of the person with mental illness as a "moral lesson" for the remainder of society was problematic, the current turn to the biological has its own set of issues:

"When science began telling us that madness was etched into our genes and our brains, what had been a flexible boundary became a closed border—with the mentally ill on the wrong side, as distant from us as ever."[227] Gold and Gold argue that the current focus on diagnosis of disorders has only heightened the already present stigma toward those with mental illness.

Various studies on stigma against those with mental illness confirm that the turn to the biological, toward diagnosis and classification of disorders, has not resulted in a decrease of stigmatizing attitudes toward those who have been diagnosed with mental illness. In fact, numerous studies exhibit that a majority of people in the United States and in many countries in Western Europe continue to harbor stigmatizing attitudes about those who have been diagnosed with mental illness.[228] In a 2002 study, Corrigan and Watson found that a diagnosis of mental disorder was linked to attitudes of fear, public avoidance, and a sense that those who were ill were somehow responsible for their illness.[229] This has resulted in behavioral impacts such as withholding of treatment, social avoidance, and advocacy for mandatory treatment in institutions. These scholars highlight potential issues that will need to be addressed by pastoral care (feminist and otherwise) as the "turn to the biological" continues.

The concept of psychiatric diagnosis functions as the principle framework that organizes and defines the environment in which the psychiatric religious caregiver operates. Yet the evolution of the concept of psychiatric diagnosis within the field of psychiatry and pastoral care reveals a complex history that is marked by debates over the origin and nature of mental illness. This debate is interrelated with the ways that such topics as health, mental illness, religiosity, and race have been constructed by society. The concept of psychiatric diagnosis has evolved toward an adherence to an increasingly "biological" model, characteristic of the Western medical model. Yet this concept is part of a larger worldview that is frequently inattentive to the racist and gendered ideology that has permeated certain theoretical assumptions in the field of psychiatry. As such, the current model of psychiatric diagnosis advances certain underlying moral values about the value of women's lives—particularly women of color. As theories of diagnosis and resulting options for treatment are developed within the framework of a white, U.S. culture, the particularities of women's lives, specifically the lives of women of color, are frequently overlooked in the process of diagnosis and treatment. The psychiatric milieu of which religious caregivers are a part includes values that overlook the myriad of stressors—both personal and systemic—that influence and define the lives of women who have been diagnosed with mental illness. These values are an intrinsic aspect of the environment in which a psychiatric pastoral caregiver ministers with women with mental illness.

The field of pastoral care has been greatly influenced by developments in the concept of psychiatric diagnosis. The current "turn to the biological" within psychiatry fomented a division among scholars of pastoral care as those who adhere to this model, elucidating potential pastoral responses to particular diagnoses and those (particularly of the feminist, intercultural and liberationist persuasions) who question overarching frameworks of health and diagnosis presumed by this model. The scholarship of this latter group will be important as we explore the voices of psychiatric caregivers who minister with women in psychiatric institutions in chapters two and three and as a framework is proposed for Just Care in chapter four.

NOTES

1. See Gary R. VandenBox, ed., *American Psychological Association Dictionary of Psychology* (Washington, DC: American Psychological Association, 2007), 277.

2. This book recognizes that there has been a resurgence in the role of spirituality in healthcare, including the positive effect that spirituality has on health, particularly in the areas of mortality, coping and recovery. There are many articles and conferences that are focused on the need for greater attention to spirituality and a more holistic approach to health and healing within the healthcare setting. Yet, based on the interviews with psychiatric chaplains (see chapters 2 and 3), this book argues that these trends have not made their way into the ethos of the state psychiatric hospital. While more geographically expansive interviews would need to be conducted to confirm this for the remainder of state psychiatric facilities in the United States, an investigation of the literature around the importance of spirituality in healthcare reveals that the majority of the books and articles focus on medical hospitals, and do not address the unique medical and spiritual needs of those in state psychiatric facilities. For more on the resurgence in spirituality in the healthcare setting, see Christina M. Puchalski and Betty Ferrell, *Making Healthcare Whole: Integrating Spirituality into Healthcare* (West Conshohocken: Templeton, 2010); John L. Cox, Alastair V. Campbell, and K.W.M. Fulford, *Medicine of the Person: Faith Science and Values in Health Care Provision* (Philadelphia: Jessica Kingsley, 2007); J. Wattis and S. Curran, "The Importance of Spirituality in Caring for Patients," *Br J Hosp Med (Lond)* 77.9 (2016): 500–01; D. Moss, "The Circle of the Soul, The Role of Spirituality in Healthcare,"*Appl Psychophysiol Biofeedback* 27.4 (2002): 283–97; Christine M. Puchalski, "The Role of Spirituality in Health Care," *Proc Baylor Univ Med Cent* 14.4 (2001): 352–57; P. Ramakrishan, "You are Here: Locating 'Spirituality' on the Map of the Current Medical World," *Curr Opin Psychiatry* 28.5 (2015): 393–401.

3. Suman Fernando, *Mental Health, Race and Culture*, third edition (New York: Palgrave Macmillon, 2010), chapters 2 and 3; Joel Gold and Ian Gold, *Suspicious Minds: How Culture Shapes Madness* (New York: Free Press, 2014), 17-51.

4. Jeffrey A. Lieberman and Ogi Ogas, *Shrinks: The Untold Story of Psychiatry* (New York: Little, Brown and Company, 2015), 203–39. While this book will primarily approach the turn to the biological from the perspective of its influence on pastoral care, Browning notes that from the perspective of psychiatry, the turn to the biological can produce both positive and negative relationships with religion. On one hand, the turn to the biological can produce a "division of labor," where psychiatry addresses mental illness that is biological in origin, while religion deals with moral and spiritual issues. Yet, "totally positivistic forms of biological psychiatry tend to reduce all human problems to their biological foundations thereby appearing to reject the relevance of religion to solving human problems." See Browning, *Religious and Ethical Factors*, 4.

5. See Edward Shorter, *A History of Psychiatry: From the Era of the Asylum to the Age of Prozac* (New York: John Wiley & Sons, 1997), 39-86.

6. Glenn Asquith, *The Concise Dictionary of Pastoral Care and Counseling* (Nashville: Abingdon, 2010), 68.

7. Considered one of the founding voices in the field of psychology of religion within the United States, James, first trained as a medical doctor, is perhaps most well known for his seminal work, *Varieties of Religious Experience* (1902). Dissatisfied with current state of philosophy of religion and liberal theology, *The Varieties* set out to "empirically" test religious faith, and to demonstrate that religious experience dramatically altered the lives of those who professed it. *The Varieties* reflected James' long-standing concern with the philosophical justification of religious faith, and served as one of the first descriptive approaches to religious phenomena.

8. Clinical Pastoral Education will be further discussed in chapter 3. It continues to this day to be a primary component of training for hospital chaplains.

9. The third edition of the *Diagnostic and Statistical Manual of Mental Disorders*, published in 1980. For more on the process behind the creation of the *DSM III*, see Lieberman and Ogas, *Shrinks, The Untold Story of Psychiatry*, 134–39.

10. According to Loren Townsend, the notion of pastoral diagnosis emerged in the mid-twentieth century, "largely as a practice that emulated psychiatry by linking problems in living to broad theological, spiritual or religious metaphors," in "Best Practices, Rethinking Pastoral Diagnosis," *Sacred Spaces: The E-Journal of the American Association of Pastoral Counselors*, vol. 5 (2013): 66–101. There were a number of scholars of pastoral care who proposed models for pastoral diagnosis; we will explore such figures as Draper, Pruyser, and Ramsay later in this chapter.

11. For instance, discussions regarding the role and necessity of a pastoral diagnosis divide scholars. See Paul Pruyser, particularly *The Minister as Diagnostician* (Philadelphia: Westminster, 1976) and Nancy Ramsay, particularly *Pastoral Diagnosis: A Resource for Ministries of Care and Counseling* (Minneapolis, MN: Augsburg Fortress, 1998) on the necessity of pastoral diagnosis, and Loren Townsend who speaks against this in "Best Practices, Rethinking Pastoral Diagnosis." Scholars such as Carrie Doehring and Emmanuel Lartey would propose a model of intercultural pastoral care in *The Practice of Pastoral Care, A Postmodern Approach* and *In Living Color: An Intercultural Approach to Pastoral Care and Counseling* respectively. These books deviate from pastoral diagnosis in their attention to interculturality, postmodernism and socio-economic factors.

12. Lieberman and Ogas, *Shrinks,* 203–39

13. Ibid., 203-238.

14. Robert H. Albers, William Meller, and Steven Thurber, eds. *Ministry with Persons with Mental Illness and Their Families* (Minneapolis, MN: Fortress, 2012); Gregory B. Collins and Thomas L. Culbertson, *Mental Illness and Psychiatric Treatment* (New York: Routledge, 2003); Dana Charry and Joseph W. Ciarrocchi, *A Minister's Handbook of Mental Disorders* (New York: Paulist, 1993).

15. See Albers et al., *Ministry with Persons with Mental Illness*, 7.

16. Two of the Christian social ethicists we will draw on heavily in this book fit into this category: Emilie M. Townes *Breaking the Fine Rain of Death: African American Health Issues and a Womanist Ethic of Care* (New York: Continuum, 1998) and Aana Marie Vigen, *Women, Ethics and Inequality in U.S. Healthcare "To Count Among the Living"* (New York: Palgrave Macmillan, 2006).

17. Bonne J. Miller-McLemore and Brita L. Gill-Austern, eds., *Feminist and Womanist Pastoral Theology* (Nashville: Abingdon, 1999), 15.

18. Lieberman and Ogas, *Shrinks,* 4.

19. Ibid., 25.

20. Ibid., 24.

21. See Fernando, *Mental Health, Race and Culture*; Theodore Millon, *Masters of the Mind: Exploring the Story of Mental Illness from Ancient Time to the New Millennium* (Hoboken, NJ: Wiley & Sons, 2004).

22. Lieberman, for example, expresses that before the 1800s, those with mental illness had either chosen to behave outside of social and moral norms, were being penalized for earlier sinfulness, or were somehow "destined" by God (or Nature) to behave in this way, see Lieberman and Ogas, *Shrinks*, 30.

23. For a more in-depth analysis, see Millon, *Masters of the Mind*, and Shorter, *A History of Psychiatry*.
24. Heather H. Vacek, *Madness: American Protestant Responses to Mental Illness* (Waco, TX: Baylor University Press, 2015), 4.
25. Millon, *Masters of the Mind*, 5.
26. Ibid. Millon positions the Judeo-Christian tradition in the demonological phase, a period when the mythological deities of former eras were placed within a larger theological system. This is important for a foray into mental illness, as the demonological period is marked by competition between a good, creative force (usually an all-good Father or God) and a destructive force (frequently demonic forces or evil). Mental illness became associated with the latter.
27. Roy Porter, *Madness: A Brief History* (New York: Oxford University Press, 2002), 10–16.
28. See 1 Samuel 16:14–13, 18:6–16, 19:9–24 and Daniel 4. King Saul was reduced to raving behavior, while King Nebuchadnezzar was forced to eat grass as punishment for his pride.
29. Porter, *Madness*, 17.
30. Ibid., 17-21. See also Gold and Gold, *Suspicious Minds*, 19.
31. Porter, *Madness*, 17–21. Albers, Meller, and Thurber also note that in the Bible, madness is often linked to a demon possession "working in opposition to the benevolent powers of God." Albers et al., *Ministry with Persons with Mental Illness*, 4.
32. For example, at the shrine of Gheel in the Netherlands, St. Dymphna was known to exercise healing powers for those of unquiet minds.
33. Vacek, *Madness*, 1.
34. Greek scholars including Thales, Pythagoras, Alcmaeon, and Empedocles laid the groundwork for the great Greek physician Hippocrates. In the work of Hippocrates (460–367 BCE), concepts of mental disorders progressed from the magical, mythical and demonologic to one based on clinical observation and inductive theorizing. The introductory notes to the Hippocratic book regarding epilepsy suggests a biological, brain-based origin of the disease, shunning those who connect illness with religious forces, such as demons, as charlatans.
35. These methods included, but are not limited to, bloodletting, exercise, dream interpretation and incubation. For more on this, see Gold and Gold, *Suspicious Minds*, 20.
36. See Porter, *Madness*, 55–61.
37. For more on these see Harriet A. Washington, *Medical Apartheid : The Dark History of Medical Experimentation on Black Americans from Colonial Times to the Present* (New York: Doubleday, 2006), 38.
38. Ibid., 46.
39. Ibid. The 1840 Census held that "1 out of every 1558 blacks in the south was 'idiot or insane''; but one of out every 144 northern blacks had similar mental problems." Washington, *Medical Apartheid*, 146.
40. Ibid., 146.
41. Ibid., 147.
42. Millon recognizes that during the Middle Ages, the ideas of Hippocrates were sidelined due to the theological belief that Satan and Satanic forces were bent on the destruction of all forms of Christianity. This belief took the form of witch hunts, not the least of which was the Inquisition. From the fifteenth to the seventeenth centuries, there was a resurgence in beliefs of demonic possession and its antidote, practices of exorcism, torture or (in some cases) death. These beliefs were adopted not only by those in positions of power, but also by the masses. See "Demythologizing the Ancient's Spirits" in Millon, *Masters of Mind*, 1-42.
43. Ibid., 4.
44. Shorter, *History of Psychiatry*, 7.
45. David J. Rothman, *The Discovery of the Asylum: Social Order and Disorder in the New Republic* (Piscataway, NJ: Aldine Transaction, 2002), 130.
46. See "The Rise of Psychiatry," in Porter, *Madness, A Brief History*, 123–56.
47. Rothman, *Discovery of the Asylum*, 133.
48. As late as the last quarter of the nineteenth century, separate Catholic and Calvinist asylums were set up in the Netherlands.

49. See "The Rise of Psychiatry," in Porter, *Madness a Brief History*, 123–56.

50. A term coined by Michel Foucault in *History of Madness* (New York: Routledge, 2006), to refer to the institutionalization of "unreasonables" (the mad, but also others regulated to the margins of society, including the prostitutes, vagrants, blasphemers etc.) in the seventeenth century. This movement corresponded with the beginning of the age of reason, where "madness" was no longer seen as linked to the possession of wisdom, but was deemed a position of moral error which needed to be separated from society and controlled.

51. Michel Foucault, *Mental Illness and Psychology* (A. Sheridan, trans., 1st ed,). (Berkeley: University of California Press, 1987), 60.

52. See Millon, *Masters of the Mind,* 74, 86.

53. Millon, *Masters of the Mind*, 92–94; Porter, *Madness*, 104–48; Shorter, *A History of Psychiatry*, 18–22.

54. Porter, *Madness*, 104.

55. Ibid., 107.

56. Ibid., 119.

57. Ibid., 120.

58. Ibid., 122.

59. See Elaine Showalter, *The Female Malady: Women, Madness and English Culture, 1830–1980* (London: Virago, 1987); Jonathan Andrews and Anne Digby, eds., *Sex and Seclusion, Class and Custody: Perspectives on Gender and Class in the History of British and Irish Psychiatry* (Amsterdam and New York: Rodopi, 2004).

60. Anne Digby, "Women's Biological Straightjacket," in *Sexuality and Subordination: Interdisciplinary Studies of Gender in the Nineteenth Century* (London: Routledge, 1989), 193.

61. Ibid.

62. Jane M. Ussher, *Women's Madness: Misogyny or Mental Illness?* (New York: Harvester Wheatsheaf, 1991), Website of the Science Museum, "Brought to Life, Exploring the History of Medicine," Accessed Feb. 2017 http://www.sciencemuseum.org.uk/broughttolife/themes/menalhealthandillness/womanandpsychiatry.

63. Washington, *Medical Apartheid*, 149.

64. Ibid.

65. For example, the state of North Carolina opened the Eastern Asylum for the Colored Insane (1880), while the state of Maryland opened Crownsville Hospital (1911). The state of Alabama created a separate facility on the grounds of the Alabama Insane Hospital. In 1897 this separate facility was reported to house 350 African American patients. For more see Vanessa Jackson, "In Our Own Voices: African American Stories of Oppression, Survival and Recovery in the Mental Health System," *Race, Health Care and the Law*, ed. Vernellia R. Randall, accessed 2 Feb 2017, http://academic.udayton.edu/health/01status/mental01.htm.

66. Vanessa Jackson, "In Our Own Voices," accessed 2 Feb. 2017, http://academic.udayton.edu/health/01status/mental01.htm.

67. Millon, Part III "Neuroscientific Stories," in *Masters of the Mind,* 159–245.

68. Shorter, *History of Psychiatry* , 26.

69. Lieberman and Ogas, *Shrinks*, 26.

70. Ibid., 49–87.

71. Ibid., 61–72.

72. Ibid., 72.

73. Ibid.

74. Ibid., 73.

75. Ibid., 85.

76. Ibid., 78. This occurred against the admonition of Freud himself. According to Lieberman, Freud cautioned against the use of psychoanalysis when dealing with those who struggled with severe mental illness, such as schizophrenia and manic-depressive illness, recognizing that his theories were less useful in these situations.

77. Lieberman, *Shrinks*, 50.

78. Asquith, *The Concise Dictionary of Pastoral Care and Counseling*, 68.

79. Ibid., 68.

80. Ibid., 52; E. Brooks Holifield, *A History of Pastoral Care in America: From Salvation to Self Realization* (Nashville: Abingdon, 1983), 16.

81. Asquith, *The Concise Dictionary of Pastoral Care and Counseling*, 52.

82. It should be noted that Holifield is neither a pastoral theologian nor a pastoral care practitioner, but a historian.

83. Holifield, *A History of Pastoral Care in America*, 16.

84. It is significant to mention that there are a considerable dearth of resources which endeavor to trace the history of pastoral care. Among the few volumes are those of John T. McNeill, *A History of the Cure of Souls* (New York: Harper Collins, 1977); William A. Clebsch and Charles R. Jaekle, *Pastoral Care in Historical Perspective*, revised edition (Lanham, MD: Jason Aronson, 1994); Thomas C. Oden, *Pastoral Theology: Essentials of Ministry* (New York: HarperOne, 1983); Seward Hiltner, *Pastoral Counseling* (New York: Abingdon-Cokesbury, 1949); and Holifield, *History of Pastoral Care*.

85. Holifield, *A History of Pastoral Care in America*, 222.

86. Asquith, *A Concise Dictionary of Pastoral Care*, 68.

87. Seward Hiltner, a student of Boisen and an American Presbyterian minister and pastoral theologian, published at least ten books and more than five hundred articles on pastoral care, including *Pastoral Counseling* (1949) and *Preface to Pastoral Theology* (1958). Hiltner was influential in bringing themes from Rogerian psychology into pastoral care, although he was careful to differentiate between pastoral care and psychology.

88. Browning, *Religious and Ethical Factors*, 4.

89. Donald Capps, *Fragile Connections: Memoirs of Mental Illness for Pastoral Care Professionals* (St. Louis: Chalice Press, 2005); Capps, *Understanding Psychosis: Issues and Challenges for Sufferers, Families, and Friends*; Harold G. Koenig *Faith and Mental Health: Religious Resources for Healing*. (Philadelphia: Templeton Foundation Press, 2005); Albers et al., *Ministry with Persons with Mental Illness and Their Families*; Collins and Culbertson, *Mental Illness and Psychiatric Treatment*; Charry, *Mental Health Skills for Clergy*; Joseph W. Ciarrocchi, *A Minister's Handbook of Mental Disorders* (New York: Paulist, 1993).

90. Boisen's own struggle with mental illness has been chronicled in memoir, *Out of the Depths: An Autobiographical Study of Mental Disorder and Religious Experience* (New York: Harper, 1960) which he wrote in his eighties. Though he was originally diagnosed with schizophrenia of the catatonic type, Boisen's diagnosis is the subject of much debate. What is known, however, is that he underwent multiple psychotic episodes, which landed him in different psychiatric hospitals, including (but not limited to) Boston Psychopathic Hospital and Westboro State Hospital. Boisen used his memoir to reflect on his own experience of mental illness from both a psychological and a religious lens. As such, he explores the causes of his own mental illness, offering both religious and psychological interpretations for his ideas of grandiosity and psychotic episodes.

91. See Capps, *Fragile Connections* and James Dittes, *Turning Points in Pastoral Care: The Legacy of Anton Boisen and Seward Hiltner* (Grand Rapids, MI: Baker Book House, 1990).

92. Asquith, *The Concise Dictionary*, 40.

93. Ibid. The statement by Boisen is also reminiscent of the theory of Carl Jung, further demonstrating the influence of psychoanalysis on the field.

94. Richard C. Cabot and Russell L. Dicks, *The Art of Ministering to the Sick* (New York; MacMillan, 1936).

95. In his seminal work, *Fundamental Practical Theology* (Minneapolis: Augsburg, 1991), Don Browning comments on the place of practical theology in seminaries. This clinical paradigm was the result of a dialogue between (and integration of) the fields of psychology and theology. It was characterized by individual relationships between caregivers and care seekers. Later scholars, particularly feminist and womanist scholars of pastoral care, argued that this model was reflective of the dominant culture (white, male, heterosexual, and liberal Protestant). As feminist and womanist scholars of pastoral care began to emphasize the importance of communal contextual and intercultural paradigms, they challenged this clinical model to incorporate an attention to dynamics of race, class, culture, power, globalization and alternative clinical methods and training. For more on this, see Nancy Ramsay, ed. *Pastoral Care and Counseling: Redefining the Paradigms* (Nashville, TN: Abingdon, 2004).

96. See Capps, *Fragile Connections*, 1. Capps does note that there are some quality books for practitioners. These will be explored in the third section of this chapter.

97. See Christie Cozad Neuger, *Counseling Women: A Narrative, Pastoral Approach* (Minneapolis, MN: Augsburg Press, 2001) for an exploration of a systemic analysis of depression. For examples of the importance of historical, cultural and social analysis and the ways this can become manifest in unique experiences of trauma, anger and grief and in the lives of African American women, see Beverly R. Wallace, "A Womanist Legacy of Trauma, Grief and Loss: Reframing the Notion of the Strong Black Woman Icon," in *Women Out of Order: Risking Change and Creating Care in a Multicultural World*, eds. Jeanne Stevenson-Moessner and Teresa Snorton (Minneapolis: Fortress, 2010); Jacqueline Kelley, "Womanist Pastoral Care Using Narrative Therapy in Addressing Multicultural Issues" in *Women Out of Order* (2010); and Teresa E. Snorton, "What About All Those Angry Black Women?" in *Women Out of Order* (2010).

98. A psychological approach which is based on the ideas of Freud and his followers, particularly Jung, Adler and Erickson. The primary components of this approach are the existence of an unconscious, which is the origin of much behavior and emotion, and a view of personality as composed of the ego, id, and the superego. Behavior, in this model, is motivated by two instinctual drives: Eros (the sex drive and life instinct) and Thanatos (the aggressive drive and death instinct). This model also includes the presence of defense mechanisms, which surface when the parts of the unconscious (the id and the superego) come into conflict with the conscious (ego) part of the person.

99. Lieberman and Ogas, *Shrinks*, 88.

100. Ibid., 89.

101. Ibid.

102. Ibid., 88.

103. American Statistical Association to House of Representatives, 1843.

104. Washington, *Medical Apartheid*, 148.

105. Ibid., 148.

106. The forerunner of the American Psychological Association.

107. The Standard became the direct forerunner to the DSM.

108. See Hannah Dekker, *The Making of the DSM III: A Diagnostic Manual's Conquest of American Psychiatry* (New York: Oxford University Press, 2013); Lieberman and Ogas, *Shrinks*, 135.

109. Lieberman and Ogas, *Shrinks*, 136.

110. Ibid., 139.

111. Ibid., 145.

112. For a more detailed version of the process by which this occurred, see Hannah Dekker *The Making of the DSM III*, and *Shrinks*, 87–149.

113. Fernando, *Mental Health, Race and Culture*, 32.

114. Ibid., particularly chapters 2 and 3.

115. Holifield, *A History of Pastoral Care in America*, and Susan Myers-Shrink, *Helping the Good Shepherd: Pastoral Counseling in a Psychotherapeutic Culture (1925–1975)* (Baltimore: John Hopkins University Press, 2009)

116. It should be noted that more theologically conservative professors of pastoral care rejected the clinical model, as well as diagnostic categories proposed by Pruyser, suggesting that pastoral care had lost its theological foundation.

117. Townsend has authored such foundational works as *Introduction to Pastoral Counseling* (Nashville, TN: Abingdon, 2009), *Pastoral Care in Suicide* (Nashville, TN: Abingdon Press, 2006), and *Pastoral Care With Stepfamilies: Mapping the Wilderness* (Atlanta: Chalice Press, 2000).

118. See Loren Townsend, "Best Practices: Rethinking Pastoral Diagnosis," *Sacred Spaces: The E-Journal of the American Association of Pastoral Counselors*, 5 (2013): 66–100.

119. Concerning mental illness in particular, Oates authored a number of works, including *The Religious Care of the Psychiatric Patient* (Philadelphia: Westminster, 1978), *When Religion Gets Sick* (Philadelphia: Westminster: 1970), and numerous other books and articles.

120. An example of this would be Oates' book *Religious Care of the Psychiatric Patient*, in which he relates that he embraces "the clinical approach to religious care of psychiatric patients." See chapter 1, 9–24.

121. Townsend, "Best Practices: Rethinking Pastoral Diagnosis," 76.

122. This is evident particularly in Wayne Oates, *Behind the Masks: Personality Disorders in Religious Behavior* (Philadelphia: Westminster, 1987)

123. Edgar Draper, *Psychiatry and Pastoral Care* (Englewood Cliffs, NJ: Prentice Hall, 1965).

124. Ibid., 31.

125. See Frank Lake, *Clinical Theology: A Theological and Psychiatric Basis to Clinical Pastoral Care.* (London: Darton Longman and Todd, 1965).

126. Townsend, "Best Practices: Rethinking Pastoral Diagnosis," 74.

127. Paul Pruyser, *Minister as Diagnostician* (Philadelphia: Westminster, 1976), 58.

128. Townsend, "Best Practices: Rethinking Pastoral Diagnosis," 75.

129. Ibid., 76.

130. Included in this category would be William Oglesby, *Biblical Themes for Pastoral Care* (Nashville, TN: Abingdon, 1980); Archie Smith Jr., *The Relational Self : Ethics and Therapy from a Black Church Perspective* (Nashville, TN: Abingdon Press, 1982); Edward Wimberly, *Using Scripture in Pastoral Counseling* (Nashville, TN: Abingdon, 1994); Merle Jordan, *Taking on the Gods* (Eugene, OR: Wipf and Stock, 2001); John Patton, *Pastoral Counseling: A Ministry of the Church* (Eugene, OR: Wipf and Stock, 1983).

131. Ramsay, *Pastoral Diagnosis*, 9.

132. Ibid., 2.

133. Ibid., 9.

134. Ibid., 2.

135. Ibid., 3.

136. Ibid., 7.

137. Carol Wise relies on ego psychology and theology to propose a model that hinged on ego processes, see Carol Wise, *Pastoral Psychotherapy: Theory and Practice* (New York: Jason Aronson, 1980). DeMarinis has constructed a model that utilizes feminist developmental psychology and feminist theology to guide diagnosis, see Valerie DeMarinis *Critical Caring: A Feminist Model for Pastoral Psychology* (Louisville, KY: Westminster/John Knox, 1993). Larry Kent Graham builds on the intersection of liberation theology and family systems theory in his contextual pastoral assessment, see Larry Kent Graham, *Care of Persons, Care of Worlds: A Psychosystems Approach* (Nashville, TN: Abingdon, 1992).

138. Townsend, "Best Practices: Rethinking Pastoral Diagnosis," 77.

139. Ibid., 78.

140. Townsend cites several studies within psychiatry and psychology to support this claim. See Townsend, "Best Practices, Rethinking Pastoral Diagnosis," 78.

141. Ibid., 83.

142. Ibid.

143. Ibid., 84.

144. Ibid.

145. Ibid., 86.

146. Ibid., 94.

147. Ibid.

148. Castellano Turner and Bernard M. Kramer, "Connections Between Racism and Mental Health," in *Mental Health, Racism and Sexism,* eds. Charles V. Willie et al. (Pittsburgh: University of Pittsburgh Press, 1995), 7.

149. Turner and Kramer, "Connections Between Racism and Mental Health," 9.

150. Ibid.

151. Ibid., 11.

152. John Townsend, "Racial, Ethnic and Mental Illness Stereotypes," in *Mental Health, Racism and Sexism* , eds. Charles V. Willie et al. (Pittsburgh: University of Pittsburgh Press, 1995), 129.

153. Vigen, *Women, Ethics and Inequality in U.S. Healthcare "To Count Among the Living,* 2–3, quoting Shankar Vendantam, "Racial Disparities Found in Pinpointing Mental Illness" *The Washington Post*, June 28, 2005.

154. See Townsend, "Racial, Ethnic and Mental Illness," 134.

155. Ibid., 133.

156. Ibid.

157. It should be noted that these studies took place prior to the 2010 Patient Protection and Affordable Care Act, which positively impacted issues of access to behavioral health services. However, an April 2015 report by the National Alliance on Mental Illness asserted that people with severe mental illness still face significant barriers to mental health care coverage, including high rates of denial for mental health care, and soaring costs of psychotropic drugs. For more information see the Public Policy Report "A Long Road Ahead," on website for the National Alliance for Mental Illness, accessed Feb. 2017. https://www.nami.org/About-NAMI/Publications-Reports/Public-Policy-Reports/A-Long-Road-Ahead/2015-ALongRoadAhead.pdf.

158. Vigen, *Women, Ethics and Inequality in U.S. Healthcare*, 3.

159. Ibid., 3.

160. Elaine (Hilberman) Carmen, "Inner-City Community Mental Health: The Interplay of Abuse and Race in Chronic Mentally Ill Women," in *Mental Health, Racism and Sexism* , eds. Charles V. Willie et al. (Pittsburgh: University of Pittsburgh Press, 1995), 219.

161. She asserts that Freud's renunciation of the seduction theory affected children by erroneously portraying the child as a sexual being, thus justifying sexual violence against children. The abandonment of the seduction theory and the resultant adoption of the Oedipus complex revealed three things: "1. Sexual molestation and abuse were infrequent 2. Children are not deeply scarred by abuse in later life and, most importantly 3. Children often lie about abuse." Elizabeth Pleck, *Domestic Tyranny* (Urbana: University of Illinois Press, 2004), 154.

162. Pleck, *Domestic Tyranny*, 159.

163. While Karen Horney attempted to propose a corrective to Deutsch by reframing masochism in light of societal factors, including misogyny and women's economic dependence on men, it was Deutsch's theory that had the most impact, as evidenced in the articles on the psychology of the rape victim that began to appear in the 1940s. See Pleck, *Domestic Tyranny*, 159.

164. Pleck, *Domestic Tyranny*, 163.

165. Carmen, "Inner-City Community Mental Health,"221.

166. Ibid., 220.

167. For a summary of several supporting studies, see Carmen, "Inner-city Community Mental Health," 221.

168. Carmen, "Inner-City Community Mental Health," 221.

169. Ibid., 223.

170. Ibid.

171. Ibid., 224.

172. Ibid., 230.

173. Townsend, "Racial, Ethnic and Mental Illness," 128.

174. Townes, *Breaking the Fine Rain*, 107.

175. The report was entitled *The Women's Health Report of the Public Health Service Task Force on Women's Health Issues* (1985), it was commissioned by the Assistant Secretary of Health of the Public Health Service (PHS) in 1983.

176. Townes, *Breaking the Fine Rain*, 110.

177. Townes, quoting Eileen Nechas and Denise Foley, *Unequal Treatment: What You Don't know about How Women Are Mistreated by the Medical Community* (New York: Simon and Schuster, 1994), 35.

178. Townes, *Breaking the Fine Rain*, 112.

179. Deborah Belle, "Poverty and Woman's Mental Health," *American Psychologist* 45.3 (1990): 385.

180. See C.R. Farnham, A. M. Zipple, W. Tyrrell, and P. Chittinanda, "Health status risk factors of people with severe and persistent mental illness," *Journal of Psychosocial Nursing*

Mental Health Service 37.6 (1999): 16–21, and J. Lynch, G. Kaplan, and S. Shema, "Cumulative Impact of Sustained Economic Hardship on Physical Cognitive Psychological and Social Functioning," *New England Journal of Medicine* 337.26 (1997): 1889–95. Lynch, Kaplan, and Shema used a sample of 2,730 adults over a seventeen-year period, found that those with the longest history of economic hardship had greater odds of having high levels of depression.

181. Lynn Bye and Jamie Partridge, "Factors Affecting Mental Illness Hospitalization Rates: Analysis of State-level Panel Data," *The Social Science Journal* 40.1 (2003): 33–47, 40.

182. R. Warner, *Recovery from Schizophrenia* (New York: Routledge, 1994).

183. Bye and Partridge, "Factors Affecting Mental Illness Hospitalization Rates," 44.

184. Townes, *Breaking the Fine Rain of Death*, 119.

185. In 1976, Even Johnstone found that the brains of schizophrenic patients have enlarged lateral ventricles (a pair of chambers within the brain that contain cerebrospinal fluid and nourish the brain). For more see Lieberman and Ogas, *Shrinks*, 210.

186. Lieberman and Ogas, *Shrinks*, 310.

187. Ibid., 306.

188. Charles B. Nemeroff and Daniel Weinberger, "The DSM Controversy. Tablet from Mt. Siani: A Step Backward or the Natural Progression of Advances in Medicine?" in *DSM 5: A Collection of Psychiatrist Views on the Changes, Controversies and Future Directions* (BMC Medicine, 2013), accessed September 2016, https://bmcmedicine.biomedcentral.com/articles/10.1186/1741-7015-11-202.

189. Nemeroff and Weinberger reveal that though the genes of various psychiatric diagnoses may overlap, this pattern also exists in such divergent clinical conditions as multiple sclerosis and Crohn's disease. For more see Nemeroff and Weinberger, "The DSM Controversy."

190. Lieberman and Ogas, *Shrinks*, 285.

191. It is notable that, according to Lieberman, this decision was a departure from the previous chairs' commitments to transparency and engagement.

192. Such as the National Alliance for the Mentally Ill, Autism Speaks, and the American Foundation for Suicide Prevention.

193. Spitzer and Frances authored an open letter to the APA Trustees published in the online section and followed with numerous articles in a variety of forums, both academic and lay. See *Psychology Today* website, accessed February 2017, https://www.psychologytoday.com/blog/dsm5-in-distress/201012/spitzerfrances-letter-apa-trustees. Also see Allan Frances, "A Warning Sign on the Road to DSM-5: Beware of its Unintended Consequences," *Psychiatric Times*, June 26, 2009 and Frances, "DSM 5 is a Guide not Bible--Ignore its Ten Worst Changes," Dec 2. 2012, *Psychology Today* website, Accessed Feb 2017 https://www.psychologytoday.com/blog/dsm5-in-distress/201212/dsm-5-is-guide-not-bible-ignore-its-ten-worst-changes.

194. Nemeroff and Weinberer, "The DSM 5 Controversy."

195. Jeffrey A. Lieberman, Allan Frances, Robert Spitzer

196. Nemeroff and Weinberger, "The DSM 5 Controversy."

197. For example, see Alan F. Schatzberg, James H. Scully Jr, David J. Kupfer, and Darrel A. Regier, "Setting the Record Straight: A Response to Frances Commentary on DSM-5," *Psychiatric Times*, July 1, 2009.

198. Allen Frances, *Saving Normal: An Insider's Revolt and Out-of-control Psychiatric Diagnosis, DSM-5, Big Pharma and the Medicalization of Normal Life* (New York: William Marrow, 2013).

199. Frances, *Saving Normal*, 77–117.

200. Ibid., 89–91.

201. Ibid., 139–69.

202. Townsend, "Best Practices: Rethinking Pastoral Diagnosis," 90.

203. Scholars such as Robert Albers, Joseph Ciarrocchi, Gregory B. Collins, Thomas Culbertson, and Donald Capps fall into this category.

204. Albers et al., *Ministry with Persons with Mental Illness*, 7.

205. Their findings are recorded in Donald Capps and Nathan S. Carlin "Mental Illness Publications in Major Pastoral Care Journals from 1950 to 2003," *Pastoral Psychology* 55.5 (2007): 593–99.

206. Capps and Carlin, "Mental Illness Publications," 597.

207. Ibid., 597–98.

208. See Stephen Pattison, *Liberation Theology and Pastoral Care* (Cambridge: Cambridge University Press, 1994); Jeanne Stevenson Moessner, *In Her Own Time: Women and Developmental Issues in Pastoral Care* (Minneapolis, MN: 2000); Neuger, *Counseling Women*; Sheryl Kujawa-Holbrook, ed., *Injustice and the Care of Souls : Taking Oppression Seriously in Pastoral Care*. (Minneapolis, MN: Fortress 2009); and Joretta Marshall and Duane Bidwell, eds., *The Formation of Pastoral Counselors: Challenges and Opportunities* (New York: Haworth, 2006).

209. Miller-McLemore and Gill-Austern, *Feminist and Womanist Pastoral Theology*.

210. See Neuger, *Counseling Women*; Doehring, *The Practice of Pastoral Care*; Kujawa-Holbrook, *Injustice and the Care of Souls*.

211. See Neuger, *Counseling Women*; Pamela Cooper-White, *Shared Wisdom: Use of the Self in Pastoral Counseling* (Minneapolis: Augsburg, 2004).

212. Miller-McLemore and Gill-Austern, *Feminist and Womanist Pastoral Theology*, 15.

213. Kathleen Greider, Gloria Johnson, and Kristen Leslie, "Three Decades of Women Writing for their Lives," in Miller-McLemore and Gill-Austern, *Feminist and Womanist Pastoral Theology*.

214. Greider et al., "Three Decades," 46–48.

215. This will be explored further in chapter 4

216. According to Harriet MacMillan, "Trauma-related and Stressor-related Disorders," in *DSM 5: A Collection* BMC Medicine (2013), accessed in September 2016 https://bmcmedicine.biomedcentral.com/articles/10.1186/1741-7015-11-202. The DSM 5 moved PTSD and acute stress disorders away from Anxiety Disorders to a new stand-alone chapter: Trauma-and-Stressor-Related Disorders (TSRD). She also notes that the three major symptom-related clusters for PTSD have been revised to four clusters, and that this is due to an increasing recognition that PTSD symptoms go beyond fear based anxiety, including dysphoria, aggression, guilt and shame. The DSM 5 also includes a new PTSD subtype, PTSD for Children 6 Years and Younger.

217. Christie Cozad Neuger, "Narratives of Harm," in *In Her Own Time: Women and Developmental Issues in Pastoral Care*, ed. Jeanne Stevenson-Moessner (Minneapolis, MN: Augsburg Press 2000), 84.

218. Beverly R. Wallace, "A Womanist Legacy of Trauma, Grief and Loss," in Stevenson-Moessner and Snorton, *Women Out of Order*, 50.

219. Traci West, *Wounds of the Spirit : Black Women, Violence and Resistance Ethics*. (New York: NYU Press, 1999), 124.

220. West, *Wounds of the Spirit,* 124. Chapter Four of this book addresses this in greater detail.

221. Sheryl Kujawa-Holbrook, "Love and Power: Antiracist Pastoral Care," in *Injustice and the Care of Souls: Taking Oppression Seriously in Pastoral Care,* eds. Sheryl Kujawa-Holbrook and Karen B. Mantagno (Minneapolis, MN: Augsburg Press 2009), 13.

222. Kujawa-Holbrook, "Love and Power," 16.

223. Ibid., 18.

224. Joseph L. Graves, Jr., *The Emperor's New Clothes: Biological theories of Race at the Millennium* (New Brunswick, NJ: Rutgers University, 2002), 5.

225. Graves, *The Emperor's New Clothes*, 8.

226. Ibid., 9.

227. Gold and Gold. *Suspicious Minds*, 13.

228. Link, "Understanding Labeling Effects," 96–112; Jo C. Phelan, Bruce G. Link, Ann Stueve, and Bernice A. Pescosolido, "Public Conceptions of Mental Illness in 1950 and 1996: What Is Mental Illness and Is It To Be Feared?" *Journal of Health and Social Behavior* 41.2 (2000): 188–207; P. Roman and H. Floyd Jr., "Social Acceptance of Psychiatric Illness and Psychiatric Treatment," *Social Psychiatry* 16.1 (1981):16–21.

229. Patrick W. Corrigan and Amy C. Watson, "Understanding the Impact of Stigma on People with Mental Illness," *World Psychiatry* Feb 1.1 (2002): 16-20.

Chapter Two

Voices of Chaplains

Seeing the "Whole Person"

Within the Western medical model, a psychiatric diagnosis in a psychiatric hospital functions as an analysis and interpretation by the practitioner of the presenting symptoms of the patient. As is evident in the previous chapter, these symptoms and signs are themselves evaluations, first by the patient (in reporting them), and then by the psychiatrist (in interpreting them). Suman Fernando, in *Mental Health, Race and Culture* (2010), suggests that the process of diagnosis can be seen as a comparison between the patient's feelings, behaviors and beliefs and the predominant values within the discipline of psychiatry.[1] As we have noted, the current values within psychiatry have been informed by numerous factors, including (but not limited to) the conception of mental illness and its treatment, which is directly related to and expressive of the named and hidden values of society as a whole. To speak about psychiatric diagnosis, therefore, is to heed the words of Fernando, that diagnosis bears the marks of the culture of which it is a product: "First, it is ethnocentric and carries in it the ideologies of Western culture, including racism; second, the practice of psychiatry, including its ways of diagnosing, is influenced by the social ethos and the political system in which it exists and works."[2]

Practically, psychiatric diagnosis arises from "the need for the practitioner to be sufficiently informed about the patient"[3] in order to prescribe what she determines to be the appropriate treatment. It is, in essence, the process by which the psychiatrist comes to know the patient, in order to assess and treat the patient's maladies. Joan Busfield, in *Managing Madness* (2014), reveals that the process of gaining this "knowledge" is informed by the Western medical model, including deference to the role of naturalistic science, as well as a view of the human body as a series of "separate independent systems" in which ill-health is viewed as the failure of one or more of these systems.[4] The psychiatrist's attempt to know the patient occurs within this model and decisions about diagnosis and treatment tend to favor the presuppositions to which Busfield is referring. The process of psychiatric diagnosis can also frequently occur with little attention to overarching cultural realities that have shaped the patient's identity and informed her current mental health crisis. As related by Fernando, even practices such as the classification by race and/or ethnicity within the mental health field brings with it certain issues, including the tendency to see the individual as embodying a group identity that may be the result of historical prejudice, stereotypes and institutionalized attitudes. In this way, the person's individuality can be lost, as the woman is seen "not as an individual, but as a carrier of various qualities assumed to be inherent in the particular category of people."[5] Other problems, such as the collapsing of ethnicity and race, also limit the perspective of the practitioner.

Shifts within psychiatric diagnosis have influenced trends in pastoral care, and in chaplaincy in particular, as explored in the last chapter. The incorporation of psychological sciences into pastoral care, now considered a central component of chaplaincy theory and praxis, as well as the predominance of a clinical model of chaplaincy, can be directly traced to the rise of the psychological sciences and shifts in psychiatry. Yet how are these trends manifested in the on-the-ground ministry of chaplains with women in psychiatric institutions? What is their connection to the underlying Western medical model and to concepts of psychiatric diagnosis?

Chaplains also engage in varied approaches that allow them to know the patient, namely a woman with mental illness for purposes of this study. Chaplains build on their relationship with the woman to determine the "central issue" or "what is really going on" and how they should proceed. Yet how do chaplains go about this process of knowing the patient and determining her needs? What are their guiding values, personal and social cues, and assumptions? What is absent from or otherwise obscures or hinders their analyses? The following two chapters will listen to the viewpoints of eighteen chaplains doing ministry at state psychiatric institutions in order to probe the ways that they embody and integrate cultural, social, and personal perspectives in their ministry.[6] These voices are important as chaplains' stories about their encounters with women ultimately provide a window into the ways that they both attempt to integrate, and struggle with integrating, wider social and political issues of justice. These voices are essential in advancing a notion of ethical pastoral care, because they provide the ground from which one can observe both the attention to and incorporation of issues of justice, as well as the gaps that one must address to advance a notion of ethical pastoral care.

The chaplains who were interviewed for this study represented different ages, genders, races, sexual orientations and education levels. Yet the chaplains were united around one assertion: their calling to see, in their words, the "whole person"[7] in a system (or on a team) that frequently engaged in a reductionist understanding of the person. For many chaplains, however, this assertion of seeing the whole person paradoxically coexisted alongside encounters with patients in which dynamics of race and/or class were difficult to address and/or "invisible." This chapter will probe the methods by which chaplains endeavored to see and know the "whole person," as well as the variety of underlying assumptions that frame their work. It will inquire about the cultural and political understandings that may inform them and ways that these assumptions interact with concepts and systems of diagnosis.

The following chapter (chapter three) will examine the relationship between psychiatric diagnosis and the assessment of psychiatric chaplains. It will discuss the role of their training and the techniques at their disposal and will explore connections between their assessments and the relationship between science and theology. It will also question the origins of their favored pastoral techniques and probe for similarities with scholars and practitioners of pastoral care. Together, these two chapters will ultimately examine the chaplains' method for making sense of diagnosis with its multivalent dimensions.

SITES

The Division of Mental Health and Addiction Services in the northeastern state[8] which I am investigating operates three psychiatric hospitals and one forensic center. The three hospitals are located in the northern, central and southern parts of the state, and offer services to those people within the pertinent geographic area. In this study I chose to visit and interview chaplains in the three psychiatric hospitals.[9]

The northern psychiatric hospital, which I will refer to as Violet Hospital, was opened in 2008 and currently has 450 beds, plus another sixty in cottages on the grounds of the hospital. It was constructed after an older hospital on these same grounds was investigated and condemned for the dilapidated state of the building, overcrowding, and various reports of assaults and other violations of patient rights. This newer hospital is considered state of the art, featuring keyless, electronic entry-ways and a wing with dedicated computer classes, art and music therapies, and other innovative approaches to group therapy. In terms of pastoral care, this hospital has a multi-faith meditation room that seats about fifteen people.

The psychiatric hospital in the central part of the state, which I will refer to as Oak Hospital, is a 450-bed hospital serving the mid-state area. It was founded by Dorothea Dix, a lifelong activist and advocate for the mentally ill, in the 1840s and retains many of the original buildings (although not all are in use). This hospital has a devoted "chaplaincy wing" as part of a larger building, which includes a chapel, chaplaincy offices, and a social space/meeting room.

The psychiatric hospital in the southern part of the state is a 532 active (709 capacity) bed hospital. I will refer to this hospital as Finch Hospital. Built in 1955, it rests on 650 acres of land. It also has a number of separate buildings and outdoor space. In terms of pastoral care, this building has a Christian chapel that is separate from other buildings and seats approximately 150. Chaplaincy offices are connected to this chapel, which remains open as long as two chaplains are present.

Visiting the Hospitals: First Impressions

The first hospital I visited, Violet Hospital, is the one in which I currently work. While I have worked there for a number of years, I will never forget the first time I entered the door, and the ways in which this particular environment has the capacity to evoke a number of emotions. While this hospital is technically located in a fairly populous part of its northeastern state, like its older counterpart, it is set back from the city of its ZIP code by numerous acres and rolling hills. In fact, in approaching the hospital, one might think she was on her way for a hike, or at least to a park. The hospital itself is up on a hill, mostly hidden from the streets that circle it. It boasts a parking lot that is the size of a small shopping area, with a welcoming, spacious, glass-plated entrance. On entering the building, one is struck by the locked doors. Though appearing inviting, one must have a badge for the sliding glass doors to open. Ringing the buzzer, I made myself known and was let in.

The process of attaining a badge was laborious and intensive. The desk was staffed by men and women in security uniforms. They inquired who I was there to see and promptly called the unit to confirm my appointment. Meanwhile, I had to produce proof of identity and have my picture taken. I then needed to log in, confirming both the time and date I had arrived, before being given a "loaner badge." I was then told to wait on a bench in the lobby.

The lobby attempted to be inviting. Semi-comfortable chairs flanked the walls and a roped-off player piano graced the entrance. Patients drifted in and out of the space, some murmuring to themselves, others lost in their own world. A few came over to inspect the newcomer: "Hey lady, who are you?" "Why you here?"

The first impression of this hospital stands in contrast to the two other hospitals, both of which were distinctly older and covered more acres of ground. Both of the other hospitals had more of a campus feel, complete with green space and (once) beautiful buildings. The hospital in the mid-state area,

Oak Hospital, was encircled with high walls and populated with red-bricked buildings reminiscent of the 1800s. As I entered this complex, I was given directions to park "by the abandoned building." I followed the circular drive around a stately building until I reached a building that could have been out of a horror movie. Windows were shattered and doorways were boarded up. Once majestic archways were crumbling and in disrepair. I walked past this building to enter the other, similar-looking building, in slightly better shape. As I was buzzed in the building, I was greeted by a narrow hallway with a security desk. I gave the name of the person I was visiting. I then needed to show identification and receive a visitor's tag. I stood awkwardly in narrow hallway, which boasted two dilapidated folding chairs against the wall, until I was greeted by the chaplain I had come to see.

The complex in the southern part of the state, Finch Hospital, seemed miles away from the nearest small town. Down a long stretch of highway flanked by cornfields, it was tucked away in a remote part of the state. It had the feeling of a sprawling campus, with squat square buildings encircling the gothic main building. At the gate to this complex, I needed to give my name and be cleared to enter the property. As I explained the reason for my visit, the guard gave me a badge and wrote down my license plate. He then offered very convoluted directions to "the chapel." I felt like I was driving through something between a college campus and a prison complex as I wound through parking lots and functionally-styled buildings to attempt to find the place where I was supposed to park. I finally recognized what looked like a chapel and parked in a lot nearby. As I got out of my car, patients, lounging on picnic tables in the sun, called out to me, asking me where I was going. When I responded with, "the chapel," some pointed me in the correct direction. Others questioned me about why I was present.

A commonality among the three hospitals was the emphasis on security. Across these hospitals, every door was locked and could only be opened with a badge and/or a key. This included not only the doors leading onto the locked wards, but also the doors separating hallways and leading into offices. At Violet Hospital, I had access to all of the locked doors because of my status as an employee. At Oak Hospital, though I was given a badge, I was not given keys and could not open most of the doors. At Finch Hospital, I was given only a nametag and could not open any of the doors.

In spite of that commonality, the differences among these hospitals did not stop with the external buildings. The chaplaincy department at each of these hospitals also differed in the amount and layout of devoted chaplaincy space. I soon realized that the devoted chaplaincy space actually said a lot about the position of chaplaincy vis-a-vis the hospital. In Violet Hospital, chaplaincy mostly occurred on the units, with one-on-one meetings and spirituality groups frequently happening in the rooms on the unit reserved for clinical groups. These chaplains sat on the treatment teams on the units and saw themselves as clinical members of the team. Violet Hospital also had the least amount of dedicated chaplaincy space, with only a multi-faith meditation room that seats about fifteen. In conversations with the staff at this hospital, they articulated that the meditation room was rarely used for the occasional group or one-on-one meeting. As it was not large enough to be used for weekly services, these services were either held in the courtroom or the auditorium. This presented difficulties, as the courtroom was also the place where patients were committed and where they could be mandated to comply with psychiatric medication, and the auditorium was a cavernous, multi-purpose space that allowed the patients to spread out so much that the worship experience lacked any positive sense of connection with the divine or each other.

The meditation room itself was an oddly shaped room which only the chaplains could access. It was painted a calming green, in contrast to the stark white walls of the rest of the hospital. The room itself, however, lacked a unifying theme. A tapestry of the symbols of the world religions hung on one wall, an abandoned communion rail graced the other. In yet another corner was a screen/barrier that was probably previously used in the sacrament of confession—ostensibly rescued from the chapel in the previous building before its demolition—now out of context and begging for explanation. When meeting with chaplains in this space, it was commonplace to have to re-arrange the plastic chairs in a formation that was more amenable to conversation; indeed, they related that this was often the case, even with patient meetings and other events. The room itself was also not soundproof, frequently one could overhear snipets of conversations in the hallway, food carts moving back and forth, and doors opening and closing. While it attempted to be a space "set apart," it seemed very difficult to forget that one was in a psychiatric hospital.

In the chaplaincy department in Oak Hospital, chaplaincy occurred both on the units and in a wing that was devoted to chaplaincy. The chaplaincy wing contained offices for both full-time and part-time chaplains, a dedicated meeting space, and a makeshift worship space. Chaplains related that they had responsibilities that occurred in both settings. Some of the chaplains viewed themselves as part of the treatment team and attended treatment team meetings on their units. Other chaplains, however, voiced views that they were "separate from" the team and stated that this was advantageous to them and to the patients. The chaplaincy wing at Oak Hospital was robust enough to house a ministry: it boasted a large room that had been purposed as a meeting space—complete with a few older couches, bookshelves with religious books, a number of tables, and a hospitality station. In a larger open space at the end of a hallway was a makeshift worship space, arrayed by metal chairs in rows, and flanked at one end by an altar covered in a tapestry. No religious symbols, however, were visible, and the windows around the outside of the space and the tiled walls were more reminiscent of a high school from the New Deal era than a worship space. I was told that the meeting space was used for chaplaincy groups, while the worship space was used for services. Indeed, as I waited in the meeting space, a patient meandered in and asked if I was leading a spirituality group. I declined, but pointed her to the office of the other chaplains.

At Finch Hospital, the chaplains had a history of sitting in on treatment team meetings. About five years ago, however, chaplains were removed from the treatment team and relegated to spirituality groups and religious services. The Director of Pastoral Care position was discontinued, prompting a reorganization that required the pastoral care department to report to the Director of Rehabilitation. All of the chaplains at this institution expressed dismay with this decision and spoke at length about the ways that they felt devalued as a professional, as well as the harm that this was causing patients. The feeling of being in conflict with the treatment team was heightened at this hospital, due to the fact that the chaplains were physically separate from the team. The dedicated chaplaincy space at Finch Hospital took the form of a free-standing chapel that seated a large number of people. The chapel, which can only be opened by chaplains, was a larger building set apart from the residence halls and other buildings. When walking in, I got the sense that I could have been entering a church circa 1950s, complete with the church lobby and bulletin board with faded announcements. Yet as I entered the worship space, it was also apparent that this space had been constructed as an explicitly Christian chapel, evidenced by wooden pews facing the sanctuary, complete with an altar and a large cross which hung from the ceiling. Stained glass windows lined the walls, and the cathedral ceiling spoke of a time when churches were built to embody the grandeur of God. I noticed that the chaplains had set up tables in the back of the church, attempting to use the space for both group meetings and worship. This, however, resulted in a disjointed feel. As I sat at one of the tables to meet with a chaplain, I frequently felt as if I should have been facing the front, out of respect for the space. The chaplains' offices were directly off of this chapel, which made them feel more like church employees and less like multi-faith chaplains. They complained of having to have two chaplains present "at all times." This policy had been put in place for safety and security should anyone want to use the chapel. In the words of one chaplain at this hospital, referring to this change in policy, "I wish it didn't shift, but a lot of times I think what happens is they . . . think that sometimes we're not, I don't know, I'm not gonna say 'important enough' or we don't have enough uh, clinical training. Or maybe they think, uh, it's not necessary."[10]

Who Are These Chaplains?

I interviewed eighteen chaplains in all,[11] with encounters that lasted approximately an hour each. The racial/ethnic breakdown of these chaplains were as follows: one African male, one African American male, one African American female, three white males and twelve white females. The ages of these chaplains ranged from twenty-five to seventy-three. In terms of education level, all except one chaplain had a college degree, the remainder had undergraduate degrees as well as masters in divinity or masters in theology or religious studies. Five of these chaplains had advanced education in psychology over and above their education in religion. All of these chaplains had at least two units of Clinical Pastoral Education, most had four units, and thirteen were board certified.

Seeing the Whole Person

These chaplains displayed a tremendous amount of diversity, not only in their race and ethnicity, but also in their opinions about the care of women with mental illness. Yet, there was one assertion around which all of the chaplains were united: their call to see the "whole person" in a system (or on a team) that frequently engaged in a reductionist understanding of the person.

For all of the chaplains interviewed, it was essential that the patient be treated with dignity and respect. While for some of the chaplains this took the form of an overt critique of the medical system in which they operated, for most chaplains, it was evidenced in their integrated view of the patient and their core assertion of the importance of the patient's humanity. This resulted in an opposition to anything that reduced this patient to a label, particularly that of psychiatric diagnosis. Chaplains, in their quest to see the entire person, also spoke of ending up in opposition to the interdisciplinary health care team of which they were a part, more commonly referred to as the treatment team. Many mentioned that the treatment team did not understand and/or value the work of chaplains; others told specific stories of their pastoral relationship bringing forth a "different side"[12] of the patient, and this being a point of contention and/or conflict with the treatment team.

Chaplains frequently spoke of seeing patients as a "whole person" worthy of dignity and respect.[13] They used such phrases as, "treating patients first as people,"[14] "helping the person recognize that they are a beloved child of God,"[15] and "treating them as I would like to be treated."[16] Alongside this, they spoke against what one chaplain termed a "categorical understanding, which limits the vastness of the person."[17] They admitted that it was challenging to attempt to see the fullness of each person in front of them. Chaplains also recognized the validity of other points of view about the patient, particularly those of the psychiatrists and/or psychologists: "Seeing someone as a whole person is recognizing that they are more than what I see/know."[18] This included recognizing the reality that while they might encounter the patient when she is in a "good space," the opinion of other team members was also valuable, even if this opinion was different that his/her own.

Yet, while every chaplain emphasized the importance of seeing the full humanity of the patient, very few chaplains (two out of eighteen) mentioned the medical model in which they operated. The two chaplains who mentioned the overarching medical model offered fairly robust critiques of it. In their opinion, this model tended to reduce patients to a diagnosis. One white female chaplain reflected: "I have a really holistic sense of what health is and I, it can, you know be frustrating to work in a medical model where diagnosis and medication are the primary framework that's used in discussion."[19] Another white female chaplain, in particular, in critiquing this model, drew parallels between the world of psychiatry and psychology and the spiritual world in she lived and worked:

> I have a fundamental understanding that the world of psychology and psychiatry is a world full of mystery, and actually as a spiritual and religious person, mystery is a concept that we are comfortable living in. As people of faith, we're people who can't empirically test things, but we believe it. In the same way, in the world of psychology and psychiatry, you can test empirically, obviously . . . but you also have . . . the human element. And we're talking about humans studying humans. . . . You can't do a blood test, for example, that tells someone exactly that they have schizophrenia. And so, it's a world full of mystery. And so, because I have that understanding, there's just a level of not, um, falling into the trap of labels. And not being presumptuous, and not, um, assuming that your religious expressions are hyper religious.[20]

This chaplain noted the constructed nature of all knowledge, including so-called "objective" medical knowledge. She also considered the gaps in knowledge: all knowledge contains an element of mystery, and must be approached with that in mind. Suggesting that the fields of psychology and psychiatry have more in common with spirituality and religion than other medical disciplines do, this enabled her to look beyond labels—not only that of diagnosis, but labels of religiosity as well.

While other chaplains did not specifically name the larger medical model, many noted that a diagnosis of mental illness was one piece of a larger, more complex reality. They spoke of mental illness as one component within the physical, emotional, and spiritual life of the patient, all of which were related to one another. Such terms as "holistic" and "wholeness" dominated these discussions, both in relationship to the health of the patient, and the goal of the interaction between themselves and the patient. When asked to define "holistic" as related to health, many chaplains voiced an integrated view, one which was attentive to all parts of the person, including (but not limited to) the spiritual. One white female chaplain offered the following explanation which was emblematic of this theme:

> Umm, yeah, I think health has a lot of different pieces. There's, you know, physical health. Do we feel well physically? Do we have any pain? Do we have any symptoms that we're experiencing physically? Umm, mental health is a little bit more ambiguous. It, you know, is how, how is our thinking and our mood affecting our daily life in some way? Is it manageable? Is it at a place where you can do the things you want to do from day to day? I think spiritual health is similarly kind of vague and ambiguous, but how are you able to connect with yourself or with others? How are you able to connect with the divine, or whatever your sense of a higher power may or may not be? But, I think connection is a big part of it for me in terms of spiritual health. Umm. And then, overall, just being able to live the life that someone would want to live. That that individual would want to live, I think is a piece of health. And I think my sense of holistic health is that all of those pieces interact with each other. You can't just isolate one and treat that. You have to be aware of how they work together.[21]

This holistic view existed alongside a recognition that, in the midst of such a complex reality, it was difficult to know where to begin the visit. Almost all of the chaplains spoke of "letting the patient take the lead." They saw their role as chaplains as broader than simply engaging the religious/spiritual dimension of the person. If the patient began the chaplaincy interaction with a physical complaint, they would engage on that issue; similarly if she began with an emotional or spiritual issue, they would follow her lead, as the following white woman expressed:

> Well, I mean, I think that as a chaplain we're called to really be concerned primarily with the spiritual. But, I think that all of the different components of a person are important. So if we're thinking about a person as integrated . . . So I consider a person as physical, emotional, and spiritual . . . all of those are interrelated. So, if there is someone who has umm let's say cancer. And, she's been traumatized. And she's got mental illness. So, there's a lot to deal with there. And umm I might just ask, "There's a lot going on right now. Is there one thing that you would like to concentrate on in this time?" So that it is more focused, but also acknowledging the . . . heaviness. And the . . . breadth of what some people deal with.[22]

The terms "holistic" and "wholeness" also made their way into conversations about the "goal" of the interaction. One chaplain said she preferred to think of the guiding question of the interaction as "What is this life we're working towards?"[23] This was echoed by a number of the chaplains, who spoke about the purpose of the interaction in terms of "the meaning of life, who we are, and where we are going"[24] or in the words of another chaplain, "What is important for them [the patients]? What do they want for themselves?"[25] A number of chaplains also noted that the patient's definition of wellness or wholeness may not be congruent with that of the treatment team. Chaplains offered different views on this dynamic; a couple said that they believed that the patient had the best sense of what she wanted for her life, others mentioned that they saw themselves as the advocate for the patient in the midst of the team.

Other chaplains spoke about wholeness as the relationship between religion/spirituality and mental health. For them, this meant that the goal of the interaction between themselves and the patient was to focus on spirituality as it related to mental health. A few spoke of wholeness as related to a sense of "hope and human potential" in the midst of systemic and personal challenges; that a goal of "wholeness" meant enabling the patient to access hope about her present state and her future.

For many chaplains, the "complex reality" that was the patient's health also included the larger systems which were at play in the life of the patient. For the chaplains who noted systemic factors, they tended to speak of the prevalence of trauma, which was frequently the result of violence against women; issues of power and powerlessness; intersecting experiences of racism, sexism, and classism within society; the gendered upbringing of women; and the challenges that come with reproduction and sexuality. The chaplains who mentioned these realities attempted to keep them in focus during the course of an interaction, and many times adopted an approach that was intersectional in nature.[26]

Frequently, the chaplains spoke of—and critiqued—the "treatment team." They admitted that they experienced "a heavy focus on illness,"[27] at the hands of the treatment team, and felt "misunderstood"[28] or "not valued."[29] They also spoke of "seeing the patient differently"[30] than the treatment team, which at times resulted in them being in conflict with this team.

Often, chaplains recognized that their particular approach resulted in a relationship with the patient that "looked different" from that of the treatment team. They frequently told stories about times when the patient had shared more intimately with them than she had with the team, or when they were privileged to be able to "see a different side of the patient."[31] Many times, the relationship between the chaplain and patient allowed for a more comprehensive understanding of the patient, enabling her access to services that were essential to her health. One African male chaplain spoke of a woman he had worked with who refused to see the gynecologist:

> V1: So I went and I talked with the patient. "Why do you want, Why don't you want to go for a physical check?" This patient explained how viciously she was raped . . . . Several times while she was a teenager. And she explained that . . . she wouldn't want . . . any man . . . Okay. This doctor is a man telling her she, uh, she needs a physical check. Okay? Observation and all the like.

> So, she says, "No. I'm not going to accept a man to come over me again!" Alright? So, now, I tell her, "Yeah, that is true. You, we, we didn't really understand. In the history, it didn't sh . . . really show that you were . . . raped. You are suffering from trauma . . . . And that, it has not been . . . it's not in your medical records. So why did you keep that for so long? "I didn't want to tell any man. Each person I met was a man."
> Interviewer: Wow. Yet, she told you.
> V1: Yeah. She said, "I didn't wanna meet a man. Each person I met was a man. Each person who wanted to interview me concerning my health was a man. I didn't want to tell this issue to a man. I just hate men." Alright. So, it is after . . . about three days of counseling . . . that we had to now sit in the treatment team and review her treatment. To, to actually go over . . . what she'd, she experienced, the trauma she experienced, and how she's facing it now. So, it took, it took our whole treatment team to convince her that uh, yes, we understand this issue, and this like this. So, "We'll get a female doctor to check you out. What about that?" It worked! So, it finally worked. She was still very uncomfortable with a female doctor to . . . to check her out, you know, but it worked.[32]

In this story, the unique relationship this woman had with the chaplain allowed her to share intimate knowledge with him, knowledge that was prohibiting her from accessing services that are essential for her ongoing bodily health. This interaction is interesting when viewed from both the perspective of the chaplain and that of the woman. One of the chaplain's first responses to the woman was that the information about this trauma was "not in the chart." This highlights an assumption that is characteristic of the Western medical model, that the chart includes the summation of all pertinent clinical information about a patient's life. The primacy and authority of "the chart" has obviously been internalized by this religious caregiver, as was evidenced in his surprise around the fact that such important, intimate information was absent from the chart. From the perspective of the woman, it is interesting that her trust in the chaplain loomed larger than his gender. The paradox of the patient's statement "I just hate men" while entrusting such a devastating detail of her life to the man across from her suggests that something about the relationship between her and the chaplain allowed the patient to share this intimate, horrifying event from her history. While the voice of this woman is not present for inquiry about what prompted her to trust the chaplain, it seems that this relationship ultimately enabled her to access medical care that was beneficial for her health. This crucial detail of her life—an experience of trauma that is essential when considering options for recovery—may have been invisible to the wider treatment team had her relationship with this chaplain not existed.

While this story exhibits a time when intimate knowledge about a woman in a psychiatric facility was accepted (and even encouraged) by the treatment team, more frequently chaplains felt that their particular knowledge of the patient—influenced not only by their assertion of the full humanity of the patient, but also by their engagement with the spiritual component of the patient's life—put them at odds with treatment team. One white female chaplain spoke of the experience of feeling like an "outsider" on the treatment team in regards to her particular view of mental health, as well as in her spiritual interventions with a difficult female patient:

> When, you know, I'm on a treatment team meeting with a patient and I'm hearing the way the doctors and the nurses are interacting with them, and I'm like, "Yeah, but . . . that's not the whole picture. That's not the only piece." Umm. I think like relationship issues and social issues are a piece that we don't often deal well with here in the institutional setting. That what's going on in their family relationships and with their friends has an effect on their mental health and we don't have a way for them to really . . . have a place for patients to talk through that, and help them see the connections between the different pieces of their lives . . . .
>
> I have one particular patient that I've been working with for . . . probably 6 or 8 months now, umm, just doing weekly, like, thirty-minute counseling sessions with her, and she's *very* disorganized. And very delusional, but her faith is really intertwined in her delusions. And one of the most reality-orienting things for her is if I say, "Okay, would you like to say a prayer together now?" And whatever she might be yelling or screaming, or responding to internal stuff, but if I say, "Would you like to pray with me?" she's right there with me in that moment. And it's so grounding for her. And that's a piece that I don't think the treatment team sees or is able to, to access with her.[33]

When questioned further about this event, particularly regarding this chaplain's relationship with the wider treatment team, this chaplain paused. She relayed that at one point this patient was on a unit with a treatment team with which she had a good relationship, but then the patient was moved. That made communication "more complicated." She found that she also wondered whether her weekly notes were attended to by the team:

> Now, do they read the notes that I put in every week? I don't know. But, I try to include that stuff in my documentation to make it clear that this is a resource for her. This isn't, you know, a religious delusion of some sort, but this is actually really grounding for her . . . . But I don't know if they read my notes.[34]

From this encounter, it is obvious that this chaplain feels that her more holistic view of the patient's mental health is not shared by the treatment team. This same team is "not able to access" the side of the patient that this chaplain sees when she engages in the spiritual practice of prayer. This chaplain wonders whether the team knows, or cares about, the insights that arise from her own interactions with the patient, interactions she finds to be crucial knowledge for this patient's well-being.

Stories like this abounded in many of the interviews, as well as notions that the team "doesn't appreciate,"[35] "doesn't understand,"[36] or "doesn't value"[37] the work of chaplains. Chaplains frequently spoke of being entrusted by patients with information that could aid the team in treatment, but either being dismissed or having difficulty communicating with the team. One African American male chaplain, in particular, articulated that his relationship with a female patient opened the door for her to share her suicidal ideations, an insight that he felt was simply overlooked:

> Was talking with her about her son. She loved the little boy. Cutest little kid. Um, but that they took the kid away from her. So that was traumatizing her, the fact that they took her kid. So, she kept talking with me about she wanted to die. So I just kept telling the treatment team, "You really need to look at her. She's, you know, she's pleasant. She's talking, you know, but she's telling me she wants to die." And they said, "Okay, thank you." I put it in her chart. And I made sure it was in there to cover my mind, cause, you know. And uhh, but within maybe two or three weeks after that, she started really acting out. And she started ripping signs down and she pulled a water fountain off the wall. She was a pretty big-sized girl. So, and, and, and, the whole time she kept doing this stuff she kept screaming, "I wanna die! I wanna see my son! I want to die, you know, if I can't have my son with me!" And that maybe could have been prevented if they'd maybe paid attention to some of the things that we say, you know?[38]

Chaplains who gave voice to the resistance of the treatment team toward them or their efforts, however, also recognized that this frequently necessitated that they become an advocate for the patient, as they may know more about the welfare of the patient than other members of the treatment team: "I find myself kind of just being a support and then an advocate as things come up. If I don't get information from the team, but then I get something from the patient, I can bring that to the team so they can be aware of . . . 'Oh she keeps complaining her foot is hurting.' 'Or going with her to talk with the nurse.'"[39] In fact, chaplains overwhelmingly spoke of the importance of being an advocate for the patient, either with the treatment team or in regard to discharge issues. In this way, the work of these chaplains extended beyond simply the spiritual or religious and instead was built on a particular view of spirituality that encompassed broader issues of justice for the patient.

A comparison of the views of these chaplains with those of scholars in the field yields insight into some of the dynamics brought up by these chaplains. John Swinton in his 2001 book *Spirituality and Mental Health Care: Rediscovering a 'Forgotten' Dimension* offers reflections on the role of spirituality in the care of those diagnosed with mental illness. His analysis offers insight as to possible reasons that these chaplains found themselves in conflict with the treatment team. Swinton argues that on the surface, spirituality appears to belong to a previous age, a way that no longer makes sense, given "our understanding of science and what constitutes the scientific truth and authentic knowledge that can be used to develop evidence-based caring practices."[40] Yet, while it appears that interest in spirituality is waning within Western society, [41] and in fact, may be fairly insignificant in the lives of many mental health service providers, he reveals that there is a rise in interest in spirituality in the lives of many with a diagnosis of mental illness.

Spirituality, however, is often pathologized or considered irrelevant by mental health providers. Swinton speaks to the influence of the medical model on mental health providers; in an "age of science" spiritual care has become associated with unverifiable "soft knowledge," as opposed to scientific "empirical" knowledge. As such, religion tends to represent "unverifiable values and beliefs," and cannot be relied upon to substantiate mental health care practices. Questions of spirituality—including issues of value, hope and meaning—are frequently excluded from the work of mental health professionals, as these professionals "look toward science as the 'new god' who can bring hope and temporal salvation in the midst of psychological storms."[42] Swinton refers to the current medical system as one of "insensitivity and spiritual blindness," arguing that the experiences of actual people with diagnoses of mental illness bear witness to spirituality as an element that fosters mental health, even in the midst of mental health problems.[43]

Swinton also explores what he considers to be the operative definition of spirituality, which he holds has migrated from the realm of religious traditions toward a more secular location. As such, the meaning of the term has broadened from something located within the structure of religious organizations toward "a more diffuse human need that can be met quite apart of institutionalized religious structures."[44] Spirituality, he argues, has become a multi-valent term with a diversity of definitions and understandings. Yet, he believes that spirituality has not become so diverse as to be meaningless; there are certain identifiable components that can be highlighted. It remains, however, that spirituality cannot be spoken of and categorized with the certainty of empirical sciences. In Swinton's reflections on spirituality and wholeness, he draws on Craig W. Ellison, professor of Counseling and Urban Studies at the Alliance Theological Seminary. Ellison defines the human spirit not simply as a component of the person, but also as "an integrative presence that permeates and vitalizes every aspect and every dimension of the human person."[45] Spirituality, in Swinton's view, recognizes that the person cannot be separated into mind, body, and emotions. Rather the person is an integrated being, who should be treated as such. For Swinton, this view has implications for mental health care, as "mental health problems are not entities that simply affect one dimension of the person: the mind. They are whole-person experiences that affect a person in every dimension of their existence."[46] Problems or issues in the psychological and spiritual realms can and do influence the physical realm, whereas spiritual problems can be manifested in one's somatic and emotional experience of illness (i.e., the lack of worth due to the stigmatization of those with mental illness can impact one's recovery and sense of self).

Swinton's description of the role of spirituality within the current medical system, as well as the reliance on science as the "new god," can shed some light on the contentious elements within the relationship between chaplains and their treatment team, as well as the ways that these chaplains speak about health and wholeness. If Swinton's analysis is correct, the lack of worth experienced by some of these chaplains could be a tangible manifestation of the reliance on empiricism and the shunning of religiosity as based on unverifiable "soft" knowledge. The "shunning" that chaplains experience could be a symbol (or symptom) of the privileging of certain types of knowledge, and a denigration of others, evidenced in the heralding of a medical model of certainty. Perhaps this dynamic is most apparent in the Finch Hospital administration's staffing decision to remove the chaplains from sitting in on the treatment teams. Each of these chaplains had stories about situations in which the treatment team had not understood the religiosity of their patients, and this had negatively affected their treatment. In one case, a female patient's Pentecostalism was mistaken for religious preoccupation; in another, a lack of understanding about funeral practices had led a patient to harbor years of guilt about stealing urns from a mausoleum, when in fact, she had stolen flower pots. The feeling of being in conflict with the treatment team was heightened at this hospital, due to the fact that the chaplains were literally separate from the team and seen as outsiders.

Swinton's description of the integrated nature of spirituality and its application in the realm of mental health is also evident in the ways that these chaplains spoke about health and wholeness. From the interviews, chaplains perceived themselves as having a much more holistic and integrated view of health than the members of their teams and advocated for this view in the treatment of their patients. They frequently addressed the social, emotional, relational and physical aspects of the people with whom they ministered, depending on which need was the most pressing. We find echoes of this approach in Swinton's assertions of spirituality as necessitating a non-dualistic approach to the person, with the implication that a diagnosis of mental health affects every dimension of the person.

Ann Bedford Ulanov, a scholar of psychiatry and religion who is known for her work on the intersection of such psychoanalytic figures as Jung and Winnicott with religion and spirituality, also speaks about the importance of an exploration of religion and spirituality for mental health. She suggests that the conversation between psychiatry and religion is one that should not be collapsed into one another, as this does not respect the space between the two disciplines. She describes this conversation as one which "mirrors the conversation between the psyche and the soul."[47] To explain this analogy, she differentiates between questions posed by the psyche, and those asked by the soul. To her, when the psyche confronts religion, questions revolve around how religion functions for the person, whether it promotes health or illness, and how this religiosity is experienced. When one approaches religious experiences from the point of view of the soul, however, one asks questions about the validity of these experiences, as well as who or what authored them and their meaning in one's life. While Ulanov focuses on the spiritual dimension, she advocates that clinicians must be conversant in both, as these dimensions permeate the entirety of the lives of both the clinician and the patient. Ulanov argues, however, that to miss the religious dimension is to "confine ourselves to efforts of recovering ego-functioning which is of priceless value but will not endure if the spiritual aspect is omitted."[48] It is in and through religion that true healing and integration can occur. If the religious dimension is not addressed in the life of the clinician (and this includes non-religion, as well as complexes concerning religion), the clinician's own religious experiences will permeate her treatment, including her countertransference reactions and her unexamined sexual images and drives. The pervasive role of religion is also operative in the lives of patients and, for that reason, must also permeate all aspects of treatment. Attention to the spiritual dimension throughout the entire treatment ensures not only emotional and spiritual healing, but also the space to create meaning: "Remembering that the two disciplines must not be collapsed into one another, that we need an exchange between the psyche and the soul, we realize it is not enough to alleviate symptoms and recover ego functioning; we also need meaning."[49] She draws on D.W. Winnicott, one of the foremost object relations psychoanalysts of his generation, noting that "the absence of psychoneurotic illness may be health, but it is not life."[50]

The chaplains that were interviewed, in one sense, echo Ulanov's sentiments concerning the value of religious experience, as well as the importance of the creation of meaning in the lives of patients. In particular, their articulation of the "goal" of the interaction as involving hope and human potential, as well as asking questions of ultimate meaning ("what kind of life" the patient is working toward), suggests these chaplains are concerned with deeper questions than simply the alleviation of symptoms. Their view of the person as integrated and multifaceted also attempts to recognize, in Ulanovian terms, "the space between the psyche and the soul." We need only turn to their descriptions of holistic health to affirm this, where many of them both describe and advocate for the integrated emotional, spiritual and physical health of their patients. While recognizing that their focus should be on the spiritual component of health, these chaplains also allow the patient to lead the interaction, even if this brings them into the terrain of physical or mental health.

Yet, Ulanov's assertion that the clinician be conversant in the language of both the psyche and the soul may or may not be attainable and/or practiced by these chaplains. As explored earlier, their training suggests that a large percentage of chaplains in psychiatric hospitals lack education in psychology and/or psychiatry, though nearly all have had at least minimal experience in CPE.[51] Some chaplains, in fact, speak to their lack of education in the social sciences as a positive, arguing that it allows them to be able to see the "entirety" of the person, in a system that reduces people to a diagnostic category. Ulanov, as well as many schools of pastoral care, might take issue with this latter claim, as both theory and practice within these spheres suggest that being able to engage with both disciplines is essential to fully navigate the landscape of the soul. On the other hand, considering that the treatment of the patient occurs in the midst of a team of professionals, Ulanov might recognize that the psychological realm is being attended to by the other members of the treatment team and advocate that the chaplain explore the religious dimension of treatment. Yet, for Ulanov, the dialogue between the two disciplines is a necessary component of caregiving. As such, she might inquire, to little avail, about the location of this dialogue within the treatment team model.

Seeing the Whole Person? Racial and Class Dynamics

For many chaplains, the assertion of "seeing the whole person" coexisted paradoxically alongside encounters with patients where dynamics of race and/or class were difficult to address and/or "invisible." While some white chaplains seemed to be unaware of the racial dynamics in their encounters, others voiced an awareness and/or concern about the racial dynamics on their staff or in their meetings with women. Yet, across the board, chaplains, particularly white chaplains, had difficulty communicating about racial dynamics in their pastoral encounters. Chaplains who were a part of racial groups of color were more able to recognize the racial and cultural dynamics at play, not only in their own encounters, but in the larger systems surrounding the pastoral encounter. Chaplains also articulated racialized dynamics in the lives of the patients with whom they worked; chaplains at every hospital voiced experiences when patients of color had delusions that they were white. In terms of class, both white chaplains and chaplains of color were for the most part united in their view that the people they served were in psychiatric hospitals because of a lack of other viable financial and social options. While they did observe the intersectional nature of class with other issues such as education and violence, most chaplains did not mention race as one of these overlapping factors.

In order to explore questions of racial dynamics, it is important to revisit the racial composition of the chaplains themselves. As mentioned earlier, out of a sample of eighteen chaplains within state psychiatric hospitals, twelve (or 67 percent) were white women. The other six people were self-identified as one African American female, one African male, one African American male, and three white males. The prevalence of white women in their chaplaincy departments was mentioned by the supervisors of two out of the three hospitals (themselves white women). In the third hospital, the statistic was reversed, as there was only one woman out of the six employed chaplains. In that case however, the white woman was one of the two full time staff chaplains.

In terms of the placement of race as a topic in the interview itself, the question regarding racial dynamics was usually over half way through the interview, after rapport had been established. It was asked in the following manner: "Are there any experiences you've had where racial and/or cultural dynamics were present in the interaction? In the person you were caring for? In yourself?" It was followed up with the following: "Are there times when these dynamics felt important? . . . Raised questions? . . . Made you feel comfortable or uncomfortable?" In the course of conversations that had more often than not become seamless, with much back and forth, this question frequently elicited a substantial pause that broke the flow of the conversation, and the response was approached with much hesitancy and caution. This was frequently followed by a series of "umms" and also punctuated by quotes like "I'm sure I have . . ."; "Hmmm. Did you say racial and cultural?"; "Give me a second to think about that."; "Well. I don't know if I've thought much about it." This response was so pervasive among the white chaplains I interviewed that I have termed it a "white response."[52]

When the two supervisors (themselves white women) were asked about issues of racial and cultural dynamics either in their departments or in their personal interactions with patients, they had varying responses. The first woman suggested that racial dynamics were not prevalent in her staff nor in her own interactions with patients, "No one has ever made a comment about my skin color."[53] She went on to note the gendered dynamics that raised their head, particularly when patients have asked for a male pastor, but suggested that racial dynamics were not at play. The other supervisor also suggested that racial dynamics were also "not a part" of the interactions she had with patients.[54] She did, however, spend a sizable amount of time reflecting on the racial composition of her staff. She expressed that part of the reason that the staff was largely white women (including all of the three full time chaplains) was that the primary feeder to the program was a seminary that "was not the most diverse community." She noted that the population of the psychiatric hospital reflected the diversity of the northeastern state in which it is situated, which is multiracial and multicultural, with many "blacks and Spanish-speaking people," and that it "would be nice to have a staff that reflected that diversity":

> We could be more intentional [about reaching out to African Americans]. Now that we're bringing this up, we could be more intentional about it. But yeah, I don't, but, the women we have had . . . work out really well! I mean, they're really good. And so that's where that whole piece comes in, that they're really good! They don't just happen to be white women, you know? They're great! They have passion, heart . . . are skillful . . . Have good professional skills, too, like showing up on time, doing what they're supposed to. And, umm, you know. So they have all of that.[55]

The interviews with the remainder of the chaplains who were white women around issues of racial and cultural dynamics indicated that the majority of white women had difficulty talking about issues of race. Of the remaining ten white women who were interviewed about times when racial or cultural dynamics raised their heads in their interactions, five answered the question about racial dynamics by shifting the topic to other issues, including socioeconomic issues, gender, sexual orientation, or religious diversity. The remaining five did offer some type of reflection on racial dynamics, but often did not spend more than one sentence on their own race.[56] Out of the twelve white women, only two offered sizable reflections on the racial dynamics in their encounters that included the influence/existence of their own whiteness.

The five chaplains who responded to questions about racial or cultural dynamics by changing the topic to other issues exhibited the characteristic "white response," marked by hesitancy, frequent pauses in the conversation, and caution. When they did answer the question, they quickly shifted the topic to another area of study and/or conflated racial dynamics with other factors, such as socioeconomic dynamics:

> That's a good question. I'm thinking about it. Ummm . . . I'm sure I have. Umm . . . you know . . . especially in the VA almost all the patients that I met with came from a different socioeconomic place than I did. So there were very few people coming from a place of privilege and, I mean, white.[57]

> You know it's actually fascinating because I think statistically, . . . uhh, we have more . . . white people in the hospital than we do like African-American or Latino or whatever. But frequently in my head, I think that our population is, the majority is African-American. And it's interesting. I have no idea why that happens, I, like, but it is, it just happens that way. And I don't know if it's because I associate a lower soc . . . socio-economic class with . . . uh, Black community, or what.[58]

Other chaplains tended to sideline racial and cultural dynamics all together by steering the conversation toward another issue of oppression, such as sexual orientation:

> Interviewer: Are there encounters or experiences where racial or cultural dynamics were present in the interaction? In the person you were caring for? In yourself?
> O2: You know I've had a number of patients come out to me. This is an especially difficult setting for that. In some cases I feel like it can be a test . . . the Church can be so traumatizing with that, I respond with warmth.[59]

A couple chaplains mentioned the racial dynamics briefly, perhaps even noting that their own racial identity might factor in the encounter, but then shifted the topic to speak about other dynamics. One noted that her sensitivity to racial dynamics allowed her to have a relationship with an African American woman that would not have been possible without this sensitivity, but then quickly moved on to a discussion of the tolerance of religious diversity necessary in a multi-religious setting. Another noted that "there are certain patients who won't meet with me because I'm white," but in the next sentence continued by saying "or the gender thing . . . or they prefer a Catholic Chaplain."[60] Another suggested that her race "does come into play" but in the same breath began speaking about the tension between the African and African American populations that exists within the hospital and the way that affected her encounters.[61]

The two white women who spent more than one sentence on their own whiteness both recognized the connection between their own racial identity and issues of power (among other factors), suggesting that their racial identity could get in the way of authentic communication with some patients. One noted that, in coming from a white, mainline Protestant denomination, her style of leadership and worship differs from the black Church:

> O4: And when you're talking about services, like, I'm certainly leading a service from a, like, white mainline Protestantism. Which is very different from a Black church, uhh, umm, or, you know, a Catholic service or anything like that. You know, so like the hymns that I choose to sing. Now I love spirituals, but then obviously, even me, like, singing a spiritual, it's the same song, same key, same time, you know signature, but it's not with the same soul. And it's not with the same like sort of . . . it's just not the same. You know? So I can sing those, "Leaning on Everlasting Arms" and stuff all the day long 'cause I love those songs, but it's just not the, it's not the same. You know? And they recognize that and they sa . . . admit that and verbally express that.
> Interviewer: What do they say?
> O4: And that's fine. I mean, it's more, it's just more, like "Oh this is the white song." Or like, "Oh, that's the, that's the whitest version of, you know, 'His Eye Is On the Sparrow' I've ever heard!"[62]

Yet, even though this chaplain noted that the humor in this situation could be a positive rapport builder, she also recognized that in groups and in one-on-

one interactions, the racial difference "could be a more painful experience." Sometimes, she noted, difference in vocabulary inhibited the relationship. She expressed that while she was familiar with many of the "regular" names of street drugs, she often did not know the slang names of the substances to which the patients were referring. This had, at times, stood in the way of connecting with them. It was in one-on-one interactions, she noted, that people tend to share their personal, (often) painful experiences, and there was the sense that because of her racial or cultural background, she couldn't (or didn't) understand what their experience was like.

The other woman who engaged with her own whiteness focused more on the ways that, as a white woman, she attempted to (as much as possible) be aware of the different racial and cultural dynamics in play. She talked about the importance of validating racial/cultural dynamics as they were named in an interaction, either by the patient or by another staff member: "And if other people disagree with it or . . . think it's just someone playing the race card . . . I'll fight against that. Because I think it's courageous to bring it up."[63] She spoke also about the importance of awareness, of "not ignoring" racial or cultural realities, because they are present, whether mentioned or not. This chaplain, echoing the observations of others, also noted that there were numerous intersections between culture and race, particularly with the racial and cultural dynamics among the staff; many of the direct care staff were from different countries in Africa, whereas almost all of the psychiatrists and psychologists were U.S. citizens. This, coupled with the racial identity of the patient, made the dynamic exceedingly complicated: "Ultimately, I just try to be aware. I just don't know what to do. And ultimately I try to be aware that I'm white. And trying to be aware of when I'm more authoritative, and when I'm being more collaborative."[64]

Yet, even after their analyses, both of these women ended their reflections with similar sentiments: "I don't know . . . I just don't know what to do."[65] The other reflected, "I don't know . . . It's a bad answer."[66]

When extending this analysis to include the two white male chaplains, these trends continued. One male, when asked about the prevalence of racial and/or cultural dynamics, said that "the racial piece comes in, but doesn't interfere with what I'm doing." He went on to discuss that he "didn't see any benefit to getting into the racial thing" even though patients would bring it up.[67] The other white male, who also identified as disabled, recognized the importance of attention to racial and cultural dynamics, yet also did not offer any reflection on the role of his whiteness within his own encounters.[68]

Chaplains of color, however, frequently found it easier to articulate the racial and/or cultural dynamics at play in the encounter. An African American chaplain began his reflection with a reflection on race in America:

> I think some people like to believe that we live in a post-racial America but I don't believe that's true. Umm, and not only post-racial, but I think women still don't have equality that they should have. So, we, we still have a long way to go. But I think sometimes people's politics has a way of sometimes uh, hindering or limiting their ability to help the patient.[69]

He continued by reflecting that he encounters people in professional caregiving positions who see patients as lazy or a drain on society, rather than people who have both psychiatric and social issues. He expressed his irritation with these views, voicing that opinions such as those "get in the way of good care and treatment."[70]

Other chaplains of color spoke about how their own embodiment and cultural location helped them to recognize the inherent racial and cultural dynamics in an encounter. One African American woman chaplain noted that her life-long experience of discrimination allows her to "read" a room and notice unspoken racial dynamics. Her practice of noting how other African Americans were received also provided her with cues as to how she would be received by the patient and the team. She recalled an instance of discrimination from a patient towards herself, and the reaction of the (white) psychologist to "attribute it to their mental illness and 'keep moving.'" When asked what she thought about that advice, she quickly and firmly dismissed the psychologist's remark, articulating "They [the patient] were always like this."[71] A chaplain from Cameroon spoke about his difficulty in "ministering across cultures." He recognized that his own socio-cultural location enabled him to notice cultural dynamics that may be hidden from others. He noted for example, that the U.S. has a "culture of abundance" which directly contradicts the values of the culture in which he was raised:

> In Africa, we're not raised with abundance. Okay? We're not raised with abundance. Even when your parents have [material goods] . . . they still make things difficult for you, in order that you become somebody who wants to fight and survive. They withhold things from you. Eh . . . in my culture, somebody who gives everything the child asks for is directly spoiling the child. Directly! And in that case, even the community steps in to talk to you about your children.[72]

This chaplain enumerated the challenges that surfaced as he attempted to process, integrate, and articulate this clash of cultural values. He revealed that at first, he assumed that everyone he was meeting was "spoiled." This led to a period where he recognized, "Maybe, it was not really that everyone was spoiled. Maybe it is (laughing) . . . maybe it is just culture." He spoke about his difficulty in ministering across cultures, which led to times when he felt that he needed to reevaluate his positions on several topics. For example, he explained his insight that perhaps it was possible to raise a child within a culture of abundance, but do so in a way that was also sensitive to the values of his own culture:

> Can you have abundance so that the child doesn't really have to be lacking, but the child, having things, may know that those things are just a privilege, not a right? So, and still raise a child that will be very functional? Yes! It's a possibility.[73]

He also spoke of the differences in gender relations between his culture of origin and the U.S. culture that he had experienced. He noted the ways that U.S. culture had challenged him to adopt a broader view of women and their capacities. He recognized that this had influenced the ways that he ministers with women. He ended the interview by noting that his particular cultural location enabled him to "minister across religious ideology, even Christian ideologies. Different Christian ideologies. So I'm able to talk to a lot of people who disagree with me."[74]

My own embodiment as a white woman must also be named within these interviews. My racial location was a factor of influence, though frequently unnamed within the context of these interviews. As a white woman, the history and present reality of white supremacy lives within current encounters, including all of the conversations I had with the chaplains. When I am honest, as white women (in particular) displayed signs of discomfort when the topic of race was raised, I noticed these feelings also arising within myself. Instead of naming the reality that was unfolding (the mutual discomfort that was occurring and the ways that this made its way into the conversation, for example, when the chaplain changed the subject), I simply moved on to the next question. That is, I frequently did not engage in deeper conversation and/or reflection around these dynamics. While I recognize that part of this decision was rooted in my commitment to allow the chaplains to speak (with as little disruption as possible), I am also aware that another part of this decision reflects my white privilege; I am able to choose when, where and how I discuss topics of race. It may have also, whether consciously or unconsciously, communicated an "it's okay" attitude to displays of white resistance to discussions of race and white supremacy.

My racial embodiment was also a factor affecting my conversations with chaplains who were of color. Their own awareness of racial realities reveals the "double consciousness" that "people of color live within order to survive in a white supremacist society."[75] People of color must be intimately familiar not only with their own cultural perspective, but with a "white perspective" of the world, particularly its tendencies to denigrate people of color. An engagement with (and understanding of) the "white worldview" aids in their survival in a white supremacist society. I wonder how my whiteness not only affected what they shared, but how they shared it. Portions of interviews with people of color were frequently spent on their explanations of systemic racism and their awareness of it within pastoral encounters—what might have filled those spaces had they not felt that they had to explain that reality to me?

Over and above the effect of their own racial and cultural identity on the encounter, chaplains also articulated racialized dynamics that were at play in the lives of the patients with whom they worked. The most obvious example of this were chaplains' stories about African American women patients who had delusions[76] that they were white. Other chaplains, however, were able to pinpoint ways in which race intersected with a variety of social and cultural factors in the lives of their patients.

More than one chaplain spoke of interactions with African American women who had delusions that they were white. The chaplains who met with these patients spoke about the racial and gendered aspect of these encounters. In one case, the delusion centered around the African American woman patient being a white male. In the other two, the African American women had delusions that they were white women. While some delusions can manifest as fleeting and fragmented, the delusions of the patients with whom these chaplains met were highly systematized and remained unaltered with medication. Given this reality, any questioning of the delusion or the delusional system usually resulted in anger toward the chaplain. While the chaplains noted that the delusions were consistent with the psychiatric diagnosis given to the woman, they also admitted that the particular racial and gendered dynamics that were raised by these delusions resulted in situations that were frequently uncomfortable for the chaplains, all of whom were themselves white women. The gender dynamic raised by the African American woman patient who had delusions that she was a white male was particularly challenging for the chaplain who worked with her:

> But it's hard for me, you know, since we're talking about dealing with women, so I have to deal with her as a woman. She is a woman. But her perception of herself is that she's not a woman . . . And you can't really, umm, contradict her delusions. So it's like you're dealing with a woman and a man at the same time.[77]

The incongruence between the perceived race of the patient and the patient's own racial identity also frequently left the chaplains in a position where they "didn't know how to respond." The chaplains also reported that the African American women patients themselves often made denigrating remarks about other African Americans. This ranged from the belief held by one of the African American women that she was being harmed by other African American patients and "only felt safe"[78] with whites to a variety of derogatory and denigrating remarks about "the blacks on the unit."[79] One chaplain recalled that she felt like it was "the twilight zone," that she didn't know how to react or what to say. Finally, she decided that she would respond with "what I would say to anyone: 'You know, it really makes me uncomfortable when you speak that way about a group of people.'"[80] Another chaplain stated that her interaction with the black woman who was experiencing these types of delusions frequently caused her to check her own cultural assumptions, and left her in a position where she "wasn't sure how to respond."[81]

Other chaplains commented on the racial dynamics in the lives of the patients with an analysis of the intersectionality of race with a variety of social and cultural factors. When chaplains were asked about the presence of issues of class in their encounters, about two-thirds of those interviewed voiced that the majority of the women with whom they met came from a "lower socioeconomic class." Many also recognized that class issues overlapped with issues such as lack of material resources, education and issues of violence. Most of these chaplains, however, did not include race as one of these overlapping factors. In fact, only three chaplains, one African American male, one African American woman, and one white woman, mentioned that race was part of these intersections.

Among those who did recognize that race was a part of the social intersections in the lives of the patients with whom they ministered, this was perhaps most deftly noted by an African American chaplain, as he spoke about the presence of many dual diagnosis patients[82] in the psychiatric hospital. He asserted the importance of asking the "why" question, as a chaplain (and as any mental health professional): "What's their background—racial and otherwise? What caused them to get to that place, you know, where they had the psychosis? Or where they were addicted to drugs?" He noted that many of the patients of color with whom he met came from poverty, and had experienced physical, emotional, and sexual abuse. He voiced his own belief about the connection between abuse and mental illness: "Maybe if we dealt more with those issues, with sexual assault, and with domestic violence issues, it could help alleviate some of the issues with psychotic behavior."[83]

Another white female chaplain also spoke about how she recognized that the woman in front of her "embodies the intersection of so many marginalizations," including race.[84] She noted "she is a woman, a woman with mental illness, in a psychiatric hospital." She also recognized that the woman was also often in the hospital due to "a lack of other financial resources or insurance options." This chaplain noted that providing care to a woman who was marginalized in so many ways was inherently challenging, and that one way she would address it was in the context of the meetings of the treatment team. She said that she would often interrupt the treatment team meeting[85] to ask the patient to voice what she was hearing from the team, "Because I think we process things differently. And that's impacted by our different experiences of the world—mental health, gender, sexual orientation, race, religious tradition, and so on. So I try to bring it back to them. But it's so hard!"[86]

Yet another African American chaplain also voiced the intersection between race and a variety of other social and cultural factors. For her, this came to light in a meeting with a woman from Korea:

> And I think that even in the state psychiatric hospital we're seeing the most marginalized, the most stigmatized patients in the entire state. And so, I think oftentimes, you know, we see, umm, homeless patients. We see patients who are estranged from their families. And, umm, one woman that I'm thinking of . . . uhh . . . who just came into admissions was, is Korean, and, was homeless, and we didn't even know what her name was.[87]

This chaplain revealed that the racial identity of this patient, coupled with her limited English and her delusions, meant that she was literally referred to as Jane Doe for a period of time. The chaplain noted how these factors had also probably resulted in her homelessness. She suggested that the lack of available information about the patient's citizenship and family affected her access to treatment and her discharge options while in the hospital.

The experience of these chaplains in regard to racial and cultural dynamics reveal that racial dynamics in the encounters between chaplains and women with mental illness are complex and multi-layered, involving such issues as the chaplain's own racial identity and embodiment and the awareness surrounding that reality, the racial composition of the chaplaincy staff and hospital staff, and the many ways that racial dynamics are at play in the lives of the patients within the hospital—including (but not limited to) their delusions, their own racial identity, and the ways that this racial identity intersects with other social and economic factors. The presence of all of these factors—named and unnamed, conscious and unconscious—are at play in the encounter between the chaplain and the patient.

While the reasons for the large percentage of white women within the field of psychiatric chaplaincy are unclear, it raises certain points for consideration and reflection. As I explored in the section on method, feminist researchers have noted that traditionally qualitative interviewers have dismissed people's hesitations, stumbling over words, and pauses in conversation as indications of inarticulateness. Yet, those statements that can be perceived as inarticulateness can also point to "a lack of fit between one's knowledge of daily practices and struggles and the hegemonic worldview."[88] In their discussions of whiteness, white dominance and white privilege, Jennifer Harvey and Traci West, both Christian social ethicists, offer insights that also may shed light on the multiplicity of responses of these chaplains to questions of racial and cultural dynamics.

When I speak of whiteness, I draw on the definition of Jennifer Harvey, a professor of religion and ethics at Drake University. In *Dear White Chris-*

tians (2014), she defines "whiteness" as "a direct and unflinching recognition of the relationship all white people have to white supremacy, along with the many ways this relationship affects those of us who are racialized as white."[89] Harvey reflects on an exercise that she uses in primarily white churches. In this exercise, she invites white people to reflect on "unique and positive characteristics that they associate with their racial identity."[90] She articulates that this frequently results in emotions of profound discomfort, distress and disarray, not dissimilar from some of the reactions I observed when I raised the question of racial dynamics with the white chaplains I interviewed. Harvey continued by recognizing that communities of color, on the contrary, easily embrace this exercise, voicing characteristics of their racial identity in which they have pride or have shaped their self-understanding. She continues to ask how white people can bring their whole selves to an encounter (her example involves the reconciliation paradigm adopted by many white churches) with those of another racial identity, if whites have no clear sense of self, let alone an ability to voice positive attributes of their racial identity.

Harvey and others suggest that the dynamic operative in this exercise, and in the responses I experienced from these white chaplains, reflects the nature of race itself. As a socially constructed reality—as opposed to a self-evident, biological category—race is interwoven with historical social, economic and political systems and relations. While race exists and is very real, Harvey suggests that it "comes to be" in the act of social relations, operative "in the interactions between different bodies and laws, economics, education, the criminal justice system, and a nearly infinite number of other institutions and processes."[91] Phenotypes that are associated with racial identities do not carry with them inherent meaning. Rather meaning is ascribed and created by social and political values attached to these features.

The social construction of whiteness is directly linked to concepts of white supremacist social structures and, therefore, to white dominance, white privilege and increasingly, white nationalism. In this way, white and non-white (or communities/people of color) are not simply parallel terms. Harvey traces the evolution of the construction of whiteness, noting that the term "white" came into existence to justify the systemic violence and oppression of those with darker skin through the institution of slavery. Christians were not only complicit in this, they used the Bible and liturgical practices to continue to justify this violence and oppression. In this way, the racial term "white" has come to mean complicity with racially-motivated violence and subjugation, resulting in material and social advantages from which white people continue to benefit. Whereas, for example, African American people have engaged in historic resistance to the tenets of white supremacy through their own narratives, religious traditions, and actions that strive for freedom (among other acts of resistance), Harvey notes that white people have not engaged in a "collective and sustained disruption and refusal of white privilege."[92] As such, to be white is "to exist in a state of profound moral crisis."[93]

This construction of whiteness is essential for an understanding of white dominance and white privilege. According to Traci West, a professor of Christian social ethics at Drew University, in *Disruptive Christian Ethics* (2006), "a basic starting point for understanding white dominance is the reality that issues of race are at play in all interactions. When there are only white people in the room, issues of race are still there."[94] Later West recognizes that, "White dominance is perpetuated through varied forms of denial—that is, by ignoring racial realities, pretending that they are not relevant in certain kinds of social interactions."[95] West and Harvey recognize that in the United States, the social construction of race "has never been morally neutral"[96] and that the values that privilege phenotypes characterized as white over those characterized as non-white undergird and inform policies of inequitable distribution of power and resources. According to West, white privilege, which is derived from white dominance, speaks to the privileging of whites when it comes to access to goods and services within society—for example access to loans and housing, education, health and healthcare. White privilege also elevates the "cultural expressions and behavioral patterns"[97] of whites in its construction of those contributions that are esteemed and valued within and by society. She notes that many theorists, "emphasize the freedom to choose whether or not to think about race as one of the main features of white privilege."[98] Again and again, West notes, white people are those who are presumed to be "normal" and do not need racial classification.

West's and Harvey's analyses of whiteness, white dominance and white privilege offer insights into the responses of the chaplains who were interviewed for this study. Harvey's examination of the historical rise of the term "white" provides a plausible explanation for the responses of white chaplains when questioned about racial and cultural dynamics in their encounters, particularly in regard to speaking about their own racial identity. Her analysis of whiteness offers a groundwork for what I have termed a "white response," characterized by pauses in the conversation, hesitancy and discomfort. It may also point to an underlying factor in the tendency of some white chaplains to "change the subject" from race to another topic. While many of the interviewed chaplains have probably been exposed to the concept of white privilege, the lack of a narrative of "white resistance" to the violence and subjugation that created the term "white" may leave whites in situations where they are speechless or uncomfortable. It may, consciously or unconsciously, cause them to shift the conversation to a topic that seems more "bearable" and less implicating. Even when white chaplains offer reflections on their own whiteness, it may leave them in situations where they doubt their own positions and feel that their answers are inadequate or "bad." One wonders if the moral judgement placed on such reflections reveals more about the feelings associated with "being white" and less about the quality of the reflections themselves. Harvey's exploration of whiteness may also point to the reasons that the chaplains of color were often able to answer questions about racial and cultural dynamics with ease and confidence. The narrative of resistance concerning their own race and/or culture could be a factor that enables them to astutely and deftly name the ways that their own embodiment intersects with the racial and cultural dynamics in their encounters with the teams and with psychiatric patients.

West's exploration of white privilege and white dominance also offers a lens through which to analyze the responses of white chaplains. Beginning with the supervisors who were white women, both voiced the absence of racial dynamics within their own interactions with patients. The quote "no one has ever made a comment about my skin color" points to two of the central components of white privilege, namely the invisibility of race for whites and the denial that race and/or racial dynamics are present in certain kinds of social interactions. The second interaction with the other white female supervisor was characterized by a certain discomfort with the racial demographics of her department. Yet, while this supervisor acknowledged "we could be more intentional," she also then privileged white patterns of professionalism and behavior as desirable behavior for chaplains. She noted that the white women on her staff "just happen to be white women," but they are really good chaplains because they "have good professional skills, like showing up on time, doing what they're supposed to." Whether cognizant of this reality or not, her attempt to portray the quality of the white women chaplains on her staff partly relied on the internalized cultural standards of white patterns of behavior, which she then used to legitimize the lack of diversity on the staff.

Yet, to simply assert that these two supervisors are guilty of ignoring racial realities is also to flatten the complexity of the encounters. Especially in the case of the second supervisor, much of the conversation included consternation with the current racial composition of her department. In the conversation, she expressed a desire to be more intentional, to have a staff that reflected the multi-cultural reality of the state in which her hospital was located. This "wrestling" with the notion of white privilege and wondering how best to address it, all while claiming that "racial dynamics were not operative" in her own encounters is characteristic of many of the white churches profiled by West. As West notes in *Disruptive Christian Ethics*, many well-meaning religious institutions harbor internalized and unnamed dynamics that advance racism in the ways they minister and structure their worship. Similarly, the white chaplain supervisors, and many of the white chaplains themselves, who endeavored to "see the whole person" also, many times could not "see" the racialized dynamics in their own encounters.

Concepts of whiteness, white privilege and white dominance also influence the racial dynamics in the lives of the patients themselves, and the complex web of social and cultural factors that the patient must negotiate. In the case of black patients who have delusions that they are white, as one chaplain noted, "I think it has to do with having the perception of who has the privilege here."[99] West notes that white privilege includes access to goods and services within society, as well as cultural and behavioral patterns. As suggested by Whaley and Hall, mental delusions are integrally connected to issues of race and culture.[100] The racism experienced by those in US society are factors in the mental health (and mental illness) of racial and ethnic minorities. While it has been noted that race-related themes often surface in the persecutory delusions of African Americans, there are many theories about the etiology of delusions, including those that they can also be connected to one's failures or shortcomings[101] or, conversely, to one's deepest desires—for community, for affirmation, for connection. It makes sense that those who are told by society that they are inferior in regards to material, social and cultural resources would internalize this racist ideology and would have delusions that they are the part of the racial identity (and perhaps also the gender) that is privileged in society.

These concepts also point to the intersectional nature of race in the psychiatric hospital. A few chaplains named the overlap between racial dynamics and other social factors, such as gender, class and the presence of violence. This intersection is theorized by Kimberle Crenshaw, law professor and one of the founders of critical race theory, in her exploration of the concept of intersectionality. Her article "Intersectionality and Identity Politics: Learning from Violence against Women of Color" sheds light on the intersectional nature of violence against women of color and also has implications for women with mental health issues. Crenshaw notes that an examination of the intersections of the categories of race and gender "disrupts tendencies to see race and gender as exclusive or separate."[102] While she focuses on the concepts of race and gender in her article, she also recognizes that this examination can (and should) be expanded to include other factors such as class and sexual orientation. She notes that intersectional subordination is frequently not "intentionally produced" however it is the consequence of "the imposition of one burden that interacts with preexisting vulnerabilities to create yet another dimension of disempowerment."[103] In her examination of the particular ways that race and gender intersect in the lives of women of color who experience violence, she notes that approaching the issue of violence simply from an analysis of race or from a gender analysis has done a disservice to women of color. The unique way that race and gender intersect for women of color has been overshadowed, as the narratives of race have been based on the experience of African American men, while those of gender have privileged the experiences of white women. She advocates for "the need to account for multiple grounds of identity when considering how the social world is constructed."[104] This was named by some of the chaplains in their recognition of the particular way that social and cultural factors intersected when considering the social world of women in psychiatric hospitals. An example was the articulated awareness that these women existed at the crossroads of "multiple marginalizations," where mental illness was yet another burden that interacted with "preexisting vulnerabilities." Yet the concept of an intersectional theory that included race was also invisible to most other chaplains, as is evidenced by their inability to name racial and/or cultural identity as one of the intersections that needed attention.

Alongside the analysis by Christian social ethicists, it is important to recognize the undeniable psychological factors in an analysis of racial dynamics in chaplaincy, particularly as it pertains to white chaplains. The nonverbal responses to the question about race, coupled with the sizable number of chaplains who could not even engage around the topic, leads to the question of what psychological dynamics may be operative in these encounters. While there could be many reasons for the verbal and nonverbal tensions that were noted in these interviews[105] it is important to recognize that these tensions, what I termed a characteristic "white response," have been found among many who have conducted qualitative research—particularly psychological research—on the subject of race.[106]

Bonilla-Silva, in a 2002 article, proposed five stylistic components that characterize expressions of what he terms "color-blind racism."[107] Color-blind racial attitudes allow whites to deny their advantage and maintain the veneer of racial equality and meritocracy. Among these characteristics are the use of projection to defend against feelings of guilt/responsibility concerning racism, as well as what he calls "rhetorical incoherence," which is characterized by "grammatical mistakes, lengthy pauses, and repetition in speech when discussing sensitive racial issues."[108]

Derald Wing Sue engages the research of Bonilla-Silva and Todd and Abrams[109] to offer possible explanations for the reactions of whites when confronted with questions regarding race and racial identity. Sue posits the existence of a "superordinate dialectical challenge" which occurs in the social conditioning of whites, which is responsible for the tensions and struggles exhibited by whites when they are asked questions about racial identity. He argues that whites are socialized from the moment of birth into two competing curriculums: one which values the inherent goodness of all people, as well as the values of liberty, freedom and democracy, and the other (less conscious) curriculum that names certain groups as inferior and to be feared. He notes that the latter serves as a justification for the structural inequality in society, while also preventing whites from acknowledging their own culpability in oppression. This leaves whites in a moral conundrum around the ultimate dialectic: They are forced to "reconcile their personal beliefs in their own morality as good, moral, and decent human beings with the horrifying realization that their unconscious prejudices, biases, and discriminatory behaviors have harmed others."[110] Sue argues that whites are in the process of overcoming and working through "nested emotions" of fear, guilt and defensiveness as they recognize that they are a part of a system that advantages themselves while disadvantaging groups of color. Sue believes that this results in whites having difficulty confronting their own racial identity, in turn resorting to avoidance, ignorance, distortion and rationalization. Whites also rely on denial, minimization and invalidation of the racial identity of nonwhites.

Sue outlines what he describes as the four major reasons that whites resist change or transformation in terms of their own racial identity: the fear of appearing racist, the fear of realizing one's own racism, the fear of confronting white privilege, and the fear of taking responsibility to end racism. These fears are at the center of the dialectical struggle in which many whites find themselves and should be taken into account when considering ways of moving forward.

While I cannot describe with certainty what undergirded the responses of the white chaplains who were interviewed, the theories of Bonilla-Silva and Sue offer two plausible explanations for a "white response" that I continuously observed among the chaplains I interviewed and in which I myself was a participant during these interactions. Sue's assertion that whites resort to avoidance, ignorance, distortion and rationalization, as well as denial, minimization and invalidation of the racial identity of people of color, was more than supported in my conversations with white chaplains.

An examination of the role of race within the dynamics of psychiatric chaplains would not be complete without an exploration of the ways that race intersects with spirituality. Earlier, Swinton's definition of spirituality proposed that interest in spirituality was waning in Western society, using such descriptions as "belonging to a previous age." Yet, an examination of spirituality as it intersects with race, particularly the African American community, reveals a different reality. Taylor and Chatters note that within the U.S. society, African Americans, Caribbean Blacks and non-Hispanic whites consistently demonstrate higher rates of religious involvement—including organizational (service attendance), non-organizational (private prayer and Bible reading) and subjective (assessed religiosity)—and spirituality than their white counterparts.[111] In fact, in their study, 93 percent of surveyed African Americans reported that both spirituality and religion were important in their lives. While there may be a variety of reasons for this, scholars note that the historical role of religion and religious institutions in the lives of African Americans reveal that African American churches "have a long tradition of spearheading social, educational and health services to their congregation and surrounding communities."[112] As African American churches have consistently been involved in advocating for the spiritual, social, and physical welfare of their members, this has translated into spirituality occupying a greater role in the lives of African Americans. When this is extended to include Caribbean Black and non-Hispanic whites, this trend continues. Taylor and Chatters note that there is "generally no significant differences" in religious involvement nor the importance of spirituality between African Americans and Caribbean Blacks, although these two groups tended to have stronger religious involvement, and claim a greater role for spirituality, than non-Hispanic whites. Again, they point to the role of the church in the Caribbean Black community in the United States as one that has "embodied an ethnic and cultural repository and safe havens for new arrivals, and providing the spiritual, social, material and psychological resources needed for adjustment to a new cultural context."[113]

When narrowing the focus to examine African American women, Taylor and Chatters' study confirms other research[114] that asserts that African American women were more likely than men to report that both religiosity and spirituality were important to them. West also points to ways that the nature and positionality of spirituality can differ in light of race, particularly when considering women who are victims of intimate violence. While West reveals that some women can feel abandoned by God in the face of trauma resulting from intimate violence, she also notes that for women for whom "socioeconomic or racist marginalization is a normal aspect of their daily lives, it is usually quite evident that God does not eliminate all the problems that these social realities bring."[115] Given this reality, for many black women God becomes a "refuge" or "bulwark of strength" in the midst of pain and suffering, a force that enables their survival despite forces that seek the contrary.[116]

These scholars reveal that one cannot analyze the role of spirituality in the encounters between psychiatric chaplains and patients without also addressing the presence of race in these encounters. Even analyses that offer a helpful potential framework for understanding the dynamic between chaplains and the treatment teams of which they are a part proceed without acknowledgement of the racial differences within the realm of spirituality.[117] A portrait of the role spirituality needs to include this essential factor.

Conclusion

Given the trends noted in chapter one, particularly the rise of the psychological sciences and the shifts in psychiatric diagnosis, how do these voices interact with these trends? The voices of chaplains reveal their tendency to view themselves as "over and against" the reductionistic tendencies of the Western medical model, in their assertions that they endeavor to "see the full humanity" of the person in front of them and to approach women's health from a holistic perspective. This often meant that chaplains were in opposition to the values of the Western medical model, which privileges a view of health that separates the person into "systems" which can then be named and treated. This was concretely manifested in chaplains' (often tense) relationships with their treatment teams. Again and again, chaplains noted that they "saw a different side of the patient" than the team on which they sat and also took on the position of advocate for the patient in the midst of this team.

Yet, particularly for most white chaplains, this holistic perspective coexisted with the invisibility of race and racial identity. The voices of Christian social ethicists and psychologists complement one another to offer possible reasons for the difficulty of white chaplains to recognize and articulate the reality of race in their encounters. The voices of chaplains of color, on the other hand, resonate with some of the scholars mentioned in chapter one who highlight the myriad ways that racism affects and interacts with mental health and diagnosis. These insights include the role of racism-induced stress in the etiology of mental illness, links between racism and institutionalization, and the fact that minorities who are in poverty and lack family and material resources seem to be overrepresented in these custodial institutions.[118] A closer examination of the ways that race and racial identity intersect with spirituality further highlights the necessity of recognizing the importance of race in any attempt to "see the whole person."

Chaplains' actions and assertions, however limited, reveal that they have both internalized aspects of the Western model, and also offer resistance to it. Yet their worldview is limited by their own social location, including their racial embodiment. This insight leads us to question the formation of these chaplains, as well as the ways that they themselves make assessments, including their training and the tools at their disposal. The following chapter will examine these realities in order to hint at a fuller picture of the relationship of these chaplains to psychiatric diagnosis.

NOTES

1. Suman Fernando, *Mental Health, Race and Culture*, third edition (New York: Palgrave Macmillon, 2010), 32.
2. Ibid., 35.
3. Ibid., 32.
4. Joan Busfield, *Managing Madness, Changing Ideas and Practice* (New York: Routledge, 1986), 16–20.
5. Fernando, *Mental Health, Race and Culture*, 19.
6. To preserve the anonymity of these chaplains, codes have been used in place of real names. The three hospital sites have been given the pseudonyms Violet, Oak, and Finch. Chaplains shall be referred to using the first letter of the pseudonym for the site where they work followed by a numeral (i.e., V1, O4, F2).

7. While I adopted this term because it was used by a number of chaplains, I also recognize that this can be an inherently problematic term. Whether any person (including the self) has access to such complete representation is debatable, particularly in light of how much can be missed in terms of racialized dynamics (as will be demonstrated in this chapter).

8. The name of this state is withheld to preserve the anonymity of the interviewees.

9. I omitted the forensic center as the approach within this center is primarily behavioral, and it does not have a sizable chaplaincy presence.

10. F1 (chaplain at Finch Hospital), interview by the author, March 9, 2016, MP3 Audio Recording (16:30).

11. 9 from Violet, 5 from Oak, and 4 from Finch.

12. O3 (chaplain at Oak Hospital), interview by the author, November 16, 2015, MP3 Audio Recording.

13. O1 (chaplain at Oak Hospital), interview by the author, December 11, 2015, MP3 Audio Recording.

14. F2 (chaplain at Finch Hospital), interview by the author, March 19, 2016, MP3 Audio Recording.

15. O2 (chaplain at Oak Hospital), interview by the author, December 11, 2015, MP3 Audio Recording.

16. O1, interview.

17. V2, (chaplain at Violet Hospital), interview by the author, February 24, 2016, MP3 Audio Recording.

18. O1, interview, 24:00.

19. O3, interview, 12:00.

20. O4 (chaplain at Oak Hospital), interview by the author, December 11, 2015, MP3 Audio Recording (37:40-48:00).

21. O3, interview, 17:00-18:00.

22. V3 (chaplain at Violet Hospital), interview by the author, October 15, 2015, MP3 Audio Recording (16:00).

23. O5 (chaplain at Oak Hospital), interview by the author, December 4, 2015, MP3 Audio Recording.

24. V4 (chaplain at Violet Hospital), interview by the author, October 5, 2015, MP3 Audio Recording.

25. O3 (chaplain at Oak Hospital), interview by the author, December 4, 2015 MP3 Audio Recording

26. This book will offer a more in-depth examination of the relationship of chaplains to intersecting systemic realities later in this chapter.

27. O4, interview.

28. V8, interview.

29. V4, interview.

30. O1, interview.

31. O3, interview.

32. V1 (chaplain at Violet Hospital), interview by the author, November 16, 2015, MP3 Audio Recording (54:00–76:00).

33. O3, interview, 14:00.

34. O3, interview, 14:30.

35. O4, interview.

36. O3, interview.

37. V4, interview.

38. F1, interview, 19:00–20:00.

39. V2, interview, 21:27.

40. John Swinton, *Spirituality and Mental Health Care: Rediscovering a Forgotten Dimension* (Philadelphia: Kingsley, 2001), 7.

41. It should be noted that Swinton does not include a racial/cultural analysis in this work. Without this analysis, it is difficult to assess whether he extends this to all races/cultures or is simply reflecting on the place of spirituality through a white, Eurocentric, Western lens. As we

will explore later, spirituality in the Black community does not share the characteristics that Swinton raises here, even though he speaks in universal terms.

42. Swinton, *Spirituality and Mental Health*, 8.
43. Ibid., 9.
44. Ibid., 11.
45. Ibid., 16.
46. Ibid., 18.
47. Ann Bedford Ulanov, *Spiritual Aspects of Clinical Work* (Einsiedeln, Switzerland: Diamon Verlag, 2004), 41.
48. Ibid., 45.
49. Ibid.
50. Ibid.
51. Whether training in CPE can be considered enough exposure to psychology to be able to preserve the dialogue between the psyche and the soul is a point that could be debated.
52. Other scholars speak of similar phenomena in their exploration of "white ignorance" and "white innocence." For more on white ignorance, see Charles W. Mills, *The Racial Contract* (Ithaca, NY: Cornell University, 1997); Eduardo Bonilla-Silva, *Racism without Racists* (Lanham, MD: Rowman & Littlefield, 2006); and Elizabeth V. Spelman, "Managing Ignorance," in *Race and Epistemologies of Ignorance*, eds. Shannon Sullivan and Nancy Tuana (Albany: SUNY Press, 2007). For more on "white innocence" and in particular the connection of emotionality to whiteness, see Cheryl E. Matias, *Feeling White: Whiteness, Emotionality and Education* (Rotterdam, Netherlands: Sense, 2016).
53. V7 (chaplain at Violet Hospital), interview by the author, March 8, 2016, MP3 Audio Recording.
54. O5, interview, 57:30.
55. O5, interview, 59:00–64:00
56. When one extends this to include all of the white chaplains, the reactions of the two white men fell into this category.
57. V3, interview, 20:00.
58. O4, interview, 27:00
59. O2, interview.
60. O3, interview.
61. O1, interview.
62. O4, interview, 29:00.
63. V2, interview.
64. V2, interview, 26:01.
65. O4, interview.
66. V2, interview.
67. V4, interview.
68. F2, interview.
69. F1, interview, 22:00.
70. F1, interview, 22:30.
71. V5 (chaplain at Violet Hospital), interview by the author, September 14, 2015, MP3 Audio Recording.
72. V1, interview.
73. V1, interview, 48:00.
74. V1, interview, 55:30.
75. Aana Marie Vigen, *Women, Ethics and Inequality in U.S. Healthcare "To Count Among the Living"* (New York: Palgrave MacMillan, 2006), xxiii. She notes that W.E.B. Du Bois brought this phrase into the mainstream, but that it had been used earlier by his teacher and mentor, William James.
76. According to the *American Psychological Association's Dictionary of Psychology*, a delusion is defined as "an improbable, often highly personal idea or belief system, not endorsed by one's culture or subculture, that is maintained with conviction in spite of irrationality or evidence to the contrary." Gary R. Vanden Bos, ed. *American Psychological Association's Dictionary of Psychology* (Washington DC: APA, 2007), 266.

77. V6 (chaplain at Violet Hospital), interview by the author, January 27, 2016, MP3 Audio Recording (33:00).
78. O3, interview.
79. V5, interview.
80. V6, interview, 29:00.
81. O3, interview.
82. Those patients who struggle with both substance abuse and severe mental illness.
83. F1, interview, 26:00.
84. V2, interview, 30:00.
85. A meeting composed of all of the mental health professionals including the psychologist, psychiatrist, and social worker.
86. V2, interview, 29:00.
87. V3, interview, 22:00.
88. Sprague, *Feminist Methodologies*, 152.
89. Jennifer Harvey, *Dear White Christians: For Those Still Longing for Racial Reconciliation* (Grand Rapids, MI: Eerdmans, 2014), 43.
90. Harvey, *Dear White Christians*, 43.
91. Ibid., 46.
92. Ibid., 56.
93. Ibid.
94. West, *Disruptive Christian Ethics*, 117.
95. Ibid.
96. Harvey, *Dear White Christians*, 47; West, *Disruptive Christian Ethics*, 117.
97. West, *Disruptive Christian Ethics*, 117.
98. Ibid., 118.
99. V6, interview, 30:00.
100. Arthur L. Whaley and Brittany N. Hall, "Cultural Themes in the Psychotic Symptoms of African American Psychiatric Patients," *Professional Psychology: Research and Practice* 40.1 (2009): 75–80.
101. See Alfred Adler, *The Neurotic Constitution: Basic Principles of Comparative Individual Psychology and Psychotherapy, Commentary Text-Critical Edition*, ed. K.H. Witte (Goettingen: Vandenhoeck and Ruprecht, 1997).
102. Kimberle Crenshaw, "Intersectionality and Identity Politics: Learning from Violence against Women of Color," in *Feminist Theory: A Reader*, third edition. Eds. Wendy Kolmar and Frances Bartkowski (Boston: McGraw, 2010), 483.
103. Crenshaw, "Intersectionality and Identity Politics," 484.
104. Ibid., 483.
105. This could even include the notion of collective perpetrator trauma. Trauma scholars, such as Jeffrey C. Alexander, Roy Eyerman, Bernhard Giesen, Neil J. Smelser, and Piotr Sztompka, recognize that trauma can and does affect communities, known as collective trauma. See Jeffrey C. Alexander et al., eds., *Collective Trauma and Collective Identity* (Berkeley: University of California Press, 2004). While individual and collective trauma are not identical, they also share many characteristics. One of the key differences in individual and collective trauma is that the subjects might not have personally experienced the particular traumatic incident. Scholars who focus on collective trauma investigate how legacies of violence and subjugation continue to shape the cultures, meaning-making and practices of communities and nations generations later. Collective perpetrator trauma, or the trauma suffered by those who inflict atrocities on other humans, is an offshoot of collective trauma. In the words of Bernhard Geisen, "Perpetrators are human subjects who, by their own decision, dehumanized other subjects and, in doing so, did not only pervert the sovereign subjectivity of the victim but challenged their own sacredness." Bernhard Giesen, "The Trauma of Perpetrators: The Holocaust as the Traumatic Reference of German National Identity," in *Collective Trauma and Collective Identity*, eds. Jeffrey C. Alexander, Roy Eyerman, Bernhard Giesen, Neil J. Smelser, and Piotr Sztompka (Berkeley: University of California Press, 2004), 115. He suggests that when a community or nation is constructed on the ideal that its founders or ancestors were heroes, yet in actuality these figures inflicted violence that violated their (and others) very

personhood, that the past is indeed traumatic. Geisen maintains that a community confronts this contradiction through collective schizophrenia, denial, or withdrawal. Recently, scholars who study collective perpetrator trauma have begun to question whether the legacy of racism in the United States, the violence of slavery that accompanied it, and the ways in which it continues to structure society, might also be an instance of this particular trauma.

106. Shawn Utsey et al, "Examining White Counselor Trainees' Reactions to Racial Issues in Counseling and Supervision Dyads," *The Counseling Psychologist* 33.4 (2005), 456.

107. Eduardo Bonilla-Silva, "The Linguistics of Color Blind Racism: How to Talk Nasty about Blacks Without Sounding 'Racist;" *Critical Sociology*, 28 (2002): 41–62. See also Bonilla-Silva, *Racism without Racists*.

108. Bonilla-Silva, "Linguistics of Color Blind Racism," 58.

109. See Nathan Todd and Elizabeth Abrams, "White Dialectics: A New Framework for Theory, Research and Practice with White Students," *The Counseling Psychologist* 39.3 (2011): 353–95. Developed from and supported by their qualitative analysis, Todd and Abrams offer the framework of six white dialectics that illustrate the tensions with which white students engage as they attempt to speak about and reflect upon their race. The dialectics are (1) Whiteness and self, (2) connection in multiracial relationships, (3) color blindness, (4) minimization of racism, (5) structural inequality, and (6) White privilege.

110. Derald Wing Sue, "The Challenge of White Dialectics: Making the 'Invisible' Visible," *The Counseling Psychologist* 39.3 (2011), 416.

111. Robert Joseph Taylor and Linda M. Chatters, "Importance of Religion and Spirituality in the Lives of African Americans, Caribbean Blacks and Non-Hispanic Whites," *The Journal of Negro Education* 79.3 (2010), 281.

112. Taylor and Chatters, "Importance of Religion," 280.

113. Ibid., 287.

114. See Robert Taylor, Linda M. Chatters and J.S. Levin, *Religion in the Lives of African Americans: Social, Psychological and Health Perspectives* (Thousand Oaks, CA: Sage, 2004).

115. West, *Wounds of the Spirit*, 60.

116. Ibid.

117. Swinton's analysis would be an example of that.

118. See Kenneth P. Lindsey and Gordon L. Paul, "Involuntary Commitments to Public Mental Institutions: Issues Involving the Overrepresentation of Blacks and Assessment of Relative Functioning," *Psychological Bulletin* 106.2 (1989): 171–83, quoted in Townsend, "Racial, Ethnic, and Mental Illness," 133.

Chapter Three

Voices of Chaplains

Practices of Assessment

As chaplains endeavored to know the patient in front of them, they were united in a central guiding value: seeing that patient's full humanity. As we have seen, for many, this assertion coexisted with the invisibility of race and racial dynamics. Given this, how do these chaplains determine the "central issue" in the encounter? This chapter examines the process by which chaplains make an assessment of the woman's needs. It will first inquire as to the role of their training and the tools at their disposal, and then will examine the relationship between their own assessment and the assessment that is privileged in the psychiatric hospital: psychiatric diagnosis. While chaplains fell along a spectrum with regard to the importance of psychiatric diagnosis in their assessment, the relationship between the two raised other questions that are relevant to ethical pastoral care. These include the presence of named and unnamed influences on their assessment models, as well as larger questions of the relationship between science and theology. An examination of chaplains' methods of assessment is essential to ethical pastoral care, as it speaks to the ways that chaplains "diagnose" their encounters and directly relates to the action that they take as a result of that assessment.

TRAINING FOR PSYCHIATRIC CHAPLAINS

One cannot look at assessment without an examination of the training of the chaplains, as training usually goes hand in hand with the methods by which the chaplains assess patients. Out of the eighteen chaplains, nine or 50 percent mentioned Clinical Pastoral Education (CPE) as one of their primary influences on their chaplaincy.[1] CPE is the primary modality by which chaplains are certified in the US. Board certification by the Association of Professional Chaplains requires four units of CPE alongside other requirements.[2] A CPE unit is usually ten to twelve weeks long. A "residency" is a year-long program that grants the chaplain from three to four units. The Association for Clinical Pastoral Education describes CPE as:

> An Interfaith professional education for ministry. It brings theological students and ministers of all faiths (pastors, priests, rabbis, imams and others) into supervised encounter with persons in crisis. Out of an intense involvement with persons in need, and the feedback from peers and teachers, students develop new awareness of themselves as persons and of the needs of those to whom they minister. From theological reflection on specific human situations, they gain a new understanding of ministry. Within the interdisciplinary team process of helping persons, they develop skills in interpersonal and interprofessional relationships.[3]

CPE is known for its psychodynamic approach,[4] and its commitment to a supervised small-group learning environment. In this environment, caregivers engage in detailed reporting of their pastoral encounters (termed verbatims) which they present to the group for feedback. Through a process-oriented approach, which includes both affirmation as well as confrontation, participants engage in pastoral reflection and pastoral formation with the goal of strengthening pastoral competence.[5] It is significant that requirements for psychiatric chaplains are identical to the requirements for other chaplains. That is, most psychiatric chaplains have anywhere from one to four units of CPE, as well as an endorsement by an organized religious body. These units of CPE, however, are usually completed in a general hospital and frequently do not include a rotation in a psychiatric setting.[6]

Of the nine chaplains who mentioned CPE as a primary influence, several spoke of the transformational quality of CPE,[7] while others focused more on the ways that CPE had facilitated the development of skills that were crucial to chaplaincy. One chaplain mentioned that CPE had imparted "an identity,"[8] while others spoke of the psychological impact, saying that it prompted them to develop self-awareness in the midst of the chaplaincy interaction: "A huge part of CPE training is, 'Where are you in this?'"[9] A number of chaplains mentioned this increased self-awareness, which was frequently manifested in a recognition of the difference between their own beliefs and the belief system of the patient. This recognition allowed them to privilege the beliefs of the patient while in the midst of an encounter. Regarding more concrete skills, one chaplain mentioned that CPE enabled her to help patients "connect to their God and not mine,"[10] while another mentioned that it "showed me the importance of not putting my dogmas out on the table."[11] Chaplains also spoke of CPE as helping them "to develop confidence and poise"[12] and giving them the skills to navigate an interaction successfully.

Shifting our focus to the 50 percent who did not mention CPE as a primary influence, it is notable that the majority of this group had advanced education in one of the social sciences (most frequently psychology) or were seeking such education.[13] While all of the chaplains with some sort of advanced education in psychology and social work mentioned the importance of education in general, they highlighted their specialized education, versus their time in CPE, as being the most influential factor on their chaplaincy. Among those who did not mention CPE, personal experience, particularly experience in therapy or with a psychological disorder such as anxiety or PTSD, was also mentioned as highly influential.

What is the relationship between training and assessment? While training is not the only factor that influences assessment, training was a predictor of the importance of psychiatric diagnosis in one's process of assessment. As we will explore in the next section, those with advanced psychological education tended to see the psychiatric diagnosis as either "one piece in the puzzle" or "very important," rather than "not important at all." Training also affected the named influences on assessment.

Psychiatric Diagnosis and Assessment

When asked in particular about their relationship to psychiatric diagnosis in their pastoral encounters, answers revealed that the importance of psychiatric diagnosis fell along a spectrum of "not important at all" to "essential." Yet, while pastoral caregivers differed in their relationship to psychiatric diagnosis, they all spoke of being able to, in some form, assess the needs of the patient and discern a way forward. Their methods of assessment and decisions about how to proceed in the interaction hinged upon a combination of a variety of factors, including (but not limited to) their training, theology and practical skills. Observation of the tools that inform their assessment alongside their actual praxis reveals the presence of certain (named or unnamed) scholars of pastoral care. Together, these elements place chaplains on a spectrum regarding the broader relationship between theology and behavioral sciences.

While all of the chaplains spoke of the necessity of seeing the entire personhood of the patient, they differed in terms of the importance that they placed on psychiatric diagnosis. On one end, chaplains placed very little emphasis on the diagnosis. This took more than one form: in some cases, the chaplain was unaware of the psychiatric diagnosis, in others, the chaplain was aware of the diagnosis, but his/her theology supplanted any clinical insights and/or recommendations. On the other end, chaplains considered psychiatric diagnosis "very important" in assessing and working with the patient. In the middle, chaplains tended to consider the patient's psychiatric diagnosis "a tool" or "piece of information," but one piece of information (among many) in their discernment of the best way to move forward with the patient.

Among those who tended to place little emphasis on the diagnosis, chaplains spoke of placing their focus on "seeing the person" versus illness. This involved actions such as intentionally meeting the person without a sense of their diagnosis, as well as focusing on empowerment rather than limitations: "So for better or worse, the person's illness rarely comes into focus for me. That is probably a strength and a really big failure, not to contextualize. Often because my instinct is to empower patients and help them see what they're capable of."[14] While chaplains in this group noted that they lacked training in mental health, they (mostly) viewed this as a positive attribute. One emphasized that her lack of training in mental health was beneficial to the patient—versus something that was detrimental—as it enabled her to complement the work of the remainder of the team, as well as to approach the patient from a different viewpoint.[15] Similarly, others noted that they didn't have training in mental health, but suggested that they brought a particular perspective that was essential to the holistic health of the person. They also admitted, however, that this lack of training resulted in difficulties in communicating with the wider treatment team. This chapter delves more into this later on.

The process of making an assessment for this group of chaplains was one which tended to emphasize and privilege their guiding theology, which included themes such as the dignity of all people, especially women. This was often characterized by seeing everyone as a "child of God." It included a recognition that women's stories about God have been historically invalidated. Relying on their skills of empathetic listening gleaned from CPE, they often rooted themselves in the spiritual assessment that had been offered by the chaplaincy department, but considered this a starting point. The tools at their disposal were overwhelmingly relational, seeing themselves as an example of "a kind, caring interaction" in a system that tends to dehumanize people.[16] They also spoke of letting the patient lead, asking open ended questions, and using listening skills that recognized and validated the person and her story. Through these relational skills, they hoped to "give them space to locate their own voice and sense of who God is"[17] while also communicating to the patient her God-given worth.

An example of a chaplain who placed little emphasis on psychiatric diagnosis was a white female chaplain who had four units of CPE, but no further education in psychology. She saw her role as empowering patients to reclaim their spirituality. She accomplished this by letting the patient lead the conversation and leaving space for the woman to talk, recognizing that violence and abuse was always a possibility in the lives of women in the psychiatric hospital. As the conversation progressed, this chaplain spoke of directing the conversation not toward solutions, but trying to help the women identify ways that they had coped thus far. This chaplain recognized that while the woman's illness rarely came into focus for her, what was important was affirming what the women were already doing and recognizing herself as a facilitator for women to support one another and to recognize the presence of God. Often she said she relied on the question, "What's been the hardest thing about this situation?" She stated that this gave women the space to "name the deepest hurt."[18]

Another white male chaplain who self-identified as disabled[19] also had four units of CPE and no further psychological training. He told a story of a woman who was "hysterical" and had issues with being "sexually inappropriate." The assessment of the treatment team was that she should not meet with male clinicians. He was aware of the diagnosis and their recommendation, yet, in his own assessment, believed that "her main problem was that she wanted love and connection."[20] He made this assessment through a process that began with the woman, stating that "I let her tell me what she needs, and tell me her story, in her own words."[21] In a process where he admittedly let the woman take the lead, he recognized that the most important part of any work that he would do was to "make her feel like a part of the human community." He based this in his theology, which recognized that "every person is a child of God." This theology undergirded his decision to meet with this particular patient, against the admonition of the treatment team. While he recognized that physical and sexual abuse was a part of her story, after a few meetings, the chaplain allowed her to hold his hand during their meetings, much to the chagrin of the treatment team. Running into her a couple of months later, after she had been transferred to a different unit, he asked her if she remembered him. "Oh," she said, "I remember you. You were the only person on that unit who treated me decently."[22]

Chaplains who tended to place little emphasis on psychiatric diagnosis admitted that there were times in encounters where they felt embarrassed or confused and/or had difficulty communicating about their ministry with the treatment team. One stated that she sometimes reached a point in interactions where "[t]here is something, like really blocking the patient emotionally, but I don't know where it's coming from." At points like that, "I just, I just don't know what will help her. I know I can be here with her. But I don't know that I can help her."[23] Others told stories of finding themselves enmeshed in situations where they felt that they were acting in the best interests of the patient, only to find that the stories the patients were telling them were emblematic of symptoms of the patient's diagnosis. They spoke of being "embarrassed" when they would approach the team about these interactions, and their body language and nervous laughter in the interview mirrored these feelings. These chaplains also noted that their lack of education in mental health could also at times inhibit their ability to communicate about their work to the treatment team, citing a "difference in vocabulary."

In terms of training, it is of note that chaplains who placed little emphasis on psychiatric diagnosis also tended to have little formal training in the psychological sciences, naming CPE as their primary influence in their ministry and assessment. Among this group of chaplains, many named "experience" as one of their teachers, as well as case studies. One noted that pastoral care classes in her seminary training were "not the most helpful," and that the practice of chaplaincy in the psychiatric hospital had taught her "more than any of those classes."[24]

Chaplains who fell in the middle of the spectrum with regard to the importance of psychiatric diagnosis tended to view the psychiatric diagnosis as helpful information to inform them about "what was going on" with the patient. These chaplains gathered information about patients from a variety of sources, including diagnosis. Yet, they frequently combined this view with an assertion that they did not allow the psychiatric diagnosis to characterize their overall sense of the patient's well-being. For a few of the chaplains in the middle of the spectrum, the importance of the diagnosis was context specific. Perhaps the patient was having physical difficulties (for example, physical pain), in which case, these chaplains would ensure that this was communicated to the team. Yet, if the patient was struggling with delusions, information about the psychiatric diagnosis would become more pertinent and helpful. Even in these cases, however, these chaplains saw the psychiatric diagnosis as one piece of information and used this to formulate their own assessment of the situation (also frequently referred to as "the core issue" or "what's really going on"). The information that they gleaned from the psychiatric diagnosis was frequently put into dialogue with their guiding theology.

Theological themes which surfaced in this group of chaplains also stemmed from the recognition that "every person is a child of God." This was mentioned by numerous chaplains, who then explained different ways of living this out: including loving unconditionally, and making people feel that they were part of a larger community. Themes of hope also surfaced in this group. Tools at their disposal included good listening, building a relationship, and meeting people "where they are at" without assumptions. Some of these chaplains also named particular psychological scholars or theories that had influenced them, including Murray Bowen's family systems theory[25] and the scholarship of Carl Rogers.[26]

A white female chaplain with two units of CPE and a masters in psychology told a story about her process of assessment that was emblematic of those who saw psychiatric diagnosis as one piece of the puzzle. She spoke about working with a woman who struggled with delusions that she had a family, even though in reality, she was alone:

> For instance, this person who has a delusion that she has a family . . . a wife and children . . . this woman, and um . . . to me it's a core of loneliness. Like this idea that she didn't have a community. You know I don't want to try to tell her that she has a community that doesn't exist. Or that the community that is real on earth isn't sufficient for her. So I think I try to . . . sort of . . . sort through I guess. It's a case by case but . . . points to how things are interconnected.[27]

In cases such as the one above, this chaplain was aware of the psychiatric diagnosis of the patient, which included delusions as one of its symptoms. She put this information in dialogue with her theological worldview, which was to live out Christ's mandate to "love unconditionally." The intersection of these two allowed her to provide her own assessment of this person's central spiritual issue (loneliness), but also to decide how she would address these delusions in a pastoral manner. She accomplished this through a method that privileged the experience of the woman. She related her goal was not to "fix" but to "come and join her in her process," to recognize that the woman was struggling not only with psychosis, but also with being in a psychiatric hospital, and many times with lack of financial resources and situations of violence. She stated that she let the woman lead the interaction, allowing the woman to define not only her needs but also what she wanted from the meeting. In her encounters, the chaplain attempted to tap into an idea of hope and human potential: "If you don't believe that someone has room to grow or that they are only their actions or their history, then they become someone you can manage."[28] She noted that she put all of this into dialogue with her knowledge of both fields and her own ability to be self-reflective.

Chaplains who fell in the middle of the spectrum—who considered diagnosis one piece of information among many—did not voice the same limitations in their conversations with treatment team as the group who placed little emphasis on diagnosis. These chaplains emphasized that, while they were not the primary clinician, they felt a certain responsibility to advocate for the patient. While their communication in one hospital was limited by the structural decisions of the hospital to remove chaplains from being active members of the treatment team, when the chaplains sat on the team, they did not express the same difficulty in communicating about their own work to and with the team.

Finally, those chaplains who emphasized the importance of the diagnosis tended toward assertions that the diagnosis was "highly influential" in formulating their approach to the patient. It is important to recognize that those chaplains who placed the largest emphasis on diagnosis also tended to have formal education in psychology, though not all with formal psychological education fell into this category. These chaplains tended to prioritize reading charts before meeting with patients, and frequently advocated for increased education in psychology for psychiatric chaplains. While they tended to privilege the psychiatric diagnosis in their pastoral assessment, they also admittedly held this in tension with their theological education and their chaplaincy; a few named their process of formulating their pastoral assessment of the situation as "putting the two fields in dialogue."[29]

Chaplains who privileged psychiatric diagnosis mentioned numerous factors—psychological and theological—that influenced their ministry.[30] These chaplains also noted that their own stories factored into this process, including their own therapy and their particular psychological history.[31] The theological theme that surfaced across the members of this group included the importance of religion/faith as a source of healing in a system that tends to be suspicious of religion. They also mentioned the love of neighbor, the importance of hope, empowerment of women, and the notion that the person is the best judge of what she wants for her life. While their tools, in general, looked similar to those in the other two groups, it was obvious that in some cases, the psychiatric diagnosis had a larger role in their assessment than the chaplains in the previous two groups.

A white male chaplain with four units of CPE and a degree in social work is an example of one of the chaplains who found psychiatric diagnosis "very important." He was quoted as saying the following:

> I'm usually aware of diagnosis. I've either talked to the team or read the chart. Dialogue with the team is important, as is what the social worker says is possible when leaving hospital. The psychological piece . . . if I don't understand it exactly I'll ask the psychiatrist to explain it to me. Borderlines are the most difficult to work with. Schizophrenics, if they're on their medication, are great. When I work with schizoaffective people, I work with them on feelings. And I want to be aware of someone who is bipolar, so I know beforehand.[32]

This chaplain emphasized the diagnosis affected not only *how* he worked with a patient, but also *the substance* of the work itself. He also related that he felt underappreciated as a chaplain in the psychiatric system, and therefore saw his role as communicating to the other clinicians the value of religion, particularly in relationship to issues of hope and hopelessness. In terms of his assessment of the issue at hand, he put his knowledge of psychology in dialogue with his theological training as a former Catholic priest. He related that when he enters the interaction, he lets the woman lead the conversation, the most important question being, "What does she want from me?" He tried to listen to what she had to say, and understand "where she was coming from." He noted that he tried to emphasize the value of community, love of neighbor and "her own power . . . the fact that they [women] are equal to men."[33] In women with suicidal ideation, he said that religious factors become "very important," especially as they relate to hope and hopelessness.

For another white female chaplain with four units of CPE and a certificate in psychology, the process of assessment involved addressing a number of different questions, both psychological and theological: "Why do they think they want to talk to me? What are the mental health issues that are presenting? What is their understanding of those issues? What does the team think their issue is? What do I think their issue is? Where are they spiritually and how do they understand this?"[34] In line with existential psychotherapy, she believed the central issue in an interaction focused around basic life issues that affect us all—hope, universal suffering, and finding meaning. She therefore made assessments with this framework in mind. She also privileged the patients as the best judges of what they wanted from their lives, with the understanding that they have coped thus far and were often simply in need of "a new learned behavior" around alternative ways of coping. She noted that she attempted to be aware of both trauma issues and the family history of the woman with whom she was in dialogue. Ultimately, one of the central questions for her in relationship to the patient was, "What is this life that we're working for?"[35]

Chaplains who placed a large amount of emphasis on the psychiatric diagnosis also did not speak of the same limitations in terms of their communication with the treatment team. This did not mean that they did not experience contentious relationships with the team; they frequently related that the team on which they worked often "saw spirituality as the problem" or "didn't respect the role of religion" in the lives of the patients with whom they met.[36] Yet, for them, religious factors were very important, and they viewed it as their job to voice this in the midst of the team. Chaplains in this category also communicated a desire to be attentive to the full humanity of the women before them and attempted to hold this in tension with the psychiatric diagnosis of these women.

Assessing the Assessors

What scholars' insights are most relevant to the responses of these chaplains? When it comes to those scholars whom the chaplains themselves mentioned as influential, it is interesting that the majority of named scholars were psychological theorists as opposed to those of pastoral care. It is notable that Murray Bowen's family systems theory and Carl Rogers were both named, as both Emmanuel Lartey and Nancy Ramsay note that these are two of the strands of psychological theory that have undergirded pastoral care and CPE.[37] We also notice the influence of both of these psychological scholars in the way that chaplains describe their assessment and the tools at their disposal—particularly in their focus on empathy and empathetic listening, a hallmark of Rogerian theory. While psychological theorists were named, however, scholars of pastoral care were notably absent. We can only conjecture at the reasons for this, especially as it is pastoral care scholars who make the link between psychological theories and theology/ministry. Although scholars of pastoral care were explicitly omitted, undercurrents of their theories present themselves in the ways that these chaplains describe their assessment process.

Searching for the impact of pastoral care scholars on the responses of these chaplains, it becomes apparent that the perceived importance and function of psychiatric diagnosis influences which scholar's thought is present. In *Introduction to Pastoral Counseling,* Loren Townsend draws on the work of Ian Barbour[38] to propose categories helpful to this discussion. The first category includes chaplains who place little emphasis on psychiatric diagnosis, tending to embrace what Townsend would claim is a stance of "independence" as it relates to behavioral science and theology.[39] A view that is characterized by independence is one in which the two realms are considered to be separate but complementary. The second and third category of chaplains—those who see psychiatric diagnosis as one factor among many and those who place a large amount of emphasis on psychiatric diagnosis—favor a more "dialogical" view, seeing theology and behavioral science as mutually informing one another.[40] Townsend also presents a fourth category of chaplains who ascribe to an "integration" view of science and religion, in which the boundary between science and theology are softened to encourage the convergence of scientific and theological knowledge.[41] Such scholars as Nancy Ramsay and Christine Cozad Neuger populate this category. Though few of the chaplains exemplify the integration view, this category is representative of the potential tools that are available as this book proceeds toward a definition of ethical pastoral care.

The stance that views science and religion as "independent" of one another assumes that each operates as an autonomous field that remains separate from the other. In this view, the two fields have different languages, methods and functions, and thus "psychologists can treat mental health problems while valuing issues of faith as a separate domain, which must be managed in a separate language and perhaps by separate practitioners."[42] Theologians, such as Paul Tillich, and pastoral care scholars, such as Wayne Oates,[43] alike exemplify this view.

As a whole, feminist and womanist scholars of pastoral care do not tend to herald this view. Most feminist and womanist scholars of pastoral care would reject this worldview as dualistic, with the potential to create a false dichotomy. This is rooted in a recognition that dualisms (such as mind/body and nature/nurture) have functioned to reduce complex issues to binaries, frequently ignoring the presence of social and cultural relationships within these issues. The commitment of feminist and womanist scholars of pastoral care to intersectionality would also question the assumption of whether science and religion should actually be viewed as "independent" from one another. When considering the complex ways that race, class, gender, and sexual orientation influence and interpenetrate the issues that women bring to pastoral care, and that these dynamics take up residence within both the psyche and the spiritual realm, most feminist and womanist scholars would tend to push back against a model that focused on separation rather than connection.[44]

Christie Cozad Neuger's critique of personality and counseling theory in *Counseling Women* (2001) serves as an example of the ways that feminist and womanist pastoral theology would push back against the dichotomy between the spheres of religion and social science. Neuger begins with the assertion that to adopt any "one lens" to discuss the complexity of the ongoing formation of the self ignores the complexity of the human personality and its relationship to wider social and cultural forces. She articulates eight critiques of personality theories from the perspective of feminism, and suggests that the minister must take these into account as he/she pursues a particular theoretical orientation in pastoral ministry. These critiques include (but are not limited to): the omission of women's experience in the construction of psychological and theological theories; the lack of an adequate definition of "mental health" for women; the dearth of sociocultural analysis in the process of "naming the problem" in the counseling situation; the tendency for personality theories to be "pathology oriented" rather than to see women's problems as adaptive to situations of sexism, racism, poverty, and other sociocultural forces; the lack of critique of the diagnostic system itself (for example, the connection between the rise of the diagnosis of borderline personality disorder and the rise of the women's movement); and the "adjustment-oriented" bias within counseling theory. Neuger asserts the necessity of keeping women's experiences at the center of theory building, "taking seriously the sexist, racist, classist and heterosexist contexts in which women live."[45] She also mandates that women must be understood from both an individual and systemic perspective. This robust critique would counter beliefs that the fields of science and religion should maintain "independence" from one another, with separate languages, methods, and perhaps separate practitioners. A view of the two fields as "independent" limits the recognition of the ways that the fields critique and challenge one another, a process which Neuger asserts must be undertaken when working with women.

Among those scholars of pastoral theology who would support the "independence" view of science and religion is Wayne Oates. Wayne Oates was a prolific author in the field of pastoral care, whose work is still highly influential today. While Oates was proficient in the theories and methods of psychology and psychiatry, he spent much energy focusing on such issues as what made pastoral counseling "pastoral," as well as using Christian resources (including Scripture and the presence of the Paraclete) to ground his method. Oates advanced a theological analysis of the human condition and pastoral care. As such, his writings addressed topics—such as pain, illness, the acquisition of material goods, and being a workaholic—from a theological lens.[46]

Chaplains in the first category—those who placed little emphasis on psychiatric diagnosis in their assessment process—tended to adopt an approach that mirrors that of Oates, seeing themselves as separate yet complementary to the treatment teams of which they were a part. In *When Religion Gets Sick*, Oates names his goal as not to put the religious understanding of the person against that of the psychiatric, but to develop an understanding of human behavior "in its direst distresses that will be readily understood and appropriated by any minister who has taken the Judeo-Christian interpretation of human life seriously."[47] This enables him to develop a scheme of religious classification, an interpretation and an approach that will not ignore the contributions of psychology and psychiatry, but will be also be unapologetically religious in nature. Oates' view of the minister is one who uses his/her specific skills to address the distinctly religious concerns of the patient. The chaplains in category one frequently made statements that are reminiscent of Oates, stating that their unique vantage point allowed them to approach the patient in a "complementary" way to that of the team, as well as in their decisions to approach the patient from a theological lens. In the examples recounted earlier in this section, chaplains relied on theological resources to frame the encounter.

Probing a bit deeper, however, an engagement with Oates would ask about the method with which these chaplains formulated their theological approach to and with the patient. For example, in the second case, the white male chaplain who self-identified as disabled adopted a theological lens that prompted him to engage in meetings with the woman, and ultimately to hold her hand, against the recommendation of the treatment team. Was the chaplain's assessment of love and connection—culminating in handholding—a legitimate theological assessment (in spite of being against the admonition of the treatment team)? Oates, in *When Religion Gets Sick*, concentrates on the functionality of religion. He notes that "sick" religion is characterized by being uncritical, self-contained and lacking humility or teachableness. Immature religion is also characterized by magical thinking, self-justification, and personal comfort. Sick religion, as it is used by Oates, is a type of belief or practice that becomes "a compartmentalized thing to be 'used' as a defense against life rather than lived as a way of life."[48] Oates also explores how religious factors can contribute to mental illness, such as isolation, idolatry, trust and distrust, hope (and hopelessness) and love (and lovelessness). Oates defines mature religion, in contrast, as that which controls motives rather than being controlled by them and is characterized by a "consistency of moral consequences of the religion itself,"[49] that is, it is a comprehensive philosophy of life.

The chaplain in the second example was quoted as saying his actions were justified by his theological convictions, specifically, to make the woman feel like a part of the human community, as "every person is a child of God." Oates might ask whether this chaplain was also aware of the way that theology functioned—both in the life of the woman with whom he was meeting and in his own life.

In terms of the woman in this example, Oates might inquire into the possible religious factors that might have contributed to her present circumstance. Though the patient expressed "you were the only person who treated me decently," a limitation of this study is that we do not have an interview with this patient to inquire about what she meant by this statement. It is a possibility that his pastoral assessment was accurate, and that the handholding she experienced allowed her to see her own dignity and worth. It is also a possibility that his pastoral assessment was accurate, but that handholding would have been confusing and/or caused regression or a stumbling block as she dealt with forming life-giving relationships in the midst of issues with her mental and emotional health. Finally, it is a possibility that both this chaplain's pastoral assessment and his decision to engage in handholding were not in service of this woman's mental health and flourishing. From Oates point of view, however, this chaplain would need to engage with the functionality of religion in the life of the woman. More of her story—including her sense of hope, her relational life, the role of religion in her life, her experience of care and lack thereof—would have to be explored in order to make a proper assessment. Oates would also probably advocate for increased knowledge of the reasoning of the clinicians in their decision to prohibit meetings with male clinicians.

Many of Oates' writings also address the formation of the person of the pastor, including issues of identity, integrity, self-understanding and professionalism.[50] Oates would probably also inquire about the personal formation of this chaplain and its relationship to his decisions with this particular patient. He would also ask about the functionality of religion in the life of the chaplain, particularly in relationship to decisions about the presence and substance of meetings with this woman, given her relational and emotional history.

Approaching these chaplains from the perspective of feminist and womanist scholars of pastoral care, many scholars might ask larger questions about some of the comments of these chaplains who described their ministry as "separate but complementary" to the work of the treatment team. Returning to the chaplain who chose to hold the woman's hand (against the admonition of the treatment team), drawing on the work of Neuger prompts larger questions about whether this chaplain had taken seriously the sexist, racist, classist and heterosexist contexts in which this woman was situated, particularly in light of the physical and sexual abuse she had experienced. While

Neuger's approach to sexual trauma is explored later in this chapter, given Neuger's earlier critiques of the current diagnostic system, her method would advocate for believing and supporting the story of this woman rather than jumping to a pathology model. Neuger's approach drives the caregiver to inquire whether the symptoms that the woman was experiencing were indeed linked to a psychiatric disorder, or whether they spoke to a need to move through and integrate the harm that she had experienced. Employing Neuger's particular method, rooted in narrative therapy, the caregiver would also ask how this chaplain had helped the woman make meaning out of this story in a way that enabled her to integrate it with her life narrative. The caregiver might then probe what mental and spiritual health would "look like" for this woman, given her particular story and circumstances.

Neuger's method also empowers the caregiver to question the maintenance and regulation of boundaries between this chaplain and the woman seeking care. In *Counseling Women*, Neuger asserts that when addressing intimate violence, the counselor must "listen with appropriate empathy, while maintaining boundaries between the counselor's story and the counselor so that the narrative doesn't take over the counseling process."[51] Given this, the following questions might be in order: Whose needs are being met by this decision? Is this hand-holding allowing this woman to seek safety and find her own voice? Might this decision to engage in hand-holding be blurring the boundaries between the two stories? Is it helping her to regain her agency and engage in prevention and resistance, both individually and communally?

The second and third categories of chaplains exemplify what Townsend would term the "dialogical" perspective of theology and science. The dialogical approach assumes that the two disciplines of theology and science mutually inform one another, as they ask, at their core, similar questions and propose similar philosophical methodologies. In this category, scholars seem to move seamlessly between theology and psychology (and psychiatry), while keeping the boundary between the disciplines.[52] The work of scholars of pastoral care such as Charles Gerkin and Paul Pruyser are characteristic of this category. Feminist and womanist scholars would, on the whole, embrace a dialogical approach to theology and science, agreeing that the two disciplines should be in conversation, as they ask similar questions and utilize similar methodologies. Yet, most feminist and womanist scholars would, at the same time, question the hard boundary between the two disciplines. Highlighting the social and cultural contexts that surround and permeate such disciplines, feminist and womanist scholars would venture a step beyond dialogue, asking instead how divergent disciplines could (and should) mutually inform, challenge, and transform one another. This will be explored in more detail in the following section on the "intregration" perspective.

For Gerkin, one's life story could be approached as a *lectio divina* of sorts.[53] Rooted in a conviction of the dignity of every person, he built on the work of Anton Boisen to argue that "each individual living human document has an integrity of his or her own that calls for understanding and interpretation, not categorization and stereotyping."[54] Interpretation, both of the life of the self and the life of the soul, is considered the "primary task of life." Writing during a time when he felt that the practice of pastoral care was becoming beholden to the social sciences, Gerkin sought to "recover" the Christian tradition in pastoral care, claiming that theological reflection was necessary to "uncover the theological problem at the core of the experience being examined."[55] Yet, Gerkin accomplished this without disavowing the psychotherapeutic paradigm; in *Living Human Document*, Gerkin proposed a model of pastoral counseling that stayed true to its theological roots without eschewing the insights gained through a psychotherapeutic paradigm. Gerkin advocated for a "dialogical hermeneutic process" of enabling the care seeker to interpret the narratives of life through the lens of theological narratives (most notably, that of the incarnation), while also maintaining dialogue with psychological modes of interpretation.[56] Gerkin argued that pastoral care, at its heart, must engage questions of ultimate meaning and value, the questions of faith. [57] In his later work, Gerkin expanded his theory of pastoral care beyond the one-on-one setting to focus on pastoral care in the context of the broader community—both the parish community and the society at large. Here, he positioned the pastor as the imaginative bridge builder between the individual and contemporary modern society.

Paul Pruyser is yet another scholar who exemplifies the dialogical view of science and theology. As explored in chapter one, Pruyser recognized that people seek aid from their pastors due to their desire to view themselves and their problem from a theological perspective. In his groundbreaking work, *The Minister as Diagnostician*, he proposed diagnostic categories based on theological needs. Yet, Pruyser was also deeply steeped in psychoanalysis. He himself stated that his diagnostic categories, while theological in nature, were based on his "own theological intuitions coupled with explicit clinical-psychological knowledge."[58] According to David Barnard, Professor at the College of Medicine at Penn State University:

> Pruyser significantly widened the scope of psychological phenomena to be included within religious studies, as well as the scope of religious phenomena to be included within psychological studies Rather than taking a particular list of predeterminedly "religious" phenomena for study, Pruyser examined the gamut of human behavioral and intellectual functioning as it appeared in religious contexts. . . . He also widened the scope of the psychology of religion by deliberately emphasizing the religious experiences of ordinary people in everyday life, rather than concentrating on religious virtuosi.[59]

Pruyser continued to build bridges between the two disciplines with *Religion in the Psychodynamic Perspective* (1991), which included such essays as "The Seamy Side of Religious Beliefs" and "Assessment of Religious Attitudes." These articles drew upon his knowledge of psychology to explore the ways that religious acts and ideas functioned as psychological coping mechanisms. Yet he also maintained an interdisciplinary approach that advocated for "sharpening rather than leveling the differences in each discipline."[60] This, he believed, was how true understanding occurred.

We notice the influence of Gerkin and Pruyser, as well as this dialogical view of science and theology, in the group of chaplains in the middle of the spectrum, who consider diagnosis as "one piece" of information in their determination of the "core issue." These chaplains acknowledged the importance of psychological diagnosis and engaged in a dialogue between the two disciplines. Yet, in the end, these chaplains allowed their theology to be the lens through which they made their decisions about assessment and how to move forward, interpreting the lives of the patients through this lens. Many times, their own interpretation of the "central issue" in the encounter was reflective of Pruyser's categories, even if they themselves were not aware of this congruence.

The theory of both Gerkin and Pruyser are evident in the white female chaplain who served as the example of this mode of assessment. In her process of naming the central issue of the woman who was experiencing delusions as "loneliness," this chaplain was aware of the delusional nature of the patient's stories, yet interpreted this through her overarching theology. Grounded in an understanding of the psychiatric diagnosis, she embraced the conviction of Gerkin to interpret this woman's life through a theological lens. While we do not know if the Incarnation, per say, was the theological lens of choice, we do know that her theology of "loving unconditionally" guided her interpretation. This led her to a place where she was able to name the central (spiritual) issue, loneliness, or, using Pruyser's terminology, to make a pastoral diagnosis based on theological categories. Her analysis is emblematic of one of Pruyser's categories, though she did not name her process as such. For example, her decision to see the delusions of the patient as indications of a greater loneliness directly corresponds to Pruyser's category of Communion, where he states that the diagnostic task is to assess whether the person "feels fundamentally embedded or estranged, open to the world or encapsulated, in touch or isolated, united or separated."[61] Pruyser connects this sense of estrangement or loneliness to internalized guilt or shame. The chaplain's recognition that she needs to work "within" this delusion to challenge this loneliness—rather than challenge the delusion itself—would reflect Pruyser's emphasis on approaching encounters with a partnership that is characterized by warmth and compassion.

Chaplains in the third category—who considered the diagnosis "highly influential" in their assessment—also at times embraced a dialogical view of religion and theology. As pointed out earlier, a few of them named their process of formulating their pastoral assessment as "putting the two fields [of theology and psychology] in dialogue."[62] When we consider the example of the white female chaplain within this category, she named the central issue in an interaction as "basic life issues that affect us all, for example, hope, universal suffering, and finding meaning."[63] She said that she tended to make assessments with those life issues in mind. She communicated, however, that she was also aware of the psychiatric diagnosis, as well as the team's assessment of the patient. This is yet another chaplain whose method of assessment bears resemblance to Pruyser's categories. Pruyser's concept of Providence addresses the three themes mentioned by this chaplain: hope, suffering and finding meaning. Providence, for Pruyser, refers to the relationship between the Divine and oneself, particularly as it relates to difficult situations. He uses an example of people who come to the pastor asking "Why? Why am I so besieged? . . . What is the 'Divine Purpose' in its intention toward myself?"[64] He suggests that Providence could relate to a desire for guidance from on high, as well as to a capacity for trust. It is, in essence, related to both the present suffering that is occurring and to hope for a greater power and a larger purpose in the midst of the suffering. It also seeks to make meaning out of the particular situation at hand through a relationship of trust with the caregiver.[65] While Pruyser's name was not mentioned in the interview with this chaplain, it is interesting that the three themes that she mentioned fit within Pruyser's diagnostic scheme.

Pruyser, however, also notes the importance of differentiating between "hoping" and "wishing," as this differentiation is "therapeutically important."[66] He defines "hoping" as having to do with "attitudes and global benefits, such as life, freedom, deliverance and salvation" and differentiates it from "wishing," which is related to specific things, such as money, rain after a drought, and expensive birthday presents.[67] Pruyser believes that one's attitude around hoping and wishing also reveals her attitude toward the Divine—the "hoper" allows "God to be God," communicating that God's presence is enough for them, while the "wisher" seeks to conform the Divine to his/her will. Pruyser might perhaps challenge this chaplain to define what she means by "hope" and to be attentive to the way that hope functioned in the life of the patients with whom she met.

It is also important to recognize that Pruyser's diagnostic scheme is larger than simply a focus on Communion or Providence, additionally including the categories of Faith, Grace, Repentance, Vocation, and an Awareness of the Holy. Yet, he also grants that these are not "static factors" to be ascertained, nor variables to be measured. His schema, rather, is composed of "multidimensional themes which, in the mind of the pastoral interviewer, provide vistas of the person's organization of meanings, at multiple levels."[68] He argues that these themes allow the caregiver to have glimpses of the presence of both beliefs and over-beliefs, and the ways that they affect one's thoughts, feelings and actions. He also maintains that they provide a tool for reflecting upon the relationship between the caregiver and care seeker.

The final perspective that Townsend presents, the "integration" perspective, softens the boundaries between the two disciplines, asking how "beliefs may need to be reformulated in the context of modern science."[69] It is reflected in the field's move toward paradigms that are communal and contextual, as it considers the implications of findings in ecology, psychology, sociology and other disciplines in formulating a vision of human life and connection. Most feminist, womanist and intercultural scholars of pastoral care would fall into this category, including feminist scholars such as Bonnie Miller-McLemore, Nancy Ramsay, Carrie Doehring, Pamela Cooper-White, and Christine Cozad Neuger. Many womanist scholars of pastoral care would also populate this category, such as Phillis Isabella Sheppard, Beverly R. Wallace, Jacqueline Kelley, and Teresa E. Snorton. As mentioned earlier, while most of these scholars engage in a dialogical view of religion and science (and/or other interdisciplinary partner(s)), they also ask larger questions about how the realities of human experience shape, penetrate and challenge theological doctrine and beliefs and vice versa.

Bonnie Miller-McLemore, the E. Rhodes and Leona B. Carpenter Professor of Religion, Psychology and Culture at Vanderbilt Divinity School and Graduate Department of Religion, speaks to this dynamic in her writings about the field of pastoral theology. When probing distinctions between pastoral and practical theology, she also explores the wider relationship between psychology and pastoral/practical theology. She notes that what is distinctive about pastoral theology (as opposed to other forms of theology) is that it begins from the location of human experience, frequently the experience of pain and/or suffering. The appropriation of psychology has enabled pastoral theology to explore those human experiences that "matter most," and to offer theological reflection on these experiences. Yet the dialogue between psychology and theology does not presuppose two static fields of thought and study. While pastoral theology inquires, "how God, faith, doctrine, and scripture make a difference in understanding and response to compelling human experience,"[70] the question also, "moves in the inverse direction, asking how assumptions about God, salvation, ecclesiology, and so forth, shape child rearing, growth, loss, love, and other loci of angst and flourishing."[71] Miller-McLemore also suggests that pastoral theology also should not presuppose that the field of psychology should always be its primary dialogical partner. She joins Neuger in a recognition of the need for an ongoing critique of the field of psychology, including its tendencies toward dehumanization and classificatory presumptions. Ultimately, she urges the pastoral theologian to keep his/her focus on what is at stake theologically in pastoral encounters. Psychology may aid in this discernment, but its appraisal requires "constant reappraisal and reinvigoration."[72]

While feminist and womanist scholars of pastoral care take as their starting point numerous aspects of human experience, one example of the ways that they privilege the "integration" perspective is their scholarship on trauma and violence against women. It is important to note that many feminist and womanist scholars of pastoral care have addressed issues of violence and trauma. This is for good reason; as Neuger notes, while we live in a violence-saturated culture, we also live in a society tainted by sexism: "Women are more likely to be assaulted in their own homes by someone with whom they have or have had a trusting, caring relationship than they are to be assaulted on the streets of the most violent American cities."[73] In order to elucidate the ways that this topic illustrates the integrative approach, we will narrow our examination to two feminist and two womanist scholars of pastoral care: Nancy Ramsay, Christie Cozad Neuger, Phillis Isabella Sheppard, and Beverly R. Wallace. These four scholars rely on different sources from divergent fields in their integrative projects on violence and/or trauma, yet also share a method rooted in practical theology that is characteristic of scholars within the "integration" category. This method begins with a commitment to begin with human experience and to formulate (and evaluate) theological principles from there. It heralds the importance of interdisciplinarity in its sources. Finally, there is an eye toward connections between theory and praxis, with the hope that praxis also leads back to theory.

Ramsay, in *Pastoral Diagnosis*, explores how the findings of psychology in the area of psychopathology affect a theological understanding of sin. She embarks on a theory of pastoral diagnosis that allows her to address constructions of authentic power within the pastoral relationship, including the structural and symbolic dimensions of such power. She accomplishes this by probing the anthropological assumptions of the pastor, taking into account his/her identity, social location and theological assumptions. As part of this constructive effort, she examines theories of psychopathology and asks how these theories both inform and alter theology. Ramsay argues that it is not helpful to simply align psychopathology with sinfulness, as has been practiced in the past. Psychopathology "diminishes at preconscious levels the relative autonomy of the person it affects."[74] It therefore alters intrapsychic structures in such a way as to affect one's ability to respond "unselfconsciously and constructively" to a variety of environmental circumstances. She then undertakes a comprehensive examination of the theological concept of sin, in which she suggests that sin arises "as a response to the tragic structures of our human condition rather than as sheer, inexplicable volition in rebellion against God and a violation of neighbor and self."[75] When confronted with situations of abuse or trauma, Ramsay argues that the caregiver must assess both the insights around psychopathology and the complexity of current scholarship around sin, freedom and agency. For her, at stake in a pastoral diagnosis is "more clarity about how psychopathology and sin limit our freedom differently"[76] as well as the ways that both sin and the victimization of psychopathology "interpenetrate, shaping each other interactively."[77] She ends by suggesting that both fields have much to offer one another around such topics as freedom, shame, power, fear, and the roots of violence against ourselves and others.

Neuger has explored the cultural and religious narratives of harm that have formed society and the church and asked how these narratives alter the pastoral care paradigm. Specifically, she focuses on the issue of trauma and trauma studies. As we alluded to in chapter one, in "Narratives of Harm: Setting the Developmental Context for Intimate Violence," she charges that women who have experienced trauma have, in previous pastoral care paradigms, been pathologized, rather than given the opportunity to process and integrate their traumatic history.[78] They have also not been given the opportunity to analyze those skills which previously helped them survive in a life-or-death situation. Knowledge of trauma challenges the models that have been foundational to the discipline of pastoral care, contributing to the creation of a paradigm of resistance that works against these core narratives.

In *Counseling Women*, Neuger uses narrative therapy to engage in an in-depth analysis of ministering with women who have experienced the trauma of intimate violence. She charges that there are three major approaches to caring for women who have been victims of intimate violence: short-term crisis needs, helping women recover from victimhood, and issues of prevention and resistance. In each of these categories, Neuger engages in a dialogue between psychology (in particular, narrative therapy) and theological principles/doctrine, asking how the two interrelate and inform one another.

Neuger begins with an exploration of theological and social issues in the church that prevent pastors and others in the church from believing women's stories of abuse.[79] She notes that these doctrines and beliefs are rooted in a patriarchal system, and if not challenged, "pastoral care cannot appropriately provide a safe and healing environment for abuse victims. Nor can it appropriately call offenders to account."[80] She follows this with an exploration of theological resources that can aid pastoral practitioners when dealing with survivors of trauma and abuse. She also offers insights regarding needed skills (mostly gleaned from psychology/narrative therapy and feminist principles) in the areas of crisis care, recovery from the trauma of intimate violence, and prevention and resistance. Yet in each of these areas she also examines the ways that familial, cultural and theological analysis are essential tools for helping the woman come to voice. Neuger ends with a challenge to church leaders to deconstruct their own "violence-laden core narratives" (evident in both theological doctrine and in praxis that condones intimate violence) in order to support the development of nonviolent alternative narratives in church and society. These alternative narratives involve naming intimate violence from the pulpit, and holding perpetrators (particularly those within the congregation) accountable.

Phillis Isabella Sheppard, the Associate Professor of Religion, Psychology and Culture at Vanderbilt University, in *Self, Culture and Others in Womanist Practical Theology*, highlights the ways that social and cultural devaluing of the black body have colonized the psyche. In her approach to issues of suffering, pain and trauma, she focuses on the importance of an intrapsychic analysis which is rooted in the reclamation of black women's embodiment. While Sheppard notes that womanist practical theology has not shied away from analysis and critique of the material, social, cultural and economic circumstances which frame and interpenetrate black women's lives, she reveals that this has often "overshadowed interest in the psyche."[81] She notes that the social context gives rise to a gendered, cultural, sexual, and racial/ethnic self, and draws on a variety of sources to inquire about the ways that the construction of the self is simultaneously a cultural and psychological experience. Specifically, she examines how experiences of suffering and pain make their way into the psyche, affecting both the self-understanding and interpersonal experiences of black women.

Utilizing a womanist self psychological perspective, she analyzes how this perspective, on one hand, challenges and speaks back to Kohut's theory of self psychology, while it also enables the experience of black women's trauma to be framed as a loss of cultural selfobjects.[82] For example, she reveals how the institution of the black church is an "ambivalent cultural institution" for many black women. While black churches have historically cared for the needs of the black community in a myriad of ways—including the creation of educational, political, economic, and social services—the black church is also "not free of sexism, abusive power arrangements, or theologies that warp the psyche and spirit."[83] The loss of the black church as a cultural selfobject necessitates mourning as a process to "move beyond trauma and as the path toward the reengagement of cultural selfobjects that are sources of self-enhancing experiences."[84]

This journey must include attention to the embodiment of black women as a central theological concern, particularly as historical and cultural forces have linked the black body with a plethora of negative associations, including, but not limited to, criminality, promiscuity, violence, lack of education, and laziness. Black women in particular are in need of an authentic experience of selfhood which creates self-love for and by black people. How might this occur? One such way is to attend to the ways that readings and rereadings of familiar texts need to be read through the lens of black women's experience. Black women also, however, need to read their experience back through the lens of Scripture, particularly in communities where they can be supported in this journey. This sets in motion a process of transformation where black women can be affirmed as being created and called by God.

Beverly R. Wallace, the Associate Professor of Congregational and Community Care at Luther Seminary in St. Paul, Minnesota, is known for her work on grief.[85] In "A Womanist Legacy of Grief and Trauma: Reframing the Strong Black Woman Icon," she notes that the grief experiences of African American women, in particular, have only recently begun to be examined. She reveals that the unique positionality of African American women, and in particular their relationship to the icon of being "Strong Black Women" influences, informs, and reinforces their experiences of grief. Putting the model of integrative grief proposed by Margaret Stoebe and Henk Schut into dialogue with the cultural icon of being "Strong Black Women," she reveals that differences in the history, experiences, and culture between African Americans and European Americans can result in differences between the grief of African American and European American women.

Wallace first examines the icon of the Strong Black Woman, drawing on Regina Romero to note that it possesses two primary themes—African American women as "strong, self-reliant, and self-contained"[86] and their role of caregiving and nurture in the family. The sociocultural phenomenon known as the Strong Black Woman can be considered "the culmination of African American women's experiences of relational losses, gains, hopes, celebrations and defiance in the context of racial and gender oppression manifested in the way that black women psychologically resist oppression."[87] The risk factors of embracing this icon, however, may include emotional and physical assaults to the person of an African American woman, as well as the tendency to supplant her own needs to those of others, particularly in the context of the family. Wallace also notes that this image is transmitted intergenerationally, as young black women are socialized to be nurturing and self-reliant as a strategy of both self protection and resistance in a racist and sexist culture. As part of this, African American women are taught to "mask their anger and internalize the experiences of the numerous micro-insults and micro-aggressions they experience."[88] Yet, this also may create situations when young women may not be able to admit (or even acknowledge) when they are in pain.

Given the unique historical, social and cultural context of African American women, this creates differences between African American grief and that of European Americans. While of course there are similarities between the two experiences, Wallace notes that more often than not, racism is a factor in African American grief experiences, and this affects the ways that African Americans grieve and cope with loss. At times, this grief is also linked to trauma, as institutional racism becomes manifest in oppression, which results in disparities in life expectancy and standards of health and wellbeing for African Americans. The oppression stemming from a racist society also impacts family dynamics, in which the icon of the Strong Black Woman creates expectations that, during times of grief, African American women should suppress her own emotions to take care of the family.

This has grave implications, first for the wellbeing of African American women, and also for the caregivers who tend to them. Wallace notes that the expectation that African American women should remain strong limits these women's ability to give expression to their grief, and possibly to heal. This also has implications for caregivers who minister with African American women, as those who lack knowledge of the cultural context of African Americans may have a difficult time understanding components of the African American grief experience, including the ways that racism has impacted grief responses, and the coping mechanisms of African American women (for example, remaining strong in the face of loss). Wallace offers a litany of things to which pastoral caregivers need to be attuned when ministering with African American women, including the impact of socioeconomic realities on the grief experience, the reality that African American women may delay expressions of grief, the ways that racial injustice and historic distrust of clinical institutions may act as a barrier to help seeking, and the necessity for the analysis both of the religious and spiritual worldview of African American women, and the social, cultural, and familial systems which keep the icon of the Strong Black Women in place. She also offers practical suggestions for spaces and techniques that might be helpful for African American women as they seek to express their grief and trauma.

These feminist and womanist scholars exemplify a method rooted in practical theology that is characteristic of scholars within the "integration" category. First, there is a commitment to begin with human experience and to formulate (and evaluate) theological principles from there. Secondly, they incorporate sources that are interdisciplinary in nature. Finally, there is a movement from theory to praxis, and praxis back to theory.

When these scholars begin with the experiences of women, particularly as this relates to violence, grief, and/or trauma, this results in a recognition of the limitations in current theological beliefs and/or praxis in the Protestant Christian church. These limitations have (and continue to) prove themselves harmful to women. Whether this takes the form of an examination of the limitations in the understanding of sin and how this has been linked to psychopathology, or the ways that theological beliefs have functioned in churches to keep women in situations of violence and/or abuse, or even the ways that the current field of practical theology has overlooked attention to intrapsychic analysis and/or embodiment and experiences of black women, these scholars recognize the ways that women's lived experience of violence, trauma, and grief reveals that certain theological principles and/or praxis has been detrimental to women's healing and flourishing.

Secondly, these scholars embark on an exploration of current scholarship in a variety of disciplines, including (but not limited to) psychology, sociology, ecology, and gender studies. While all of the named authors draw upon psychological resources, they also incorporate familial, cultural, racial, sociological, and embodied analyses in their arguments. Ramsay, Neuger, Sheppard, and Wallace draw upon larger systemic analyses not only to highlight limitations in theological beliefs and/or praxis, but also to engage in robust critiques of non-theological resources, which have frequently been inattentive to these dynamics. Whether this is a critique of Heinz Kohut's theory of self psychology in light of womanist theology, or an analysis of current research on grief and cultural analysis as it relates to the lived experiences of African American women, feminist and womanist scholars engage in interdisciplinary analyses to name and explore the implications of gaps in this conversation which diminish the flourishing of women.

This interdisciplinary analysis culminates in an openness to how these theories might influence—and even change—theological theory and praxis in the field. In the case of Ramsay, for example, she considers both how psychological theory and systemic social analysis intersects with theology. This results in a move toward "communal-contextual paradigms that consider ecological, interdependent, and multileveled theological visions of human life."[89] Sheppard explores how a womanist self psychological approach might bring embodiment to the center of analyses, while also prompting alternative, liberative readings and re-readings of Biblical texts. Wallace examines how analyses of racism, coupled with awareness of the cultural icon of the Black Strong Women, might change the ways that pastoral caregivers approach African American women who struggle with grief.

While we do not see a direct correspondence between the examples of chaplains who were interviewed and the "integration" category of scholars, the method of these scholars could provide an interdisciplinary approach that would enable caregivers to embrace contextuality within their theology and ministry. It begins to name some of the issues of justice that are present and analyzes the ways that current theological beliefs and practices function in relationship to these issues. It then offers constructive proposals for how to move forward, and does this with an eye towards the ways that this method and analyses alter current theological theory and praxis.

I believe there would be an openness toward the "integration" viewpoint among many of the chaplains I interviewed. Many chaplains mentioned the influence of other factors on their theology and praxis and also noted the role and frequency of abuse/trauma in the lives of the women with whom they met. They wondered about the implications of violence and abuse, both theologically and psychologically, and spoke of their challenge in addressing this all-too-pervasive reality. The feminist and womanist scholarship explored above offers a method and praxis that enables a more comprehensive, contextual systemic approach to chaplaincy with this population.

Conclusion

From this chapter on assessment, particularly in light of psychiatric diagnosis, it is evident that chaplains voice divergent views on the role of psychiatric diagnosis within their own assessment of care seekers. At the same time, regardless of their position on psychiatric diagnosis, every chaplain named a particular way of assessing the issue at hand and proposed a method for moving forward. Whether these caregivers are engaging in an isolated "pastoral diagnosis" or tend toward Townsend's notion of "pastoral engagement with interdisciplinary diagnostic practices" could be debated, as there are variations in the tools at their disposal and the ways they privilege these tools. What is apparent, however, is that the western medical model, with its emphasis on the practice of diagnosis, has influenced the praxis of these caregivers, whether stated or not. Across the board, chaplains were exceedingly aware of the pervasive presence of psychiatric diagnosis. Whether they saw themselves as "complementary" to it, said that they "put the two fields in dialogue," or considered it "very important," they recognized that this was the primary reality with which they needed to engage in the environment of the psychiatric hospital. Given that over half had little to no training in mental health, one even wonders about the validity of statements such as "putting the two fields in dialogue." How might chaplains go about this process, given their lack of training? In turning to the integrationist perspective, which presupposes knowledge in a variety of fields and a commitment to analyzing how this knowledge might alter doctrine and praxis, one also wonders if the chaplains have the tools to engage in this wider, interdisciplinary dialogue.

While questions about chaplains method(s) of assessment remain, the importance of being able to "diagnose" the "central issue" and to construct a method for addressing it was paramount. The method, sources and praxis of their assessment varied widely—from privileging theological categories for their assessment to privileging the diagnosis as constructive of how they should proceed—yet the importance of assessment was never questioned. What *is* notably missing from these conversations around assessment, however, is the presence of race. When speaking about the process of assessment, descriptions of the racial identity of the care seeker were not mentioned, nor were insights regarding how the racial identity of the caregiver might have influenced the interaction. Given the exploration in the previous chapters about the numerous ways that race is a factor in diagnosis, as well as the insight that race is *always* present in encounters (even when not mentioned), the absence of any acknowledgment of race when speaking about assessment is in need of attention.

The concrete practices of these chaplains reflect different approaches to the relationship between science and religion and incorporate, explicitly or implicitly, different scholars of psychology and pastoral care. Most of the chaplains fell into the dialogical view of religion and theology, that is, formulating their pastoral assessment of the situation by putting the two fields of pastoral care and psychology in dialogue. While this view is characteristic of numerous preeminent scholars of pastoral care, it also maintains a separation between the fields of psychiatry, psychology, and pastoral care. Townsend would argue that this separation allows the fields of psychiatry and psychology to define the norms for spirituality, as well as grant spirituality professional legitimacy.[90] One wonders if and how the "integrationist" position, advanced by feminist and womanist scholars in the latter part of this chapter, might complicate the dynamic about which Townsend speaks, or at least grant chaplains and scholars of pastoral care (and ethics) a larger role in the conversation around spirituality as it relates to mental health. We will examine this further as we propose a framework for ethical pastoral care, Just Care, in chapter four.

NOTES

1. As we noted in chapter one, Clinical Pastoral Education was founded by Anton Boisen and his colleagues.
2. According to the Association of Professional Chaplains, the standards for board certified chaplains include a Masters degree in theological studies, endorsement of good standing in accordance with the applicant's faith tradition, four units of CPE from an accredited institution, a minimum of two thousand hours of work experience as a chaplain prior to completion of the CPE units and demonstration of current competency standards via written materials and interview. Association for Clinical Pastoral Education, https://www.acpe.edu/ACPE/_Students/FAQ_S.aspx. Accessed February 2017.
3. Association for Clinical Pastoral Education, https://www.acpe.edu/ACPE/_Students/FAQ_S.aspx. Accessed February 2017.
4. See Amy Elise Green, "Critical Components in the Formation of Clinical Pastoral Education Supervisors" (DMin diss., Ecumenical Theological Seminary, 2011), 28–33.
5. Pastoral competence is defined as "pastoral function, pastoral skills and knowledge of theology and the behavioral sciences." Association for Clinical Pastoral Education, https://www.acpe.edu/ACPE/_Students/FAQ_S.aspx.
6. The exception to this are CPE programs that are held in psychiatric hospitals. In the state in which I interviewed chaplains, one hospital hosted a CPE program, and another was attempting to offer a CPE program, but had not yet been successful. The third hospital did not offer a CPE program on their grounds.
7. This "transformation" usually referred to their own inner world and not to broader systemic dynamics.
8. V8, interview.
9. O5, interview.
10. V5, interview.
11. V1, interview.

12. V8 (chaplain at Violet Hospital), interview by the author, February 22, 2016, MP3 Audio Recording.

13. Among the degrees held by these chaplains are the following: a masters in counseling, a social work degree, a certificate in abnormal psychology, an online masters in psychology. Another chaplain was leaving chaplaincy for a doctoral program in psychology.

14. V8, interview.

15. O1, interview.

16. O3, interview.

17. V8, interview.

18. V8, interview.

19. He self identifies as disabled due to being classified as "legally blind."

20. F2, interview.

21. F2, interview.

22. F2, interview.

23. O1, interview, 30:00.

24. V8, interview.

25. According to the APA Dictionary of Psychology, family system theory is a broad conceptual model that focuses on the relationships between and among family members. Any systemic change must not be concerned simply with the individual, but must consider the entire family system. Family systems theory is one of the psychological theories that has made its way into pastoral care. Examples include the work of Ron Richardson, *Creating a Healthier Church: Family Systems Theory, Leadership and Congregational Life* (Minneapolis, MN: Augsburg, 1996); Mpyana Fulgence Nyengele, *African Women's Theology, Gender Relations and Family Systems Theory, Pastoral Theological Considerations and Guidelines for Care and Counseling* (New York: Peter Lang, 2004).

26. Carl Rogers is regarded as the founder of the person-centered approach, manifested in person-centered psychotherapy. This approach holds that the most important factor in successful therapy is the relationship between the therapist and client. Three factors that contribute to a relationship that facilitates positive change include congruence, unconditional positive regard and empathy. This theory has also made its way into pastoral care and is particularly noticeable in pastoral care's increased emphasis on empathetic listening. For examples see Carrie Doehring, *The Practice of Pastoral Care: A Postmodern Approach,* Expanded and Revised Edition (Louisville, KY: John Knox Press, 2014); Glenn Asquith, *The Concise Dictionary of Pastoral Care and Counseling* (Nashville, TN: Abingdon, 2010).

27. V2, interview, 21:27.

28. V2, interview.

29. V4, interview; O5, interview.

30. This included existential psychology and philosophy, family systems theory, trauma studies (including a knowledge of PTSD), psychological rehabilitation, lived theology, feminist and liberationist theology, and the theology of their parents.

31. One mentioned that he himself was a veteran with PTSD, and this informed his knowledge and assessment of others, notably veterans; another mentioned that her own therapy has helped her to assess the situation at hand.

32. V4, interview, 21:30.

33. V4, interview.

34. O5, interview.

35. O5, interview.

36. F1, interview; V4, interview.

37. See Emmanuel Lartey, *In Living Color: An Introduction to Intercultural Pastoral Care* (London and Philadelphia: Jessica Kingsley, 2003), 84-86; Nancy Ramsay, *Pastoral Diagnosis: A Resource for Ministries of Care and Counseling* (Minneapolis, MN: Augsburg Fortress, 1998), 18-24.

38. Ian Barbour, who earned both a doctorate in physics from University of Chicago and a divinity degree from Yale, is credited with providing a framework within which science and religion could relate to one another. His seminal work, *Issues in Science and Religion*, was first published in 1966, and subsequent works (including *When Science Meets Religion* [2000])

continued to explore his proposed categories of conflict, independence, dialogue and integration.

39. Loren Townsend, *Introduction to Pastoral Counseling* (Nashville: Abingdon, 2009), 79–83.

40. Ibid., 83–86.

41. Ibid., 86-90.

42. Ibid., 82.

43. Ibid. While Townsend maintains that Oates falls into the "independent" category, an argument could also be made that Oates embraces a correlational view in order to formulate his theological assessment; that is, the insights from both psychology and psychiatry inform his assessment of "sick" religion, and he does not see religion as totally separate from psychology and psychiatry. Oates, *When Religion Gets Sick*, 20–24. While I will follow Townsend on this point, it is important to recognize that Oates may indeed fit into both categories.

44. A possible exception to this would be Ann B. Ulanov, whose writings on women and feminism tended to accentuate the dualisms exhibited in Jungian psychology. See *The Feminine in Jungian Psychology and in Christian Theology* (Evanston, IL: Northwestern University Press, 1971), *Receiving Woman: Studies in the Psychology and Theology of the Feminine* (Philadelphia, PA: Westminster Press, 1981), *Transforming Sexuality: The Archetypal World of Anima and Animus* with Barry Ulanov (Boston, MA: Shambhala, 1994). Her view of science and religion followed this, as she saw them as two distinct disciplines which remained complementary to one another.

45. Neuger, *Counseling Women*, 40.

46. See Thomas Chapman ed., *A Practical Handbook for Ministry: From the Writings of Wayne E. Oates* (Louisville, KY: Westminster/John Knox Press, 1992).

47. Oates, *When Religion Gets Sick*, 21.

48. Ibid., 180.

49. Ibid., 31.

50. See Chapman, *Practical Handbook for Ministry*.

51. Neuger, *Counseling Women*, 122.

52. Townsend, *Introduction to Pastoral Care*, 85.

53. Arthur Pressley, unpublished lecture, Drew University, June 2016.

54. Charles V. Gerkin, *The Living Human Document* (Nashville: Abingdon Press, 1984), 38.

55. Charles V. Gerkin, *Crisis Experience in Modern Life: Theory and Theology in Pastoral Care* (Nashville, TN: Abingdon, 1979), 16.

56. Gerkin, *Living Human Document*, 38.

57. Gerkin, *Crisis Experience in Modern Life*, 14.

58. Pruyser, *The Minister as Diagnostician*, 83.

59. David Barnard, "Paul Pruyser's Psychoanalytic Psychology of Religion," *Religious Studies Review* 16.2 (1990), 126.

60. Pruyser, *The Minister as Diagnostician*, 110.

61. Ibid., 74.

62. V4, interview; O5, interview; V2 interview.

63. O5, interview.

64. Pruyser, *The Minister as Diagnostician*, 64.

65. This trust encompasses the caregiver's character, that he/she is worthy to receive this care, and the caregiver's relationship with the Divine.

66. Pruyser, *The Minister as Diagnostician*, 65.

67. Ibid., 66.

68. Ibid., 67.

69. Townsend, *Introduction to Pastoral Counseling*, 89.

70. Bonnie J. Miller-McLemore, "Also a Pastoral Theologian: In Pursuit of Dynamic Theology (or Meditations from a Recalcitrant Heart)," *Pastoral Psychol* (2010) 59: 813–28, 825.

71. Ibid., 826.

72. Ibid.

73. Neuger, *Counseling Women*, 93.

74. Ramsay, *Pastoral Diagnosis*, 147.

75. Ibid., 147.
76. Ibid., 148.
77. Ibid., 171.
78. Christie Cozad Neuger, "Narratives of Harm: Setting the Developmental Context for Intimate Violence," in *In Her Own Time: Women and Developmental Issues in Pastoral Care*, ed. Jeanne Stevenson Moessner (Minneapolis, MN: Augsburg Fortress Press, 2000): 65–86.
79. These include God imagery, theological ownership, glorification of suffering and those qualities which have been idealized for Christians (and applied to women). For more on this see Neuger, *Counseling Women*, 97–102.
80. Neuger, *Counseling Women*, 102.
81. Sheppard, *Self, Culture and Others*, 61.
82. Sheppard draws on Heinz Kohut's definition of selfobject here, defining it as "creative persons in 'religion, philosophy, art, and the sciences' who, in the case of group illness, are in 'empathic contact with the illness of group self and, through their work . . . mobilize the unfulfilled narcissistic needs and point the way toward vital change. These creative persons give form to the cultural malaise and social conditions that perpetuate group illness.'" Sheppard, *Self, Culture and Others*, 114–15, drawing on Kohut, *Self Psychology and the Humanities: Reflections on a New Psychoanalytic Approach*, ed. Charles B. Strozier (New York: W.W. Norton, 1985), 84. She adds to this definition the insight that cultural selfobjects are not simply individuals, but that they also encompass the symbols, language, institutions, and cultural productions that meet the needs that are "sometimes embodied by individuals." She notes that given Kohut's particular social and cultural location, a womanist understanding of selfobject must grant greater attention to the social, relational, and contextual aspects of the development of the self.
83. Ibid., 137.
84. Ibid., 127.
85. For more see P. Rosenblatt and Beverly R. Wallace, *African-American Grief* (New York: Brunner Routledge Press, 2005), and "A Black Widows' Journey Toward Living Life Anew" in Sabra Robinson, ed., *Widowed but Not Wounded—The Hustle and Flow of 13 Resilient Black Widowed Women* (Nehemiah, 2017).
86. Wallace, "A Womanist Legacy of Trauma, Grief and Loss," 46.
87. Ibid., 47.
88. Ibid., 49.
89. Townsend, *Introduction to Pastoral Counseling*, 89.
90. Townsend cites numerous studies within psychiatry and psychology to support this claim. See Townsend, *Introduction to Pastoral Counseling*, 78.

Chapter Four

An Alternative to a Diagnosis-Focused Approach

Just Care

This book proposes a model of ethical pastoral care for women in psychiatric hospitals, Just Care. Just Care brings together contributions from the fields of feminist and intercultural pastoral care and feminist Christian social ethics with the voices of psychiatric chaplains in a unique blend that undergirds its key theoretical foundations and its essential components and guidelines. Psychiatric chaplains were united in their assertion that they aimed to see and honor the "whole person" in a system (and on a team) that tended to reduce women to their diagnosis. Just Care follows scholars of feminist and intercultural pastoral care in its proposition that ethical pastoral care that addresses the entirety of the person—from her personal history, hopes, and dreams, to the larger culture in which she lives—must include both a personal and systemic analysis of her life. When considering the particular social and cultural place of women in psychiatric institutions, it asserts that a commitment to justice is *foundational* for ethical pastoral care. As such, a systemic analysis rooted in a commitment to liberation, such as one advanced by scholars of Christian social ethics, must be an essential theoretical foundation for Just Care. Yet, as a form of pastoral care, Just Care also must necessarily include attention to the encounter between the caregiver and the care seeker. The voices of feminist and intercultural pastoral theologians bring attention to the role of culture in the lives of both the care seeker and the caregiver, as well as the unique cultural ethos of the psychiatric hospital within U.S. society, and the institutional culture that exists inside the hospital walls. Just Care builds upon these sources of knowledge to propose that ethical pastoral care with women in psychiatric institutions must account for *both* institutional-personal and societal-systemic elements. In sum, the theoretical framework for Just Care that rises out of feminist and intercultural pastoral care, feminist and womanist Christian social ethics and the approaches of psychiatric chaplains must be rooted in a commitment to justice and an emphasis on the role of culture within the encounter.

In previous chapters, this book examined the ways that preeminent scholars in the field of pastoral care, including those who self identify as feminist, womanist, and intercultural pastoral theologians, scholars from feminist and womanist Christian social ethics and the voices of psychiatric chaplains troubled concepts of psychiatric diagnosis. Yet, how do these three sources of knowledge come together to offer theoretical foundations for Just Care? And why is it essential to rely on these sources, as opposed to others? As mentioned in the section on method, this book privileges experience as knowledge. Interviews with psychiatric chaplains reveal that, in the particular setting of the psychiatric hospital, racial, and cultural dynamics in the encounters between chaplains and women with mental illness are complex and multi-layered. These dynamics include such issues as the chaplain's own culture, racial identity, and embodiment (and her awareness surrounding that reality), as well as the racial and cultural composition of the chaplaincy staff and hospital staff and their surrounding socio-cultural location. This intersects with the many ways that racial and cultural dynamics are at play in the lives of the patients within the hospital—including (but not limited to) their own racial and cultural identity, and the ways that this identity intersects with other mental, emotional, spiritual, social, and economic factors. In this chapter, I show that Just Care draws on feminist, womanist, and intercultural care to recognize and privilege the presence of these overlapping and interwoven cultural pieces. It is rooted in the acknowledgement that culture is not static and that membership in a culture does not necessarily imply an endorsement of the variety of aspects of that culture.[1] Just Care further recognizes the importance of privileging the presence of these cultural dynamics within an encounter. As such, Just Care draws on feminist, womanist, and intercultural care to affirm the basic principle of contextuality: every behavior and belief must be considered in light of its context.[2] It does this within the context of a psychiatric hospital, which admittedly has its own institutional culture, as well as being rooted in the culture of the United States at large.

Just Care also draws on intercultural care to affirm that a cultural awareness requires more than just information about culture, for true change comes from encounter. It affirms that encounters between the psychiatric caregiver and the woman must first be rooted in Lartey's concepts of multiple perspectives and authentic participation.[3] Lartey's principle of multiple perspectives asserts that, "*equally rational* [italics mine] persons can examine the same issue and yet arrive at very different understandings."[4] Multiple perspectives is important for intercultural care as it maintains that every perspective is important and worthy of being both articulated and heard. This principle stands against monocausal explanations of phenomena, that is, the stance that there is "one total explanation for any experience."[5] Intercultural pastoral care notes that monocausal explanations are usually intertwined with power dynamics; they have been handed down (and enforced) by the powerful to the powerless.

While Just Care recognizes the importance of the concept of multiple perspectives in pastoral care, it also departs from portions of this definition. As it stands, Lartey's description of multiple perspectives would exclude those individuals who may be suffering with symptoms of severe mental illness, as in many instances these people are not given the descriptor of "equally rational." Instead, Just Care follows the insights of on-the-ground chaplains who are committed to the entire humanity of the women with whom they minister. A commitment to the "whole person"[6] recognizes that, though the woman in the psychiatric hospital may be experiencing delusions or hallucinations, her voice within the context of the entirety of her humanity needs to be honored and believed. We will delve more into the importance and varied understandings of "belief" later in this chapter. Along with this commitment to multiple perspectives, Just Care affirms the right of each person to participate in the discussion and to examine the issue from her own perspective.[7] This may be especially challenging in the context of a psychiatric hospital, where a patient's perspective might deviate from normative societal beliefs and values. Just Care privileges the voices of chaplains many of whom commented on the importance of meeting the patient where she was and following her lead in the conversation. While the praxis of these chaplains revealed that following this premise was often difficult to embody,[8] Just Care holds that this is a valuable assertion nonetheless. As conversations with these chaplains revealed, sometimes Just Care may mean addressing issues that appear outside of the boundary of "religion or spirituality," such as communicating with the patient about a physical ailment. Other times, following the patient's lead may be manifested in "entering into her delusion" and naming the underlying dynamic therein.[9] Yet, drawing on Lartey, Just Care asserts that the combination of privileging a deeper notion of multiple perspectives, while also honoring the authentic participation of both the caregiver and the patient is essential.

Just Care also suggests that within an encounter itself, the caregiver needs not only to "believe" another culture, but also to "come to understand it both cognitively ('thinking with') and affectively ('feeling with')."[10] How does one embrace a cognitive and affective approach to another culture within an encounter, particularly within the context of a psychiatric hospital? Just Care builds on feminist, womanist and intercultural pastoral care to assert that pastoral care must include components of listening, empathy, and respect.[11]

It also, however, follows Lartey in his proposal of "interpathy" as one of the necessary components of pastoral care.[12] Interpathy involves bracketing one's own beliefs and values in order to temporarily enter another's system of beliefs. It seeks not only to recognize the other, but to attempt to share in "that otherness," as much as the caregiver is able.[13] This requires a commitment to a three-fold view of the person as simultaneously sharing in the common humanity of all people, while being formed by social and cultural forces, and also having experiences that can be attributed to the individuality of each person.[14] Just Care, drawing on intercultural care, lives at the intersection of these three views of the person. It recognizes that a commitment to interpathy relies on simultaneously holding these views in tension with one another, recognizing that cultural difference between the caregiver and care seeker can also create situations in which the caregiver becomes cognizant of a gap between her own cultural experience and that of the woman in front of her. In these situations, interpathy can also result in a recognition on the part of the caregiver that she may not be the best person to accompany the woman through a particular situation.

Just Care also recognizes that a commitment to interpathy, in the context of a psychiatric hospital, requires emotional and spiritual groundedness. When the care seeker expresses beliefs that are widely outside of normative experiences, it can be uncomfortable to voluntarily enter this belief system. A commitment to share in the "otherness" of women in psychiatric institutions can be exceedingly emotionally and spiritually challenging. As such, Just Care's assertion of the importance of interpathy also includes a commitment on the part of the caregiver toward self-care and self-awareness.

Just Care builds on feminist pastoral care, particularly Pamela Cooper-White, who notes that self-care must come first in a pastoral interaction. While self-care is not a prominent theme in Cooper-White's work, her definition is helpful to this discussion. Cooper-White defines self-care as "claiming some time and space, seeking the safe support she needs to process her [the caregiver's] initial reactions and responses."[15] Just Care recognizes that this can take many forms: professional resources such as personal psychotherapy, spiritual direction and professional consultation; personal resources such as prayer, yoga, and practices devoted to spiritual growth; simply taking days off to enjoy life-giving activities, such as hiking or painting; and seeking and enjoying racially and culturally diverse interpersonal relationships that are grounding and nurturing. Yet, self-care needs to ground pastoral care, it cannot be an afterthought or something that happens when the caregiver "has time." For Cooper-White, self-care, coupled with attention to countertransference, are the central components of pastoral assessment. She proposes a definition of countertransference as, "the sum total of thoughts, feelings, fantasies, impulses and bodily sensations, conscious and unconscious, that may arise in the pastoral caregiver in relation to any person who has come for help."[16] Just Care maintains that an examination of countertransference, as it is presented by Cooper-White, is crucial to ethical pastoral care. First, Cooper-White's notion of countertransference nods to a more mutual, intersubjective approach to encounter, one that builds on a notion that sees the caregiver and care seeker as "reciprocal subjects" rather than as a subject-object interaction.[17] In the relationship paradigm proposed by Cooper-White, countertransference is viewed not as a "threat,"[18] but rather as a means by which meaning is constructed and shaped between the caregiver and the care seeker.[19] Just Care, in following Cooper-White, stands against the view of the encounter between the caregiver and care seeker as one in which the caregiver possesses knowledge that she needs to "impart" to the care seeker; rather it proposes a model of relationship where both members are contributing to the construction of something larger than either one of them. Just Care recognizes that both are changed by the encounter. In acknowledging the importance of both self-care and attention to countertransference, Just Care also creates the space for the caregiver to examine her own internal life, as well as her physical, mental and emotional reactions. This hopefully prepares the caregiver to respect and honor the life and culture of the care seeker, rather than projecting her own life and culture on to the care seeker.

Yet Just Care also goes beyond Cooper-White's analytical approach to privilege an interrogation of the caregiver's own social and cultural positionality, as well as the social and cultural assumptions embedded in the ethos of the psychiatric hospital. While Cooper-White does recognize the importance of wider systems on the life of the caregiver, in her text *Shared Wisdom*, she devotes only a few pages to this.[20] Whereas she suggests that the reader should "play with difference" by asking "[h]ow might this case play itself out differently if each individual in the narrative were [this race], [this gender], [this sexual orientation]," she does not suggest that the process of naming social/cultural positionality is a central component of pastoral care, nor does she speak to the role of systemic analysis as it informs and surrounds the encounter. For example, interrogating the ways that the social and cultural location of the larger institution (i.e., in the case of Just Care, the psychiatric hospital) might also change the interaction. Just Care names this exploration of one's own social and cultural positionality, and the power dynamics attached to that positionality, as essential. This exploration affects whether and how the caregiver hears and assesses the woman in front of her.

Just Care advocates for an engagement on the part of the caregiver with Doehring's concepts of self reflexivity and theological reflexivity[21] in order to name the caregiver's own social, cultural and theological positionality. This includes an awareness of the cultural dominance of Christianity, and the frequent misuse of the Christian God to define other religions, recognizing that this participates in assimilation and colonialism. Just Care also follows Doehring's assertions, explored in *The Practice of Pastoral Care: A Post-*

modern Approach, Revised and Expanded Edition, that the caregiver needs awareness of both her own culture, social position, power, and embedded and lived theologies, as well as the culture, social position, power (or lack thereof), and embedded and lived theologies of the woman in front of her

Yet, Just Care also recognizes that the caregiver's attentiveness to the social and cultural positionality (of both herself and the care seeker) can become exceedingly complicated in the atmosphere of a psychiatric hospital, which has its own social and cultural ethos. Goffman's study of psychiatric facilities reveals that psychiatric hospitals, in particular, have a "totalizing" effect on those who live in them.[22] In this institutional setting, patients can feel completely isolated from the world, particularly as their day-to-day activities depart from the basic social and cultural structure of Western society, in which the individual tends to "sleep, play and work in different places with different co-participants, under different authorities and without an overall rational plan."[23] Goffman recognized that psychiatric patients who were forced to live a regulated, institutionalized existence in a closed system, separated from the remainder of society, undergo what he termed a "mortification of self, through physical and social abuse, which then leads to the loss of their usual identity."[24] Just Care supplements Goffman's analysis with its emphasis on the practice of diagnosis that takes place within the setting of the psychiatric hospital. As this book has explored, the psychiatric hospital is defined by the values of the Western medical model. These values are reflected in the practice of psychiatric diagnosis, which itself is frequently inattentive to larger dynamics of race and culture. In the psychiatric hospital, it is particularly easy to lose sight of the cultural understandings that are institutionally reinforced and regulated in the lives of the care seeker and caregiver. Just Care advocates for the flourishing of the entire self and recognizes the tendency for institutions to erase the complexity and humanity of patients. It serves as a disruption to the institutionalization and resultant depersonalization that can occur in institutions, asserting that it is incumbent upon the chaplain to stand up against a totalizing institutional culture. Yet, this must stand alongside the chaplain's commitment to honor the racial and cultural understandings that inform both the life of the chaplain herself, and the life of the woman who seeks care. Instead of the questions proposed by Cooper-White, which inquire how interactions might play out differently if either (or both) of the individuals in the encounter were [this race], [this gender], [this sexual orientation], a Just Care practitioner might ask the following: What is my obligation to intervene and/or advocate for the woman in front of me? How might an anti-racist critique alter the perception of this person's diagnosis and how might that affect this encounter? How is culture—both the cultures of the caregiver and care seeker and also the culture of the psychiatric hospital—present and/or invisible in this interaction?

Feminist and womanist Christian social ethics, with its focus on lived commitments to justice and systemic analysis, is an integral and necessary partner in providing the theoretical foundations for Just Care. Why? Just Care recognizes that the commitment of feminist Christian social ethics to approach ethical analysis from a place that takes seriously the place of power, race, gender and class as "necessary theoretical tools"[25] in an analysis of the presence (and absence) of justice is essential when approaching care for women within a psychiatric hospital. As the chaplains noted, the women in front of them were "at the intersection of so many marginalizations"[26] : they were women, frequently of color, the majority of whom had a history of violent abuse. Many were admitted to a state hospital because they had "no other social or financial options."[27] On top of this, these women were struggling with the symptoms of severe mental illness. In such an extraordinarily disempowering situation, Just Care asserts the importance and centrality of a commitment to justice.

To say that feminist and intercultural scholars of pastoral care do not focus on larger systemic dynamics would be inaccurate, as we have explored. Scholars of feminist, womanist and intercultural pastoral care have focused on the power dynamics between the caregiver and the care seeker, emphasizing the importance of awareness of the caregiver's and care seeker's own social position and embedded and lived theologies. They have interrogated diagnostic systems, noting how women (in particular) have been pathologized rather than given the space to integrate violence and/or trauma. Others have noted that differences in culture between African American women and European American women can result in differences in experiences like grief or anger.[28] All of these have implications for the practice of psychiatric diagnosis, which on the whole tends to ignore larger issues of culture and race. Yet, these intersectional analyses, particularly those focused on the impact of race and racialized dynamics, have yet to be applied to the particular situation of women caught in the culture of the psychiatric hospital, who struggle with severe mental health issues alongside (and sometimes as a result of) other situations of oppression and/or marginalization. An analysis such as this is crucial for ministry with those with mental health challenges, and particularly women within the psychiatric hospital, as they exist at the nexus of their own social, cultural, and racial location and a culture informed and permeated by the values of the Western medical model. As has been established earlier, the latter culture is frequently inattentive to larger systemic analysis and the issues of justice raised by these concerns and critiques. Referring specifically to pastoral care within psychiatric hospitals, Pattison notes that:

> The individualism of hospital medicine and the clinical approach to illness create a milieu into which . . . ministry fits comfortably. This means that

> hospital work may proceed faithfully and effectively (by present criteria) without influencing the institution. The essential power structures are untouched by the chaplain. Indeed he may feel impotent in the hospital . . . and not see how the structure itself denies what he wants to say.[29]

Just Care needs the theoretical partner of feminist and womanist Christian social ethics for this very reason—the emphasis on justice brought by feminist and womanist Christian social ethics, is crucial to name and trouble the "essential power structures" not only of the psychiatric hospital, but also of the society that surrounds it. The dual focus of justice as inclusive of both the systemic and the particular within feminist and womanist Christian social ethics is essential as a foundation for Just Care, especially in light of a discipline such as pastoral care, which has been historically focused on the particular and can still fall prey to this at times, even with the greater awareness raised by communal-contextual and intercultural paradigms of pastoral care. Just Care asserts that a commitment to justice is *foundational* for ethical pastoral care with women in psychiatric institutions, and that a systemic analysis that is rooted in justice must be an essential starting point to fully and accurately see the "whole person."

Just Care relies on Christian social ethics, as a theoretical tool, to expand the conversation from the personal encounter between the caregiver and the care seeker, toward an analysis that includes the ways that a diagnosis-focused approach has been informed by—and continues to intersect with—issues of power (including provider bias),[30] stigma, racism, gender, socio-economic realities, and institutional realities. It reveals that the current "turn toward the biological" within psychiatric diagnosis turns a blind eye toward socio-political and theo-ethical realities that undergird the system and practice of psychiatric diagnosis.

The place of feminist and womanist Christian social ethics as a necessary partner to feminist, womanist and intercultural pastoral care allows Just Care to note that practices of diagnosis are also connected to issues of power—personally and socially. Psychiatric doctors themselves exercise substantial power in issues related to diagnosis—such as the type of diagnosis, which (and whether) pharmacological interventions will occur, and whether someone is institutionalized and for how long. And all of this is lodged within insurance policies, issues of health care access and other such practices around health and healthcare that are linked to (and the result of) social oppression. Yet practices of diagnosis are also integrally connected to issues of social power, which are manifested in the racial-ethnic inequalities in the area of mental health, both in involuntary institutionalization rates and treatment options.[31] Just Care troubles the recent "turn to the biological" as it relates to potential cause(s) of mental illness and the diagnostic scheme, revealing that the onset of mental illness is also frequently linked to social forces, particularly those stressors that tend to be more common among women, such as intimate violence and other threats of violence.

Just Care maintains that questions around race, ethnicity and diagnosis are also extremely important in questioning the diagnostic-focused approach of the psychiatric hospital. As this book has noted, the insights of Townes and Vigen reveal that the current standards for diagnosis, in their silence around race and ethnicity, can result in misdiagnosis:

> A standard that assumes White American culture as the norm and as generalizable to other cultures means mis- and underdiagnosis. Even more deadly is when certain cultures are labeled pathological rather than simply different. Such mental health issues as high rates of undiagnosed stress, stress and substance abuse—issues that may be, and often are, related to issues of interstructured oppression—are often left fallow in many African American communities.[32]

Insights such as the one above point to the injustice and potential harm that is wielded by an approach holding to a standard of diagnosis that excludes significant portions of the population. What is unspoken is that with misdiagnosis also comes ineffective treatment, which translates to people of color, particularly women of color, being more likely to receive ineffective treatment (pharmacological and otherwise) than whites. Yet to simply blame these conditions on provider bias is also to miss the role of the social, political and economic history in the construction of diagnosis.

Just Care relies on Christian social ethics to propose a more expansive analysis of the social and cultural role of the institution within a Western society by putting this in historical perspective. Just Care would recognize that the psychiatric hospital exists within a society that has adopted deinstitutionalization[33] and, some would argue, trans-institutionalization.[34] This raises questions about the justice of who is institutionalized (and who is not). Just Care would also necessitate an investigation between deinstitutionalization and the incarceration rate of the mentally ill, including questions of justice around the validity of this incarceration, and the overlap between the psychiatric population and those who have been incarcerated. It also notes the indisputable ties between the practice of psychiatric diagnosis and the commercial interests of the pharmaceutical industry, including the pharmaceutical industry's role in the development of specific diagnoses in the *DSM-5* and the ties between psychotropic drugs and commercial organizations with for-profit business goals.[35] Just Care asserts that insights and questions such as these are an integral component of holistic ethical care for women with mental illness. The addition of feminist and womanist Christian social ethics as a partner alongside feminist and intercultural pastoral care provides the framework to engage with questions such as these.

Ultimately, Just Care relies on the marriage of feminist, womanist and intercultural pastoral care and feminist and womanist Christian social ethics to highlight that the encounter between a caregiver and care seeker within a psychiatric institution is permeated and surrounded by the injustice of a system in which women, particularly women of color who are in poverty and have been subject to violence or other stressors, are both the ones most likely to develop mental illness and also least likely to seek out treatment. When (and if) these women end up in a mental health facility (to which they may be forcibly referred by the legal system), they are more likely to end up misdiagnosed than their white counterparts, increasing the likelihood that they will receive pharmacological intervention rather than other forms of therapeutic intervention. When they are discharged, they are more likely to reside in settings plagued by poverty, endure poor living conditions, and/or have issues with their physical health.[36] Given this reality, justice, alongside an attentiveness to race, gender, class and culture, must be foundational to ethical care with women with mental illness. Yet, what is the operative definition of justice that undergirds Just Care?

THE "JUST" IN JUST CARE

While there are a variety of definitions of justice, and scholars differ as to the "problem" that ultimately needs prioritization, a concern for justice unites Christian feminist ethicists and scholars of feminist, womanist, and liberation pastoral care. As Just Care directs attention to both the systemic and the particular, it is important to advance a definition of justice that encompasses both of these realities. To arrive at this dual focus, Just Care draws on the definitions of justice from three Christian social ethicists, Aana Marie Vigen, Traci West, and Kate Ott, in combination with one another.

Vigen emphasizes that as a Christian social ethicist, she is not comfortable with a notion of justice that simply emphasizes giving each individual "his/her due." Rather, "justice means loving rightly—seeing and regarding one another rightly."[37] For her, love is an expression of this justice and is expressed in "actively working for the care and healing of all of God's creation—every bit of it. Nothing and no one is expendable; no person can be spared or discarded."[38] She applies this notion to health, by suggesting that a collaborative effort is needed—including a multiplicity of voices and faith traditions, secular laws, and emotional and embodied knowledge—in order to understand "what it means to be human and how to treat one another humanely."[39]

West applies the concept of justice to Christian faith communities, asserting that the appropriation of Jesus Christ as truth involves more than an intellectual assent, but a commitment to praxis that privileges "knowing and doing": "This 'knowing and doing' involves an interactive process of becoming empowered. . . . To recognize what is truly just, Christians rely on their ability to access power from God, their communities of accountability, and resources within themselves."[40] She notes that justice requires "literal engagement with distorting human realities such as violence, white supremacy, and male dominance."[41] It means an enfleshment of the work that brings about the wholeness and dignity of all human people.

Ott proposes a definition of justice that challenges feminist ethicists to address the limits that exist within the worldview of each person.[42] These false limits mar people's ability to recognize the structural and systemic nature of justice. Ott draws on the parable of Jesus and the Syrophoenician woman to highlight the interplay between a person's own limits and her ability to "see" clearly and respond. As she illustrates, even Jesus needed another to challenge him to recognize that the borders he had placed around his ministry were causing injustice! Justice, for Ott, needs to be approached systemically, rather than individualistically: "It is not only teaching the woman to fish, it is ensuring clean water, protecting the area from over-fishing, providing safe access to the body of water, attending to her mental and physical health so she can continue to work, etc."[43] In order to become cognizant of these dynamics, Ott draws on Beverly Harrison's concept of "critical consciousness," which requires the acknowledgement of "the social contradictions which shape not only our collective existence but our personal lives as well."[44] She notes that this consciousness can often only be awakened in concrete engagement or struggle. Justice, for Ott, is action oriented. It calls people beyond themselves to engage with the other and is experienced as "power-in-relation." It is both personal and political. Yet justice in its fullest sense can only be experienced when one fosters an awareness of her own limits and entitlement and develops a "faithful imagination."[45]

This dual focus of justice as both outward and inward, including both the systemic and the particular, is essential as a foundation for Just care. As has been noted, pastoral care has been historically focused solely on the particular, though feminist, intercultural and liberation scholars of pastoral care have advocated for inclusion of a systemic analysis as well. Just Care, in its focus on justice and liberation for those institutionalized with mental illness, must have a notion of justice that is large enough to account for the systems that impact the practice of diagnosis and particular enough to address the ways that justice functions within the lives of *both* the care seeker and the caregiver. These three definitions of justice, drawn from Vigen, West, and Ott, include personal, political, and systemic dimensions and, as such, are appropriate to undergird Just Care.

Non-negotiable Epistemological Assumptions That Ground Just Care

After proposing an operative definition of justice to ground Just Care, it is also important to examine necessary underlying assumptions about the sources of knowledge within Just Care, more specifically what we know and how that knowledge is gathered. As this book argued in the section on theoretical foundations, Just Care asserts that knowledge, at a minimum, must be drawn from feminist and womanist Christian social ethics and pastoral care, and the chaplains' own voices. While the sources of knowledge could be expanded to include insights from other fields, these three sources are the constitutive epistemological elements for Just Care. An absence of any of these perspectives creates a gap in knowledge that results in a distortion of the reality of the lives of women in psychiatric institutions, as one cannot endeavor to propose ethical care for the entirety of the person without knowledge that is attentive to her communal and societal context, as well as her emotional, psychic, spiritual and physical reality. For Just Care, the importance of privileging the voices of the chaplains who are "on the ground" providing care for women in psychiatric hospitals at the same level as the scholarly discourse on feminist and womanist Christian social ethics and feminist, womanist, liberation, and intercultural pastoral care cannot be overstated. These chaplains' voices provide insight into the care that is already occurring, both its strengths and the gaps that need to be addressed. The practices, questions and silences of psychiatric chaplains are a critical foundation from which Just Care must proceed.

Just Care: Psychiatric Caregiving at the Center of Moral Discourse about Care

The intersection of these two fields with the experience of psychiatric chaplains culminates in Just Care. As has been evidenced, Just Care, or ethical pastoral care with women with mental illness, is not based on objectivist moral claims about care or caregiving. Rooted in the actual experiences of caregivers in psychiatric institutions, it places these experiences at the center of ethical pastoral care. As such, it positions the care for women in psychiatric institutions as central to moral discourse about pastoral care and caregiving with women with mental illness.

The decision to position psychiatric care at the center of discourse around systemic pastoral care is based on the insight that this care has historically been relegated to the margins of scholarly conversations within both pastoral care and Christian social ethics. Psychiatric care is not sizably represented in pastoral care research; it is not incorporated into the training of chaplains; it is often regarded as peripheral to pastoral care. Pastoral care for women with mental illness, often subsumed under "care for women" or "intercultural care," frequently assumes that the core components of pastoral care are generalizable across gender, racial and ethnic boundaries. In terms of Christian social ethics, while much has been written about care and healthcare, conversations concerning the specific care of women with mental illness are also frequently pushed to the outer edges of the ongoing scholarly conversation. As has been noted, women with mental illness are usually positioned as examples in a larger discussion of ethical health or healthcare.

This book has enumerated the ways that women in psychiatric institutions exist at the intersection of numerous dehumanizing forces, both personal and systemic. The process of diagnosis can, as we have explored, reduce these women to a one-dimensional diagnosis, while at the same time remove communal responsibility for the moral harm that can result in symptoms of mental illness. These women, however, share the same equality and dignity as every other human being. To put the care of these woman at the center of an ethical system needs no special permission or warrant. In fact, it could be argued that if justice is central to Christian social ethics, one must place the *most* marginalized at the center of one's ethical system to gauge whether this system is addressing their unique situation. Similarly, if pastoral care is directed toward the flourishing and wellbeing of *all* people, the care of women with mental illness should function as a measure for whether pastoral care is truly embodying those aims. As such, the ethical move to put these women at the center of moral discourse about pastoral care is imperative, especially in light of the goals of liberation and human flourishing that are foundational to both disciplines.

While necessary for both disciplines, this ethical move prompts a greater realignment and expansion of the moral center and norms that underlie pastoral care with women. Norms represent acceptable and unacceptable behaviors among groups, while also reflecting their core values and beliefs. Yet, norms are not merely descriptive, they are also prescriptive. According to Jürgen Habermas, norms are acceptable as long as they equally and fairly represent and advocate for all of the members of the group.[46] Just Care maintains that the norms upon which pastoral caregiving relies do not at present fairly represent women in psychiatric institutions. At the same time, it challenges Christian social ethics to recognize that any approximation of justice must include attention to the particular situation of women in psychiatric institutions. Given this reality, it is essential to examine the central components and guidelines of Just Care that prompt the development of alternative norms for pastoral caregiving.

HOW DO CHAPLAINS PRACTICE JUST CARE? WHAT ARE THE COMPONENTS/GUIDELINES?

Just Care proposes that ethical pastoral care for women in psychiatric institutions, at its core, recognizes that the factors which prop up a diagnosis-focused system based on the Western medical model must be named as dehumanizing and unjustifiable to those women who are subject to them. Just Care acknowledges that the psychiatric chaplain has an unusual and unique role in this situation. As chaplains indicated in their interviews, they were both part of the treatment team and separate from it. Yet they were also united in their stance of being opposed to anything that might function as reductionistic in the life of the woman. Chaplains are also symbolic of a discipline that is, in the words of one chaplain, "familiar with mystery."[47] In light of this, how can chaplains be bridge builders between the world of the psychiatric hospital and a more holistic way of seeing, being and believing?

The core components of Just Care offer guidelines for a care that is attentive to both the individual and to broader systemic realities in its aim toward liberation from injustice. Just Care is care that begins with the woman and also embodies an awareness of the chaplain's own social positionality along with the chaplain's embedded and lived theologies. It is both communal and individual, and is attentive to the intersection of culture, gender, race and class. Finally, Just Care is rooted in the power of encounter. It has an expansive view of health and healing and puts spirituality at the center of its care. Each of these components will be elucidated in turn.

Care that Begins with the Woman

> "What is important for them [the patient]? What do they want for themselves?"[48]

> "You are suffering from trauma. And that, it has not been . . . it's not in in your medical records."[49]

Just Care first and foremost recognizes the beauty, sanctity and dignity of each woman who resides in a psychiatric hospital. It recognizes that care in service of these women must begin with them—the entirety of their humanity, their hopes and dreams as much as their struggles and trauma. It must begin with their narrative, the ways that they make meaning of their existence in the shared space that is the encounter between themselves and the chaplain. The recognition, noted by many chaplains, that these women are the best judge of what they want for their lives is crucial to Just Care.

Just Care is rooted in a fundamental respect for the immense stressors under which women live. Yet, it also recognizes that many of these stressors are frequently a result of a larger culture that can reduce and infantilize them due to their gender, race, mental illness, or socioeconomic status. Many times it is a combination of these factors—rather than simply one—that creates the psychic, physical or spiritual disequilibrium with which these women struggle. It is for this reason that an examination of these stressors must be central to Just Care. While pastoral care historically frequently recognized the importance of the examination of the personal history of the woman, this personal history must also be put into dialogue with the communal and societal analysis, utilizing tools from feminist and womanist pastoral care and Christian social ethics. Just Care respects the ways that these women have coped with these stressors thus far and holds in tension the particular narrative of the woman and the communal context in which this narrative was created.

Alongside the recognition of the beauty and complexity of these women is the assertion that any one source, particularly those produced by the psychiatric hospital—be it the chart or the psychiatric diagnosis—does not tell the entire story of a particular woman. At worst, this source may be erroneous or neglect important and crucial details of a particular woman's life. Recall the male chaplain who met with a woman who had never told anyone that she was raped. This is an all too familiar scenario in psychiatric chaplaincy. The chart or the diagnosis cannot be regarded as a full narrative of the woman's life. Similarly, the "on the ground" interaction between the woman and the chaplain also falls short of encompassing the full beauty and mystery of this woman. The life and reality of the woman is always larger, deeper and more complex than any official or unofficial source can express.

Awareness of the Chaplain's Own Social Position, Cultural Context, and Embedded and Lived Theologies

> "And ultimately I try to be aware that I'm white. And trying to be aware of when am I being more authoritative and when am I being more collaborative. Just watch myself . . . like . . . I don't know."[50]

As has been noted in the theoretical foundations, Just Care builds upon scholars of feminist, liberation, and intercultural pastoral care in their emphasis on a commitment to fostering the self-awareness of the caregiver. This includes intentional exploration of the caregiver's own social positionality, cultural context and embedded and lived theologies, particularly those factors that cause her to see the other through the lens of her own experience. As we have noted, this can be extremely challenging in light of the particular social and cultural ethos of the psychiatric hospital.

How might one go about this? As Ott reminds us, all caregivers are limited by their own worldview.[51] As it is often difficult for one to see the limits of her own worldview, as well as to name her own power, caregivers need the aid of groups to foster awareness and accountability. A commitment to Just Care recognizes that the caregiver often needs the aid of community to engage in these processes with integrity. Doehring also speaks to the importance of accountability groups among ministers to help to identify privilege. For Doehring, she suggests that these groups be composed of colleagues who can aid the minister in engaging with her own emotionally-charged "default" theology, as well as her social advantages and disadvantages.[52] While Just Care recognizes that communities of colleagues can function as a safe supportive space in which to engage with social, cultural and power dynamics, it further recognizes that having a community composed of individuals of different social and cultural positionality might have the capacity to reveal these dynamics in undiscovered ways. While social and cultural diversity may be reflected in a community of colleagues, there may need to be an intentionality around the composition of this community. The core insight here is that Just Care urges caregivers who endeavor to keep these social, cultural, and power dynamics in view to surround themselves with an intentional, supportive and challenging community. While this may not happen in a linear fashion (as sometimes it is engagement with the other that prompts awareness in one's self), this engagement with self and culture needs to be an intentional process that is undertaken with the aid of others who are committed to justice.

Furthermore, Just Care follows feminist and womanist pastoral care to challenge caregivers to engage both with their own culture, social positionality and embedded and lived theologies, and also with the culture, social positionality and embedded and lived theologies of the woman in front of them. As noted by Jacqueline Kelley, in "Womanist Pastoral Care Using Narrative Therapy," "it is important for counselors to become knowledgeable about how race, culture and gender affect communication styles, and seek to obtain additional training in a variety of theoretical orientations and approaches beyond those that are formally taught."[53] She highlights that effective ministry with culturally diverse populations must involve both knowledge of theory (whether this be education, counseling, or other forms of caregiving) and also knowledge of the particularity of the person/group with whom the caregiver is ministering. Using the frame of narrative therapy, she offers examples of deconstructive questions that can be used within an encounter to explore cultural differences concerning the mysteries of human existence. While, as Kelley notes, tools of narrative therapy provide one method for engaging with the cultural difference of the care seeker, Just Care would hold that this is an essential component regardless of one's chosen tool(s).

Care That Is Both Communal and Individual

> "What's going on in their family relationships and with their friends and in their communities has an effect on their mental health and we don't have a way for them to really . . . have a place for patients to talk through that and help them see the connections between the different pieces of their lives."[54]

Just Care embraces the expansion of the concept of care from the individual to the communal, that is, "from care understood as counseling to care understood within a wider social, religious and political context."[55] Yet, it also holds the two in tension, recognizing the overlapping, interrelated nature of communal and individual care that is essential to ethical pastoral care.

Communal care recognizes that the social and cultural position of women in a society marked by intersections of patriarchy, racism, and classism renders certain groups of women stigmatized and disenfranchised in intensely complicated ways. They are more likely than men to be in poverty due to workplace inequality, to be the head of single-family households (and thus have the stress of caring for dependents), and to be victims of intimate violence, among other factors. The social and material disparity that women experience can lead to feelings of helpless and hopelessness, as well as create immense stress in their lives. Any one of these factors can result in mental illness.[56]

Communal care recognizes that the system of psychiatric diagnosis has evolved within this society and, as such, can often reduce and ignore these factors and/or offer an incorrect assessment of a woman's situation. In instances of intimate violence for example, a healthy response to emotional trauma has the potential to be masked as a diagnosis, while some diagnoses ascribed to the woman can imply collusion in her own abuse.[57] A diagnosis of severe mental illness can also provide the admission criteria and justification for the separation of "problematic" women from the wider society, and women with such a diagnosis frequently end up either incarcerated or in psychiatric institutions. Finally, diagnosis can also function as a tool for dismissal of communal responsibility.[58] Just Care, in its commitment to communal care, asserts the moral responsibility of communities—the community of chaplains, as well as church communities—to challenge those structures that create stressors in women's lives which may culminate in the mental illness and institutionalization of women. Just Care also reminds members of the wider society of their communal responsibility to care with and for the vulnerable members of society, particularly those women who have been diagnosed with mental illness. It further stands against forces that project the responsibility for care solely on psychiatric chaplains and other caregivers, as this enables the remainder of society to remain unchallenged and to keep this reality (literally) at a distance. Just Care, with its emphasis on communal care, demands that these negating and dehumanizing forces be named, articulated, and challenged in order that action can be taken to redress these situations.

Just Care also heeds that both communal and individual care are necessary to care for institutionalized women with mental illness. The individual care that occurs in relationship, particularly the one-on-one relationship between the chaplain and the woman, has the potential to be transformative in the lives of both the care seeker and caregiver. Individual care is enfleshed in taking the time to sit with a woman, to listen to her story, and to journey with her, while at the same time embracing a communal care that advocates for transformation of the structures that oppress and diminish her humanity. Feminist and intercultural scholars of pastoral care note that many times it is chaplains who can gently point out the relationship between systemic injustice and the story of the woman in front of them, whether this be through examination of her embodied responses and/or exploring harmful (and hopeful) narratives that she has internalized about herself. Just Care advances principles of individual care that include this systemic dynamic. While listening and empathy are crucial components, they must be coupled with an awareness of the larger systems that have culminated in the presence of the woman in a psychiatric hospital.

Just Care also recognizes the power of a sustained relationship, as opposed to relationships that may happen in medical hospitals. Many times, due to the lengthy stays that can occur in psychiatric institutions, the pastoral relationship can span months or even years. These sustained relationships have a depth that goes beyond crisis care, creating a space of exploration of the underlying stories and experiences that are foundational to this woman's self and theology. This indeed is sacred work, involving the utmost respect, empathy, interpathy and compassion. It is also work that has great potential. Together the caregiver and the care seeker discover the numerous ways that the care seeker engages in meaning-making, particularly around her religious beliefs and worldview, and assess whether the care seeker's lived theology is functioning in life-giving or life-limiting ways. In these sustained relationships, it is not uncommon to address God-imagery, beliefs about sin and grace, and forgiveness, as well as questions of ultimate existence and meaning. For many women in psychiatric institutions, an interaction with a chaplain comprises the first time that they have had sustained and intentional one-on-one engagement around these topics. This sacred space is the ground on which the chaplain is invited to trod. It is the power of the individual relationship, a generative relationship of safety and trust, that allows these conversations to unfold. In this space, the caregiver and the care seeker can together sift through and examine her embedded and lived theologies, noting those beliefs and/or practices that remind her of her inferiority, as well as those that reinforce her God-given dignity and worth.

Care Attentive to the Intersection of Culture, Gender, Race, and Class

"The person in front of me is the intersection of so many marginalizations."[59]

This book has engaged in an in-depth exploration of the necessity of care that is attentive to culture, gender, race and class. It is therefore grounded in the theory and methods offered by feminist and intercultural approaches to pastoral care, yet at the same time reaches beyond these proposals. Pastoral care that is attentive to intersectionality asks about the ways that these various forces have intersected in the particular lives of the women who are now institutionalized. It also notes that these forces—racism, sexism, heterosexism, and classism, to name a few—overlap in every part of her life, not simply in her hospitalization and diagnosis. Just Care recognizes that the analysis of each encounter will look different depending on the unique circumstances of the woman, including (but not limited to) her racial identity, socio-economic status, experience of violence, sexual orientation, personality, spirituality, experience of religion, and family upbringing. It also, however, notes that these issues intersect in a particular way in the lives of women who are institutionalized in a psychiatric hospital. In light of Goffman's insights about the "totalizing" nature of the psychiatric environment,[60] the chaplain must maintain an awareness of the ways that the regulated culture of the psychiatric environment might be influencing (and/or rendering invisible) any of the aforementioned factors in the woman's life.

Feminist and intercultural scholars of pastoral care, while advocating for an attentiveness to gender, race and class, have proposed methods that do not encompass the totality of this assertion. For example, Neuger recognizes that women make decisions in the midst of complex and oppressive situations. Thus, she attempts to aid women in viewing their problems as symptomatic of the forces that are harmful to women in the surrounding culture, rather than as purely individual psychic issues. Yet, while she maintains that "it is the responsibility of counselors to have a complex enough understanding of the cultural dynamics around sexism, racism, classism and heterosexism that they can place the particular stories of counselees in the context of those dynamics,"[61] her examination of the racist, classist and heterosexist forces that continue to form the lives of women lacks the robustness of her examination of sexism. Furthermore, in her attempt to expand the analysis of the causes of mental illness to include the prospect of intimate violence, she unwittingly engages in a one-to-one correspondence between the presence of particular symptoms and the prospect of intimate violence: "Consequently, any pastoral counseling with women who have problems with relationships or who experience depression, anxiety or phobias, eating disorders, addictions, or a host of other seemingly unrelated symptoms needs to assess the possibility of a past history (or current experience) of intimate violence."[62]

While Just Care recognizes the need for increased attention to intimate violence within the pastoral encounter, it pushes back against Neuger's analysis to question whether statements such as the ones above can be generalizable across race and culture. For example, in light of the particular ways that race and culture intersect in the lives of African American women, these women may exhibit different signs and symptoms of depression (and/or of the presence of intimate violence in their lives) than those deemed "typical." That is, the embodied responses of African American women may differ from a standard that puts white women at the center.[63] A theory that correlates certain "symptoms" with the presence of intimate violence, while well meaning, must also contain a racial and cultural analysis as part of this assessment process. Similarly, this racial and cultural analysis must be present when it comes to every part of the interaction, be it the delusions the woman is experiencing, the voices she is hearing or any other symptom that may be disrupting her life. The presence of this multi-layered analysis enables the caregiver to make connections between the forces of sexism, racism or classism, and the ways that the woman's struggle against these forces is currently being manifested in the symptoms she is experiencing.

Taking our example a bit further, consider the likely scenario (in light of the racial composition of the interviewed chaplains) of a white caregiver and an African American woman in a psychiatric hospital. Given the historic racial subjugation at the hands of white people, might a black woman be resistant to the exploration of her depression (perhaps the result of intimate violence) with a white caregiver? This, coupled with black women's possible inclination to protectively portray the black community dynamics (and especially represent black men) in a favorable light in front of whites,[64] could result in hesitancy and/or non-disclosure of the intimate details of her life that involve abuse. Her embodied responses might vary depending on multiple overlapping and interrelated factors, including the different ways that black women experience depression,[65] anger,[66] grief,[67] and a host of other emotions. Her responses may also possibly differ given the gender of the caregiver. Any one of these potential dynamics could ultimately hinder the African American care seeker from exploring crucial and formative life experiences with a white caregiver, while also keeping the white caregiver from making an accurate assessment of the "core issue." While feminist and intercultural concepts of belief, affirmation, education and interpathy are important, one cannot cognitively "envision and experience another's thoughts and feelings" without an awareness of the overlapping, intersecting dynamics that are forming (and informing) the current encounter. Multiple grounds of subjugation also require a healing process that addresses this overlapping, intersecting marginalization. West draws on interviews with victim-survivors of intimate violence to illustrate that even in therapy groups whose attendance is solely black women, the presence of oppressive, dehumanizing forces is never absent. One participant noted that a comprehensive healing process must address not only her emotional and spiritual health, but also tangible, recurrent concerns (such as employment and housing discrimination). If the healing process does not incorporate material realities, it "will be perpetually unsatisfactory and insufficient."[68]

On the other hand, Just Care cannot slide into an overemphasis on race, class or gender. West notes that "generalizations about the uniform, devastating consequences of racism can lend credence to stereotyped claims about the innate pathology of blacks."[69] While attention to intersectional dynamics of sexism, racism and classism is a necessary component of Just Care, it must always be balanced with a respect for the individuality of each woman. Each woman's personality and spirituality will intersect with forces in society to create a narrative that is uniquely hers. It is the mission of the caregiver to faithfully and intentionally accompany her as she explores this narrative.

Care That Recognizes the Power of Encounter

> "Good caregiving means you Listen. Really Listen. And just be with her."[70]

As has been noted, Just Care builds upon Emmanuel Lartey's concept of interpathy, that caregivers need not to just "believe" another culture, but also to "come to understand it both cognitively ('thinking with') and affectively ('feeling with')."[71] We have just discussed how this concept needs to be grounded in an intersectional approach to the systemic issues that frame and inform the encounter. Yet, this intersectional exploration culminates in an encounter, whether this be an encounter in community or a one-on-one encounter between the caregiver and care seeker.

Unique to encounters between chaplains and care seekers in a psychiatric hospital is an emphasis on belief. The intersection of gender, race, and class with mental illness is a unique set of circumstances that can further silence women whom society has already been working to silence. The fact that the women in psychiatric institutions may "hear voices" or "see things" not visible to most people, sets up a situation in which she is frequently "not believed." Neuger notes that belief in what the woman is saying is fundamental to helping someone gain "voice and agency."[72] This is even more true in the case of chaplains in a psychiatric setting. In sharing her narrative, the woman entrusts the chaplain with the truth of her (frequently terrifying) reality. Belief in her narrative and in her experiences as *true to her* (whether they can be externally verified) is essential to creating an encounter in which trust and healing can occur. It also aids the woman in gaining agency in the midst of a situation that is frequently totalizing and disempowering.

What about a woman who is experiencing psychosis? Belief builds on the contention, supported by many researchers, that refuting or outright denial of delusions and/or hallucinations is rarely therapeutic.[73] While a variety of psychotherapeutic approaches have been found to be effective with psychosis,[74] most of these techniques are rooted in a relationship marked by empathy, one who "seeks to find the essential human being lost in the seemingly uncanny."[75] A commitment to belief builds on this contention. The chaplain is one who enters into the world of the woman experiencing hallucinations or delusions in order to affirm the humanity of the one who is experiencing this world. Belief is also rooted in research that links adverse life circumstances with the etiology of psychosis. As noted by Longden and Read, though illnesses such as schizophrenia have historically been linked to the biomedical model of illness, current research has revealed that a wide variety of life stressors is linked to the onset of psychotic symptoms and schizophrenia.[76] While the link between childhood abuse and psychosis is widely known, Longden and Read reveal that less-known factors such as discrimination, domestic violence, poverty, inequality, material deprivation, and lack of social support have been proposed as predictors of psychosis. Belief is linked to the realization that psychosis can be the mind's way of coping with the inhumane circumstances in which one has been immersed.

It could be argued that the chaplain, as someone familiar with the concept of belief in a religious context—that is "having faith" in religious doctrines that cannot be materially verified—occupies a space that renders her more receptive to and capable of practicing the concept of belief as advanced by Just Care. For example, beliefs such as the existence of bread and wine which, at a certain point in the Roman Catholic liturgy "become" the body and blood of Christ,[77] reveal the chaplain as a figure who is, in the words of one chaplain, "comfortable with mystery."[78] Yet chaplains within a psychiatric hospital also (ostensibly) embrace the findings of science. This was evidenced by the statements of many chaplains regarding their assessment process, in which they revealed that they put their knowledge of the social sciences in dialogue with theology. The role of belief that positions chaplains as figures who stand at the crossroads—of science and theology, mystery and verifiable material reality—reveals their potential as bridge builders between the world of the psychiatric hospital and that of the woman.

This comfortability with mystery is also important in regard to the role of spirituality in their encounters between themselves and women in psychiatric institutions. Just Care holds up the power of an encounter that is focused on an exploration of one's spirituality. It names these encounters as generative of something larger than each of the participants, aiding both parties in an exploration of relationship with themselves, one another, the wider world, and a transcendent reality (however this is named). In the words of Cooper-White:

> Instead of one expert and one client, both subjectivities are honored, and both contribute to and, in fact, construct the knowledge shared between them. From a theological perspective, such shared knowledge participates in the "infinite conversation" of which Buber wrote, "extended, the lines of relationships intersect the eternal Thou."[79]

This encounter can encourage both integration and expansion of the self, a self-discovery that encourages the solidification of the disparate and cut-off parts of the woman's narrative, as well as a groundedness that enables her to reach out to the wider community and world. It is the foundation from which both parties can explore right-relationship with themselves and with others. This encounter, as is noted, is also generative. The interaction between the caregiver and the care seeker creates not only shared meaning, but also knowledge about the lives and needs of those in psychiatric institutions. Ironically, sometimes it is in the lack of knowledge that these encounters become knowledge-producing! For instance, those times where chaplains admitted that they "didn't know what to do"[80] often provided information about areas in need of further exploration in psychiatric chaplaincy.

Yet, it is also important to recognize dynamics of power in encounters between chaplains and women in psychiatric hospitals. The two parties are not equal, in fact, there is an "asymmetry of roles"[81] between the two. Caregivers must learn to recognize and monitor power dynamics in a relationship. When these are not monitored, this "can lead to abuse and neglect."[82] Just Care draws on Doehring's notion of a "process theology of power"[83] to ground the caregiver. It privileges this theory over others as it probes how power is connected to the social positionality and privileges of the caregiver. Doehring begins by recognizing that all relationships are infused with power and involve both agential and receptive power. For her, agential power "influences, guides and shapes," while receptive power "receives and takes in."[84] She proposes that pastoral relationships are life-giving when there is a "role-appropriate intertwining of receptive and agential power, with caregivers assuming responsibility for monitoring the ways that their role and social advantages inflate agential power."[85] She notes that the more that agential power is propped up by social and professional privilege, the greater the danger of misusing this power, through social status or "professional" knowledge that is inaccessible to the care seeker.

Doehring advocates for the use of agential power in the beginning of an interaction in order to monitor and name "contracts of care,"[86] which should be based on professional standards and ethical codes. She indicates, however, that caregivers need to intentionally shift into receptive power as the interaction proceeds in order to respect the mystery of the other and to be able to truly receive her story. Doehring notes that the exchange of power is "like a dance"[87] in which each person alternates between taking the lead and following the other. She reveals that often caregivers need to shift to agential power to bring theory and research into dialogue with their assessment of the situation. Yet, she also notes that "agential power that draws on theory needs to be continuously monitored,"[88] as theory can be used to categorize the care seeker and eclipse her full humanity. Just Care notes that dynamics of agential and receptive power can be complex to monitor. As such, it relies upon communities of accountability (explored previously) to keep one's social and cultural positionality, as well as the inherent power dynamics, in view.

Care That Has an Expansive View of Health and Healing

> "My sense of holistic health is that all of those pieces [the physical, mental, emotional and spiritual] interact with each other. You can't just isolate one and treat that. You have to be aware of how they work together."[89]

We have explored that chaplains frequently held a commitment to a notion of health that is larger than diagnosis. This commitment to the interconnected and expansive nature of health, as well as resistance to anything that seeks to reduce the woman's health to a one-dimensional concept, is an important component of Just Care. Just Care seeks the health and well-being of the entire woman—mental, emotional, spiritual and physical. It asks about the *interrelationship* of these various components, as opposed to a model that seeks to understand health by focusing on the separation of the body into its various components. It rails against value systems and worldviews that seek to silence or ignore any one of these factors. In this way, proponents of Just Care may find themselves in opposition to the overarching medical system that governs the psychiatric hospital. Just Care also builds upon Townes to propose that "health is not simply the absence of disease—it comprises a wide range of activities that foster healing and wholeness."[90]

Just Care's advocacy for this expansive notion of health is grounded both in the particular and the systemic. That is, the experience of a woman's health that is revealed in a one-on-one encounter is just as important as an inquiry into the systemic, socially-constructed nature of health. Just Care explores, and is attentive to, historic and current trends that have created a system which privileges the culturally-constructed Western medical model. It is also attentive to the ways that this model has been enfleshed, and the resulting socio-economic disparities in health and healthcare. Just Care recognizes the presence of these trends in the practice of psychiatric diagnosis. It pushes for a definition of health that includes an expansive notion of the self, which includes a woman's racial identity, gender identity, sexual orientation, and culture, alongside of her physical, mental, emotional and spiritual health. It recognizes that care for these various aspects of the woman must reflect both particular and systemic realities.

For example, addressing the woman's emotional health involves a culturally-sensitive exploration of her narrative, but also an examination of disparities in education, employment access and housing which limit her emotional and social development. To address her spiritual well-being, Just Care must both explore her embedded and lived theologies, but also the systems that have influenced the development of this theology, as well as the church communities that continue to advance theologies that limit the woman's sense of self and spirituality by condoning patriarchy and/or not actively resisting intimate violence. Questions of her physical well-being include not only her physical pain, but also an exploration of environmental and other factors that have affected her physical health. While Just Care may focus on one or more of these issues at a time, it also attempts to hold the others in view.

The contention that health and healing are greater than the simple "absence of disease" is also important for Just Care. For many women in the psychiatric hospital, mental illness is something with which they will struggle for the remainder of their lives. While some medications may lessen the symptoms of these illnesses, these medicines can lose their effectiveness over time. Other forms of mental illness may be unresponsive to medications and talk therapy. In situations such as these, Just Care advocates for a notion of health and healing that is rooted in relationships and activities that foster dignity and wholeness *in the midst* of mental illness. Perhaps the woman's delusion cannot be "cured," but Just Care would endeavor to aid in the healing of the lack of self-worth or loneliness at the heart of this delusion. Perhaps another woman perennially struggles with anxiety, but Just Care would offer compassion-based spiritual practices[91] to aid in emotional regulation during episodes of high anxiety.

Care That Is Advocacy-Oriented

> "I find myself kind of just being a support and then an advocate as things come up. If I don't get information from the team, but then I get something from the patient, I can bring that to the team so they can be aware of . . . 'Oh she keeps complaining her foot is hurting.'"[92]

Chaplains overwhelmingly spoke of the importance of being an advocate for the patient, either with the treatment team or in regard to issues of discharge. In this way, chaplains saw their work as connected to broader issues of advocacy and justice for the patient. While chaplains voiced different methods of advocacy, this theme surfaced in many interviews.

Just Care recognizes that voices of resistance are frequently subsumed in larger bureaucracies and that institutional goals of self-perpetuation frequently serve to flatten and de-politicize dissenting voices. At the same time, Just

Care follows the lead of Stephen Pattison and his recommendation that advocacy within the hospital involves embracing what many chaplains are already doing—that is, dis-identifying with the treatment team when their view of patients is reductionistic, as well as advocating that the patient be taken seriously when decisions about the patient are being made.[93] In Pattison's view, chaplains enjoy a certain independence of hierarchies in the hospital, and this can aid them in providing an alternative view of the current situation, as well as prompting the staff toward a more critical evaluation of their role.[94] Advocacy for patients within the hospital also includes both exposing and protesting against instances of patient abuse, dehumanization and reductionism, as well as supporting those who risk their lives and positions to expose these things. While Just Care recognizes that this advocacy may not change the larger bureaucratic culture, it strives to provide resistance in the midst of the bureaucratic system of the psychiatric hospital.

Yet, Just Care also notes that sometimes the best avenues for advocacy occur through fostering relationships with the wider team. Even if the chaplain disagrees with the approach of the treatment team, showing respect for the common humanity, as well as the training and clinical insight, of team members creates an atmosphere in which this team may become more open to hearing the chaplain's advocacy on other matters. For example, recall the chaplain who made the decision to meet with the woman and to "hold her hand" against the admonition of the team. While he himself might have seen this as a form of advocacy for the woman, Just Care would necessitate that he ask certain questions, both personal and systemic, before proceeding with this decision. Personally, has he engaged in self-care? Are his emotional and spiritual needs being met elsewhere? Has he assessed his own countertransference as it pertains to this relationship? Is he offering care that is truly "beginning with the woman," as Just Care proposes—with her story, her history, her needs—or is the interaction more about gaining something for himself? Is he aware of the power differential, and how is he monitoring the power dynamics during his interactions with the woman? Systemically, has he investigated his own social and cultural positionality?[95] Was the decision to meet with this woman informed by an analysis of the ways that gender, culture, race, and class informed her present situation, as well as the role of abuse in her life?[96] On what was his assessment based, and what form of health/healing informed this decision? How was the present atmosphere and ethos of the psychiatric hospital informing this encounter? Is this a situation that necessitated advocacy on the part of the chaplain (that is, what were the factors that led the team to make this decision that she should not meet with male clinicians)? Were there issues of justice/injustice that needed to be addressed? If so, was this the optimal way to address these issues?

While these questions reveal that advocacy (and decisions around advocacy) within the hospital can be a complicated process, Just Care also asserts that advocacy is a crucial component of Just Care. It suggests that this advocacy must also extend beyond the walls of the hospital. Though psychiatric chaplains frequently spoke of advocacy, it was usually limited to those issues—physical, mental, or emotional—about which the patient needed help communicating. A commitment to advocacy as a component of Just Care prompts chaplains also to engage in social and political activities that influence the wider society. Advocacy includes efforts that direct society's attention and resources toward women who are mentally ill. In particular, this involves the education and mobilization of church communities.

Care That Puts Spirituality at the Center

> "One of the most reality-orienting things for her is if I say, 'Okay, would you like to say a prayer together now?' And whatever she might be yelling or screaming, or responding to internal stuff, but if I say, 'Would you like to pray with me?' she's right there with me in that moment. And it's so grounding for her."[97]

One of the hallmarks of chaplaincy (as distinctive from psychotherapy or counseling) is the place of religion and spirituality within the encounter between the caregiver and care seeker. While there are many definitions of spirituality, Just Care follows Ulanov in her assertion that to miss the religious dimension is to "confine ourselves to efforts of recovering ego-functioning which is of priceless value but will not endure if the spiritual aspect is omitted."[98] Just Care holds that it is in and through religion and spirituality that true healing and integration can occur. While this does not preclude other sources of healing and integration, Just Care privileges the role of religion and spirituality as a primary source of healing in psychiatric chaplaincy. This means that the religious dimension needs to be respected and addressed in both the life of the caregiver and in that of the care seeker.

Just Care privileges definitions of spirituality that follow the work of Swinton and Lartey. Spirituality, in Swinton's view, recognizes that the person cannot be separated into mind, body and emotions, rather the person is an integrated being, and should be treated as such.[99] Any definition of spirituality must build on this view of the human person. Lartey recognizes that from the intercultural perspective, spirituality refers to the "human capacity for relationship with self, others, world, God and that which transcends sensory experience, which is often expressed in the particularities of given historical, spatial, and social contexts, and which often leads to a particular form of action in the world."[100] For Lartey, spirituality functions as the "integrating center" for both an individual and a people.

Privileging the centrality of spirituality, Just Care recognizes that mental illness, like spirituality, is a "whole-person experience that affects a person in every dimension of their existence."[101] The emphasis on spirituality as an "integrating" center underlines the potential not only for emotional and spiritual healing with self and others, yet also as a place where meaning can be created. Just Care recognizes that spirituality is a source of strength for many women who experience mental illness, particularly for women of color. For other women, the presence of mental illness can cause them to feel that they have been abandoned by God or to question the spiritual aspect of their lives. In either case, spirituality provides an entry point from which to commence the analysis of meaning, a way in which the care seeker can begin to make sense of her journey, quest, purpose and relationships in her life. It is in and through this spirituality that healing can ultimately occur, although this is always mysterious in nature.

Just Care also recognizes that spirituality has a functional impact for the woman, meaning spirituality can function in both life-giving and life-limiting ways. Caregivers must first work to be able to identify both the shared and unique aspects of the woman's spirituality. This involves the recognition that every person has a unique spirituality that provides "a particular way of negotiating, interpreting and understanding the world."[102] As such, one's personal spirituality will always deviate, in some ways, from the commonly held tenets of the religious tradition to which she adheres. This deviation, however, should not necessarily be equated with pathology. Just Care necessitates an approach to the woman's spirituality that honors and respects all of the aspects of her spirituality, even if it is drastically different than that of the caregiver. Returning to the insights of several of our scholars of pastoral care,[103] the caregiver seeks to journey with the woman to uncover those aspects of her spirituality which draw her closer to her "source of meaning, value, hope and transcendence"[104] while also being able to name those aspects which draw her away from emotional, spiritual, and psychological health (the terms life-giving and life-limiting could also be used here). While Oates and Pruyser have proposed specific tenets of "sick religion,"[105] Just Care acknowledges that both of these proposals are written from a Eurocentric perspective marked by Western views of culture and knowledge. For example, Oates maintains that "sick" religion is characterized by being uncritical, self-contained and lacking humility (or teachableness), as well as by magical thinking, self-justification, and personal comfort.[106] Just Care maintains that its commitment to justice alters characterizations of "sick religion." It recognizes that assessments of the "health" of religious beliefs must be contextual and informed by analyses that are attentive to racial, cultural, gendered and socio-economic factors. For example, the tenets of religion that would need to be interrogated for a woman of color raised in a church community that prohibited women from positions of leadership would be different than those of an upper-class white woman from a progressive Christian church that thoroughly reflected gender equality at all levels of church leadership. These would also differ from those of a first-generation Korean woman who had been attending a Korean-speaking Christian church since she immigrated to the United States. Yet, Just Care would maintain that in any of these circumstances, religious beliefs that do not emphasize women's inherent dignity and self-worth would need to be interrogated. In contrast to Oates, it may be that, for some of these women, "healthy religion" would be a view of religion that *aided* in their own justification of themselves and sense of comfort!

Just Care's commitment to the central role of spirituality in the pastoral encounter also requires an intentional awareness and fostering of the chaplain's own spirituality. Particularly important are the gifts of courage and humility. Just Care, in its very subject matter, as well as in practice, requires the gift of courage. As chaplains noted, working with those with severe mental illness is not easy.[107] There can be frequent emotional outbursts that culminate in physical harm (whether this be self harm or harm towards others), painful and heart wrenching stories, and times when the chaplain will be insulted, dismissed or even physically attacked. Courage allows the chaplain to acknowledge her fear and call on her spirituality as a source of resilience in these circumstances. Just Care also requires courage to be able to name systemic dynamics that may or may not be received with openness. Yet, this courage must be rooted in humility, which would allow the chaplain to recognize her own limitations, to be attentive and aware of timing in a conversation, and to practice ways of asking questions that open up the conversation and encourage exploration. Her humility needs to recognize that the systemic dynamics that the chaplain may name as present in an encounter may not be the ones that are most prominent for the patient. Healthy humility can allow the chaplain to integrate these experiences without allowing them to render her hopeless or defeated. Humility engenders the sense that one is finite, that much about life, spirituality and mental illness is mysterious. Finally, psychiatric chaplaincy can create situations that are difficult for the chaplain to tolerate, emotionally and spiritually. The chaplain must foster an active spirituality to ground her in these encounters and must be intentional about the implementation of spiritual exercises that enable emotional regulation, especially in difficult circumstances.

Alternative Norms for Pastoral Caregiving

The guidelines of Just Care expand current norms for pastoral caregiving. Doehring reflects that pastoral caregiving draws on numerous religious sources and norms of authority to undergird its praxis.[108] Scriptures, liturgy, and doctrines would function as a source of authority in pastoral care. For Doehring, modern and postmodern theologies provide the norms for interpretation of said Hebrew and Christian texts, liturgy and doctrines. Pastoral care also draws on "narrative sources and norms of authority."[109] For example, the encounter between the caregiver and care seeker would be considered a narrative source, which would be interpreted through norms such as the social sciences, a variety of psychological perspectives, and cultural studies. She also notes that a variety of theological perspectives, including feminist and womanist perspectives, also provide norms for the interpretation of the encounter between the caregiver and care seeker. While Doehring advances an approach that brings these sources into dialogue,[110] the sources at the table are limited to those aforementioned. The presence of Just Care expands the norms of interpretation for pastoral caregiving. Just Care asserts that pastoral caregiving must also involve a wider, systemic analysis, such as the one advanced by feminist, womanist Christian social ethics, to fairly represent the life of women in psychiatric institutions. It argues that the present tools for the interpretation of the woman's life are not expansive enough to encompass the fullness of her humanity. The absence of a systemic analysis as a norm that governs pastoral care presents an incomplete, possibly erroneous portrait of the underlying factors governing this encounter between caregiver and care seeker, one that may result in an inaccurate assessment of the central issue in the encounter. To truly address "the whole person," Just Care advocates for a care that includes analyses of gender, race, class and culture as necessary norms of interpretation for ethical pastoral caregiving.

A RETURN TO PSYCHIATRIC DIAGNOSIS

What differentiates psychiatric chaplains from chaplains in other settings is the presence of a psychiatric diagnosis of mental illness. We have explored the ways that feminist and womanist Christian social ethics and feminist and intercultural pastoral care trouble a diagnosis-focused approach. What then, should the chaplain's relationship be to psychiatric diagnosis? As has been revealed, Just Care begins by emphasizing the importance of knowledge about the wider systems of power that accompany the practice of diagnosis. The systemic, intercultural analysis that has been explored in this book would be an important starting point for chaplains. It would be essential that chaplains understand the ways that gender, power, provider bias, race, and class correlate with the ways that diagnoses are administered in psychiatric institutions. This intersectional approach should guide and inform the chaplain's interactions and advocacy.

As explored in chapter three, chaplains fell on a spectrum as to the importance of this diagnosis in their assessment processes. Yet, those who placed very little emphasis on the stated diagnosis often found themselves in situations in which they had difficulty communicating with the treatment team. Their assessment often relied solely on theological resources or on practical skills they had learned in CPE. If Just Care is advocacy-oriented, it also requires a knowledge of the central components of diagnosis as expressed in the *DSM*. It is difficult for a chaplain to embrace a stance of advocacy, which may include challenging the treatment team, if she has little to no knowledge of their language and their field. Similarly, one questions whether a chaplain can make an accurate assessment of the situation at hand, which would optimally require knowledge of the intersection between gender, culture and diagnosis, without at least a preliminary knowledge of all of these concepts.

Yet, knowledge of diagnosis must always be held in tension with the reductionistic tendencies of the diagnostic process within the Western medical model. Some chaplains who considered psychiatric diagnosis "very important" also related that they had determined what issues to address before even meeting the woman herself! Just Care would also find it important to examine the relationship between theology and behavioral science. Many of the chaplains who were interviewed favored a more "dialogical" view between theology and behavioral science, viewing the two as mutually informing one another. While this is a valid perspective, and one touted by many in the realm of pastoral care, Townsend also presents a third view of science and religion, the "integration" view, which softens the boundary between science and theology, encouraging the convergence of scientific and theological knowledge.[111] As has been noted, most scholars of feminist and womanist pastoral care would fall into this category. While few of the chaplains exemplified this view, this approach could be valuable for practitioners of Just Care. Just Care asks how the insights of both Christian social ethics and feminist, womanist and intercultural pastoral care shape and ultimately transform both the psychological and theological theory that undergirds pastoral care in psychiatric institutions.

And what of the label itself? Neuger recognizes that a label such as that of psychiatric diagnosis can be helpful or hurtful: "We can use labels to better understand, normalize and counsel with the women who come for pastoral counseling or we can use them to objectify, simplify and dismiss them."[112] She relates that diagnostic criteria are "helpful" insofar as they help build solidarity around suffering and aid in "building a better set of skills for helping women resist depression in the present and in the future."[113] They are hurtful when they reduce and objectify women. Just Care would add that diagnostic labels are also hurtful when they are products and expressions of the sexism, racism and classism of society. Without an exploration of the ways that an intersectional, systemic analysis challenges the diagnosis-focused approach that exists in psychiatric hospitals, chaplains are not providing adequate or comprehensive pastoral care.

Just Care also would ask how the dialogue between these fields changes the ways that chaplains themselves go about assessment of the central issue at hand. Given the importance of a contextual approach that emphasizes culture, Just Care would agree with Townsend's assessment that the practice of pastoral diagnosis is a process that is hierarchical and insensitive to culture, privileging the knowledge of the chaplain over that of the patient.[114] Just Care would advocate for a process of assessment that is interdisciplinary, contextual, and collaborative, while remaining sensitive to intersectional dynamics of gender, culture, race and class. While chaplains noted that they were frequently "putting the two fields [of psychology and pastoral care] into dialogue," what would assessment look like when putting three (or more) fields into dialogue? What would assessment look like if it were collaborative, rather than a solitary practice?

In one sense, some of the central tenets of theological assessment, for example insights from Charles Gerkin regarding interpretation of the life of the self and the life of the soul,[115] are still relevant. Just Care would build upon scholars of pastoral care who seek to frame the central issue in theological and spiritual terms, while also emphasizing that in an interdisciplinary approach this may not be the sole way of framing these issues. Just Care also alters the "tools at the table," that is, the frameworks that are operative in the process of discernment and assessment. The presence of intersectional, systemic analysis means that questions of the intersectionality between gender, race and class must be integral components of the process of assessment. Neuger provides an example of this regarding a gender analysis by asking how internalized beliefs of the woman are reflective of larger dehumanizing myths about women and their place in the world. Her recognition that culture "plays a major role in providing the interpretive lenses by which people make sense of their lives"[116] applies here. How does the caregiver sift through those cultural narratives? Doehring suggests that embodied responses provide insight into the ways that larger cultural narratives have been integrated into the person's lived theology. The caregiver "keeps the political dimension of the care seeker's crisis in view, mindful of ways that intersecting systems of social privilege and oppression shape lived theologies."[117] Embodied responses such as fear, guilt and shame provide insight into the ways that cultural messages have been integrated, and it is the caregiver's job to sift through and identify the ways that these embodied responses correlate with larger systems that privilege some and disadvantage others.

Yet the intersectional racial, gendered and cultural analysis of Just Care at the same time complicates Doehring's approach. Revisiting the example of the white caregiver and the African American woman who had experienced intimate violence is helpful here. Perhaps the African American woman is experiencing the embodied response of anger. Is this anger a result of internalized sexism, internalized racism, internalized classism, a mixture of all three of these dynamics, or none of the above? Might the anger be related to the stereotype of the "strong black woman" that she has been encouraged to embrace throughout her life? Or perhaps the anger reflects the fact that this woman might be evicted from her apartment while she is institutionalized, because she is presently unable to secure or maintain a job, and there is no one else to pay the rent? Might her anger be surfacing due to the internal voices and/or hallucinations with which she has struggled throughout her life? Once expressed, this woman might feel guilt and remorse for this anger due to numerous cultural and religious factors, including the controlling image of the "angry black women" painted by the dominant culture, and/or the ways that the Christian tradition has historically linked anger with sin.[118] If the caregiver is white, s/he "may not know what to do" when the care seeker's anger surfaces. The white caregiver might erroneously interpret this emotion as inappropriate or extreme. The caregiver may also lack awareness that what might be needed is encouragement for the black woman to embrace her anger as constructive and rooted in a sense of empowerment: "When a black woman feels safe enough to express her anger, it is to be celebrated, not feared."[119]

Just Care complicates approaches that imply that one can easily or quickly identify the larger systemic dynamics at play in the life of the woman. It necessitates the importance of a contextual assessment, one which is both informed by knowledge gleaned from gendered, racial, cultural and psychological analyses, but also recognizes the particularity of each individual encounter. This includes an awareness of the inherent limitations in any analysis that a caregiver may undertake. Why? The very factors that we have examined throughout the course of this book are present and embodied in the encounter itself. In the same way that the chart is not "the full story," every assessment will be limited by the ways that larger forces of racism, sexism, and classism are present and absent in the embodiment and social location of the two people sitting in the room. Together, the caregiver and care seeker will engage in a construction of knowledge that will enable them to explore the issues at hand and to attempt to name and identify the forces beneath embodied and emotional responses. This will require courage, self-awareness, and humility on the part of the caregiver, as it may raise issues that are difficult to hear, and difficult to articulate. Like all encounters, however, Just Care recognizes that the caregiver's knowledge of the woman will be partial and incomplete. It will be limited not only by the ways that racism, classism and gender are present in the current encounter, but also by the simple fact that no encounter can fully encompass the mystery of the woman in front of the caregiver. In its attempt to be attentive to larger, complex dynamics, however, Just Care is a step toward recognizing the sacredness of the woman's life.

WITH THE FOREGOING GUIDELINES IN MIND, WHAT MIGHT ETHICAL PASTORAL CARE—JUST CARE—LOOK LIKE ON THE GROUND? HOW MIGHT JUST CARE CHANGE THE CHAPLAINCY OF PSYCHIATRIC CHAPLAINS?

The components of Just Care become enfleshed in the tangible, ethical practice which alters the current education and training of chaplains and challenges the racial and gendered composition of chaplaincy staffs. It invites chaplains to embrace a relational, communal model that also privileges the individual encounter.

Education about Mental Health for Clergy

As this book has explored, there are many books that seek to educate clergy on issues of mental health. A number of these books focus on the articulation of certain diagnoses in terms understandable to the caregiver, as well as offering suggestions for pastoral interventions based on these descriptions. As helpful as these resources might be, books that simply elucidate diagnoses are not enough. Just Care must include educational initiatives that also highlight an approach that is characteristic of Christian social ethics, one which links the practice of psychiatric diagnosis to gendered, racial, social and economic analysis. Both of these types of education are necessary for Just Care. Neither can exist at the expense of the other. If chaplains are truly to engage in care that is both communal and individual—that is attentive to dynamics of gender, race, and class, but that also appreciates the power of encounter, advocacy and spirituality—they must have educational opportunities and training in all of these areas.

Training for Psychiatric Chaplains

As it stands, training for psychiatric chaplains looks identical to training for hospital chaplains. This includes four units of Clinical Pastoral Education, as well as a Master of Divinity and endorsement by one's particular denomination. Yet, many chaplains can complete four CPE units without spending any time in a psychiatric hospital and/or on a psychiatric unit. Beyond the Masters of Divinity, there is no requirement for any other advanced training, so many psychiatric chaplains enter their positions with little to no formal training in psychology. Though insights from several schools of psychology have made their way into pastoral care theory, chaplains receive little to no formal training that focuses on counseling skills that are necessary in long-term pastoral relationships.

Just Care notes that requirements for the training of chaplains reveal priorities for ministry. While questions exist as to whether CPE should remain the gold standard for chaplaincy training and certification, the lack of emphasis on psychiatric chaplaincy is obvious within the current model. Just Care advocates that all clergy, especially chaplains, should be required to participate in a mandatory mental health unit as part of their CPE training. This time in a mental health setting should be extended to at least two units for those who endeavor to minister in psychiatric facilities. Just Care would also advocate for some sort of advanced education in psychology (including counseling skills) for psychiatric chaplains. Returning to those chaplains who were interviewed, while all of the chaplains with some sort of advanced education in psychology and social work mentioned the importance of their education, they highlighted *that* education, versus their time in CPE, as being the most influential factor on their chaplaincy. Advanced education in psychology would also enable a psychiatric chaplain to be a more engaged and active team member, as she would have a more complete understanding of the concept of diagnosis and the system of which she was a part. It would also grant her more legitimacy to critique the current system of diagnosis.

Just Care would also question the primacy of CPE as the sole model of training for chaplaincy. Much has been written about the ethnocentrality of CPE, and the fact that it is based on a white, individualistic Euro-American model.[120] Those who have implemented CPE in other countries have voiced concern for the development of "culturally appropriate programs, including supervisory training," recognizing that the Western cultural and medical norms which undergird the CPE process have come into conflict with the norms of students from other cultures, specifically around such topics as models of personhood, health and community.[121] Just Care, with its attention on interculturality, would advocate for a training model which is more sensitive to issues of race and culture, not only in other countries, but also in the United States. It would call for training that incorporates an intersectional analysis focused on justice, alongside components from pastoral care.

Communities of Accountability

The formation of the person of the chaplain, including such issues as identity, integrity, self-understanding, social positionality, and attention to power dynamics, is extremely important for Just Care. To promote positive formation of the person of the chaplain, Just Care advocates that a key part of this ongoing formation for caregivers is membership in a community of accountability. This community is intended to be a space for the caregiver to explore her own embedded and lived theologies and social and cultural positionality. It is also an opportunity for caregivers to process their caregiving with others. As one chaplain noted, "psychiatric chaplaincy is just . . . really difficult."[122] Too often psychiatric chaplains feel alone in their work, and/or "in over their head," due to working in an inherently interdisciplinary environment. Some of the challenges of working with women with severe mental illness are also drastically different from many, if not all, of the ones that caregivers have encountered during their training. It is important for chaplains working in this context to have communities of both accountability and support. These communities also function as forums where chaplains can bring systemic dynamics into dialogue with the particularity of encounter.

These communities would serve as a venue for chaplains to bring their assessments along with an articulation of the presuppositions that undergird their decisions. Here, the caregiver could participate in a communal process of assessment in a safe and supportive space. Communities of accountability function as places for chaplains to receive the feedback of others who are also in psychiatric chaplaincy, particularly as this pertains to issues of assessment. This would not only enhance their ministry with women in psychiatric institutions, but would also aid in the caregiver's own formation.

Clergy Embracing Their Stance as Advocates for Patients They Serve

As alluded to earlier, advocacy for adherents of Just Care takes place both within the hospital walls and outside of them. Advocacy within the walls of the hospital begins with a commitment to the full personhood of the patient, which is manifested in advocating that the patient be taken seriously when decisions about the patient are being made. This also involves being an advocate within the current climate of deinstitutionalization. Many times patients are discharged to places that may or may not be a good fit for them given their social and cultural positionality. For instance, women who have struggled with drug or alcohol addictions are often discharged to neighborhoods that are riddled with drugs, while women with trauma histories may be discharged to a co-ed group home. Part of advocacy is taking the time to accompany women on visits to potential discharge sites and to participate in assessing whether this might be a good fit for the patient. It involves reporting back to the team on the material conditions of discharge and community sites. It is committing to be a voice for justice in the midst of frequently dehumanizing material conditions.

Outside of the hospital walls, advocacy may look as varied as the chaplain. Important to Just Care is the recognition that ethical analysis of the relationships between gender, race, class and psychiatric diagnosis must inform this advocacy. Communally, this may take place in and through the chaplain's church community. Individually, however, advocacy outside of the hospital also must address the position of the chaplain vis-a-vis the discharged patient. In order to protect the rights of the patient, chaplains who work in psychiatric facilities are not allowed, by law, to have contact with patients upon discharge. Given this reality, the patient may request that the chaplain recommend a welcoming religious community. Researching and fostering connections with religious communities open to those with mental illness as well as with pastors who understand the intricacies and interconnections between race, gender, trauma and diagnosis is essential for a chaplain engaged in Just Care. This might also involve working with congregations to create welcoming environments for women who are discharged from a psychiatric hospital. Finally, advocacy on the part of the chaplain can also involve advocacy for any of those issues that intersect with a diagnosis of mental illness, whether this be work for racial justice, women who have experienced intimate violence, equal housing, stigma involving matters of employment, and/or funding for mental health community residences. Chaplains are in the unique position of carrying both the stories of the women with whom they have met and the endorsement of a particular denomination. Fostering bridges between these two worlds in relationship to issues of psychiatric diagnosis is essential to advocacy.

A Commitment for Diversity on Chaplaincy Staffs

Recall the chaplain supervisor who expressed her staff was largely white women (including the entirety of the full time chaplains) in part because the primary feeder to the chaplaincy program was a seminary that "was not the most diverse community."[123] She noted that while the population of the psychiatric hospital reflected the diversity of the state in which she resided, her staff was not representative of that diversity. This supervisor concluded by saying that they "could be more intentional" about reaching out to African American chaplains.

Just Care recognizes the importance of a chaplaincy staff that reflects the diversity of the hospital. Diversity is important for many reasons (most of which will not be explored here). When approached from the perspective of a woman who is a patient in a psychiatric hospital, diversity allows the patient to recognize herself and her culture in the chaplains who surround her. One of Just Care's guiding theoretical foundations is the importance of culture. If chaplaincy departments do not make a commitment to represent a variety of cultures, they risk becoming irrelevant to a large portion of the psychiatric population. Chaplains of the same race and culture as the patient may be able to offer services that are more familiar to the patients, as well as to speak from a similar cultural context. Recall the white female chaplain who noted that her rendition of spirituals was "the whitest version" that the patients had ever heard. Conversations between a patient and chaplain who is of the same race as herself may also address previously mentioned issues such as systemic racial oppression. For example, a black woman may feel more comfortable sharing situations of intimate violence with someone of the same race and gender, as she may not feel the pressure of having to protectively defend her race to whites. Yet, Just Care refrains from viewing the commitment to racial and cultural diversity as a panacea. For example, to propose that African American women should only be ministered to by African American women chaplains is also to dismiss the presence of inter-group dynamics and to flatten the individuality in every encounter. Furthermore, even in therapy groups composed solely of black women, concrete obstacles (such as job and housing discrimination) and unique gifts must also be addressed for healing to be comprehensive and effective.

In order to address diversity on chaplaincy staffs, Just Care advocates for an awareness of the historical circumstances that have created the racial disparity that is now manifested in the composition of chaplaincy staffs. This may involve asking difficult questions about the current racial and gendered makeup of the staff. For example, what are the primary theological feeder institutions to the hospital, and how were the bonds between these institutions forged? When, and by whom? How could state psychiatric institutions be more intentional about drawing from numerous theological institutions that are representative of gender, theological, racial, and ethnic diversity?

Finally, Just Care would also advocate for diversity training for current chaplaincy staffs. Noting the large number of white chaplains who had difficulty acknowledging and speaking about race, Just Care would emphasize the importance of educational opportunities for current chaplaincy staffs on issues of race and racial justice. This would better equip chaplains to be able to name and recognize issues of race and culture in their encounters. Together, all of these components are essential when addressing questions of intentionality about racial, ethnic, and gender diversity on psychiatric chaplaincy staffs.

Future Directions and Implications for Just Care

What sort of implications might it have to teach and/or practice Just Care? And what can be envisioned when looking to the future? Just Care, if taught in seminary, might influence future pastors, as well as chaplains, to consider ministry with women with mental illness as a component of ministry that necessitates their attention, time and energy. If Just Care were both taught and practiced, these ministers would also have on-the-ground ministry experience with those with mental illness. This could influence churches to become places of advocacy and education about the construction of mental illness, specifically as this relates to connections between white privilege, socioeconomic realities, violence against women and diagnoses of mental illness. This might also involve opportunities for churches to investigate societal stigma against mental illness and to live out the call to be tangible bastions of love and acceptance in the midst of a society that prefers containment and separation.

The implementation of Just Care might prompt an examination of the ways that churches respond to women with mental illness, which would require that they explore certain questions concerning aspects of their own liturgy and theology.[124] Just Care's advocacy for an intersectional analysis around issues of mental illness might influence churches to incorporate attention to mental illness into already existent trainings/educational opportunities, such as those on white privilege, race, poverty, and/or violence against women, further highlighting connections between the construction of mental illness and other issues of justice.

An implementation of Just Care might prompt churches to examine their own stereotyping and stigma of congregants who are mentally ill within their congregations. It could invite churches toward reflection on the ways that they are addressing the other, intersecting issues that overlap with mental illness. It might prompt them to advocate for people with mental illness by engaging with larger systemic issues of justice, which could include advocacy efforts around dispelling erroneous connections between violence and mental illness, as well as the overlap between the incarcerated population and those who have been diagnosed with severe mental illness.

Just Care could prompt both churches and chaplains to foster connections between religious bodies and community and national organizations who address mental illness[125] or to make themselves aware of legislative efforts on behalf of the mentally ill. In sum, Just Care may aid in raising awareness and fostering justice-oriented action in church communities around issues of women with mental illness.

Just Care might also encourage an inherently more interdisciplinary approach to the fields of both Christian social ethics and pastoral care. It might invite more students to put these fields in dialogue, in both their academic work and in their on-the-ground ministry. As such, it might contribute to ministerial approaches that are more attuned toward seeing the full humanity of the people in front of them.

CONCLUSION

Just Care proposes that ethical pastoral care must, at its foundation, embody a commitment to justice and a respect for culture. As such, Just Care challenges current norms of pastoral caregiving by intentionally placing psychiatric chaplaincy with women at the center of its moral discourse about care. Rooted in a method that privileges the voices of the psychiatric caregivers, coupled with the systemic analysis of feminist and womanist Christian social ethics and the insights of feminist, womanist, liberationist, and intercultural scholars of pastoral care, Just Care ultimately advocates for an anti-racist-psychosocial-spiritual model of ethical pastoral care that privileges the presence of concerted cultural, racial, gendered and class analyses as *constitutive* of pastoral care with women in psychiatric institutions. Just Care proposes that these systemic analyses expand and frame the encounter between the caregiver and care seeker, while the contributions of feminist, womanist, and intercultural pastoral care highlight the necessity of privileging the role of culture in the particularity of every encounter.

The theoretical foundations of Just Care are enfleshed in the components of Just Care, which include care that begins with the woman but does not end there. This care must also embody an awareness of the chaplain's own social positionality and embedded and lived theologies. It must be both communal and individual and attentive to the intersection of culture, gender, race and class. Finally, Just Care must be both rooted in the power of encounter and also advocacy oriented: it must embrace an expansive view of health and healing that puts spirituality at the center of its care. These components challenge the training and educational requirements of psychiatric chaplains, as well as their praxis.

Returning to Denise and the description of the encounter in the introduction to this book, Just Care offers a care that would enable the caregiver to ask larger questions about the context enveloping the pastoral care encounter with Denise, questions that place justice at the center. Given that Denise is an African American woman living within U.S. culture and its historic legacies of racism and sexism, how might an in-depth analysis of race, gender, class and culture, along with insights about the practice and values of psychiatric diagnosis within the culture of the psychiatric hospital, change and challenge the pastoral care provided for her?

Just Care would recognize that the encounter with Denise is both permeated and surrounded by the injustice of a society and medical system in which women, particularly women of color who are at the nexus of multiple forms of oppression, are both the ones most likely to develop mental illness and also least likely to seek treatment. A larger analysis such as the one prompted by Just Care would first highlight that the onset of mental illness is frequently linked to social forces, particularly those stressors that tend to be more common among women of color, such as intimate violence, poverty and racism. It would question how Denise arrived in the psychiatric hospital. Was she referred by the legal system? It would also look closely at her diagnosis and treatment options, noting that she is more likely to end up misdiagnosed than her white counterparts, and also more likely to be a recipient of pharmacological intervention than other forms of therapeutic intervention. It would inquire how an anti-racist critique might alter the perception of Denise's diagnosis, and how this may affect the encounter between Denise and the pastoral caregiver.

Just Care would also require an analysis of the social and cultural role of the psychiatric institution within Western society, recognizing that the psychiatric hospital exists within a society that has adopted de-institutionalization and trans-institutionalization. It would be cognizant of the totalizing culture within the psychiatric hospital, including the ways that the values and reductionism of the Western medical model may have influenced and limited Denise's perception of herself. Just Care would advocate for the flourishing of Denise's entire self, recognizing the tendency of this institution to erase her complexity and humanity.

When considering the beauty and mystery of Denise herself, Just Care would necessitate the use of a contextual lens. It would inquire how Denise's particular history, religion, race, gender, embodiment, and class might be informing and influencing the current encounter. It would note that standards of behavior and diagnosis which privilege the white experience frequently overlook the unique ways that an African American woman might experience and express emotionality. It would explore and name the privileged place that religion and spirituality might have in her life, placing this within a historical and cultural analysis.

When engaging in an assessment of the "issue at hand," Just Care would privilege an "integration" approach, one which both engages in dialogue between the fields of religion and science, and asks how the two might mutually inform and/or challenge one another. It would also invite the caregiver to engage with interdisciplinary sources, including historical, cultural, familial, and social analysis in her assessment. Once undertaken, this analysis might reframe the goal of "treatment" to include not only the treatment of the care seeker's symptoms but also to instill a greater sense of self and sacredness of her embodiment. It would prompt questions concerning what health, wholenesss and well-being might look like in the midst of her mental health challenges. It might seek ways for Denise to draw on her spirituality as a source of strength in the midst of treatment, rather than simply equating her spirituality with pathology. It could potentially invite the pastoral caregiver to partner with Denise in a model of relationship where both members were contributing to the construction of something larger than either of them. This relationship would enable Denise, with the support of the pastoral caregiver, to discern and embrace life-giving spiritual practices within her religious tradition, and to name those that might be life-limiting.

Just Care would also be consistently inviting the caregiver to ask questions about the ways that her own embodiment, particularly her race and gender as a white woman, might be impacting the encounter. It would necessitate that the caregiver foster awareness of the limitations that may be present in the current encounter given their different racialization. It would invite the white caregiver to confront the presence of white supremacy within the encounter, and to inquire whether she was the "best" person to accompany Denise. Should the relationship move forward, Just Care would also necessitate that the caregiver surround herself with a community of accountability to aid her in monitoring her own intersecting social and cultural privileges and personal needs. It would encourage the caregiver to continue to engage in self-care and to monitor her own agential power, while ensuring that she was allowing Denise to take the lead in the conversations.

Finally, Just Care is a practice of care in which advocacy would necessarily coexist with the intimacy of this encounter. It is care in which the caregiver would be encouraged to accompany Denise on visits to potential discharge sites, and to engage in larger efforts to create more welcoming churches for Denise when she is discharged. This might involve calling and/or visiting potential churches before recommending that Denise attend this church. Ultimately, it would invite this caregiver to work toward a more welcoming society for all women diagnosed with mental illness. Just Care, however, would also remind members of the wider society of their communal responsibility to care with and for the vulnerable members of society, particularly those women who have been diagnosed with mental illness. It would stand against forces that project the responsibility for care with Denise solely on this pastoral caregiver. It would not overlook the culpability of the larger society for the systemic harm that can create situations where women, particularly women of color like Denise, are caught in the midst of dehumanizing systems and find themselves in a psychiatric facility with a diagnosis of mental illness.

Just Care ultimately endeavors to provide care that, in the words of psychiatric chaplains, respects the “entire humanity” of the woman in front of them. It asserts that the position of the pastoral caregiver, when informed by feminist and womanist Christian social ethics and pastoral care, allows her to see the woman as a holistic person whose diagnosis has been informed by, and continues to intersect with, issues of power, stigma, racism, gender, socio-economic realities, and institutional realities. From this perspective, the relationship between the individual pastoral caregiver and woman stands against the characteristic reductionism of the Western medical model through an awareness that the woman exists in the web of larger systemic factors and constraints. Just Care enables the pastoral caregiver to reimagine and reframe pastoral care with the woman as one that allows for advocacy and social analysis to coexist with the intimacy of an encounter that is respectful of the inherent mystery in every woman struggling with mental illness.

NOTES

1. Emmanuel Lartey, *In Living Color: An Introduction to Intercultural Pastoral Care* (London and Philadelphia: Jessica Kingsley, 2003), 31.
2. Ibid., 33.
3. Ibid.
4. Ibid.
5. Ibid.

6. O3, interview.

7. This is similar to Lartey's concept of "authentic participation." Lartey, *In Living Color*, 33–34.

8. There were a few examples of chaplaincy in which it seemed that their own internal reactions might have been an obstruction to the conversation. For example, recall the chaplain who voiced her own discomfort with a black women who was speaking in a derogatory manner about other blacks. V6, interview.

9. Recall the interview in which the chaplain named "loneliness" as the central issue in a delusion about family. V2, interview, 21:27.

10. Lartey, *In Living Color*, 34, quoting David W. Augsburger, *Pastoral Counseling Across Cultures* (Philadelphia: Westminster Press, 1986), 26.

11. Lartey, *In Living Color*, 81–112; Christie Cozad Neuger, *Counseling Women: A Narrative, Pastoral Approach* (Minneapolis, MN: Augsburg Press, 2001), 229–39; Carrie Doehring, *The Practice of Pastoral Care: A Postmodern Approach,* Expanded and Revised Edition (Louisville, KY: John Knox Press, 2014), 56–71.

12. Lartey, *In Living Color*, 93–94.

13. Ibid., 94.

14. Ibid., 36.

15. Pamela Cooper-White, *Shared Wisdom: Use of the Self in Pastoral Counseling* (Minneapolis, MN: Augsburg Fortress, 2004), 67.

16. Cooper-White, *Shared Wisdom*, 5. Cooper-White details how this definition departs from classical definitions of countertransference throughout the book, but particularly in chapter 1, "Countertransference, A History of the Concept," 9–25.

17. Cooper-White, *Shared Wisdom,* 25.

18. Ibid., 11. She relates that Freud saw countertransference as a threat, "not only to individuals in treatment but also to the reputation of psychoanalysis as a profession." This was such because subjectivity was viewed in a negative light, as the goal of the helping professional was to maintain objectivity.

19. In this model, the caregiver uses his or her self, "not only as a channel of information about his or her inner knowledge but equally as an empathetic receiver of the other's affective state and the shared meaning that is emerging between them." Cooper-White, *Shared Wisdom*, 56. To allay fears that this may influence professional boundaries between the caregiver and care seeker, Cooper-White emphasizes that there is an asymmetry of role and responsibilities due to the contractual trust that has been established around the purpose of the relationship: to help the care seeker. For more see Cooper-White, *Shared Wisdom*, 59.

20. See Cooper-White, *Shared Wisdom*, 64–66, in which she draws on family theorists Betty Carter and Monica McGlodrick to note how external stressors, such as social and economic conditions as well as race and gender, have extrinsic influence on the dynamics of a relationship (i.e., type and quality of education), while also operating intrinsically in each individual's sense of self. She notes that racism and other forms of oppression may also operate at the level of the unconscious.

21. Recall that Doehring defines self-reflexivity as the use of second and third order language to help the caregiver reflect upon "how the self and theological knowledge reflect our social location, advantages, and disadvantages," particularly one's racial privilege. Doehring, *The Practice of Pastoral Care,* 22. Theological reflexivity applies the method of self-reflexivity to one's theological meaning-making, asking how one's social location, formative experiences, and status influence one's (childhood) embedded theologies and (adult) deliberative theologies.

22. See Erving Goffman, *Asylums: Essays on the Social Situation of Mental Patients and Other Inmates* (New York: Anchor Books, 1961), 1–124. Erving Goffman in his ethnographic study of psychiatric patients, coined the term "total institution" to refer to the life of the patients he observed.

23. Goffman, *Asylums*, 17.

24. Winnie S. Chow and Stefan Priebe, "Understanding Psychiatric Institutionalization: A Conceptual Review," in *BMC Psychiatry* (2013), accessed in January 2017, https://bmcpsychiatry.biomedcentral.com/articles/10.1186/1471-244X-13-169, quoting Goffman,

Asylums. The culmination of this process is in the individual abandoning his/her previous roles in order to adopt a purely institutional role. Later scholars prefer the term "institutionalism" to speak about the social position and resultant depersonalization that can occur in modern psychiatric institutions. This includes (but is not limited to) a paternalistic relationship between staff and patients, and a loss of independence that may hinder patients' re-integration into society. For more see Frank M. Ochberg, Vincent P. Zarcone, and David Hamburg. "Symposium on Institutionalism," *Comprehensive Psychiatry* 13.2 (1972): 91–104; David L. Rosenhan, "On Being Sane in Insane Places," *Science* 179.4070 (1973): 250–58.

25. Townes, *Breaking the Fine Rain of Death*, 1.

26. V2, interview.

27. O3, V3, O4, interviews

28. For more on this, see Snorton, "What About All Those Angry Black Women?" in *Women Out of Order* (2010).

29. Pattison, *Pastoral Care and Liberation Theology*, 187, quoting Michael Wilson, *The Hospital: A Place of Truth* (Birmingham, UK: University of Birmingham Press, 1971), 107.

30. Aana Marie Vigen, *Women, Ethics and Inequality in U.S. Healthcare: To Count Among the Living* (New York: Palgrave Macmillan, 2006), 44–48.

31. As was noted in chapter one, both blacks and Hispanics are more likely to be diagnosed with schizophrenia than whites. See Vigen, *Women, Ethics and Inequality*, 3. As Vigen notes elsewhere, "Both U.S. and British psychiatrists are more likely to prescribe antipsychotic medications, hospitalize involuntarily, and place nonwhite patients in seclusion once hospitalized than their white counterparts, independent of appropriateness of clinical factors." Vigen, *Women, Ethics, and Inequality*, 48, quoting Michelle Van Ryn, "Research on the Provider Contribution to Race/Ethnicity Disparities in Medical Care," *Medical Care* 40 no. 1 (2002): I-140-I-151, I-142.

32. Townes, *Breaking the Fine Rain of Death*, 155-6.

33. Beginning in the 1950s, deinstitutionalization refers to the closing of large inpatient psychiatric facilities, and the shift in the responsibility of care for the severely mentally ill from the state government to the community. This was codified by the Mental Health Centers Act of 1963, which stated that "only individuals who posed an imminent danger to themselves or someone else" could be committed in state psychiatric hospitals. See Jeneen Interlandi, "A Madman in Our Midst," *The New York Times,* June 24, 2012, accessed in February 2017, http://query.nytimes.com/gst/fullpage.html?res=9402E0DE1138F937A15755C0A9649D8B63&pagewanted=all. This massive deinstitutionalization effort, however, has not been uncontroversial. While some studies report positive outcomes of deinstitutionalization, others report that the mentally ill who reside in independent community settings are plagued by poverty, poor living conditions, and issues with physical health. For more see, Enric J. Novella, "Mental Health Care and the Politics of Inclusion: A Social Systems Account of Psychiatric Deinstitutionalization," *Theoretical Medicine and Bioethics* 31.6 (2010): 411–27.

34. A theory maintaining that deinstitutionalization has forced the criminal justice system to become a panacea among poorly-funded community housing alternatives. The deinstitutionalization effort has created a system in which state psychiatric hospitals and criminal justice systems have become "functionally interdependent," with those who used to reside in psychiatric hospitals now being forced to live in other institutions—most notably in prisons. See Prins, Seth J. "Does Transinstitutionalization Explain the Overrepresentation of People with Serious Mental Illnesses in the Criminal Justice System?" *Community Mental Health Journal* 47.6 (2011): 716–22; Dustin DeMoss, "The Nightmare of Prison for Individuals with Mental Illness," *Huffington Post,* March 25, 2015 (updated May 25, 2015), accessed in February 2017, http://www.huffingtonpost.com/dustin-demoss/prison-mental-illness_b_6867988.html.

35. For more see Allen Frances, *Saving Normal: An Insider's Revolt against Out-of-Control Psychiatric Diagnosis, DSM-5, Big Pharma, and the Medicalization of Ordinary Life* (New York: HarperCollins, 2013).

36. See Novella,"Mental Health Care," 411–27.

37. Vigen, *Women Ethics and Inequality*, 9

38. Ibid.

39. Ibid.

40. West, *Wounds of the Spirit*, 198.
41. Ibid., 199.
42. See Kate Ott, "Feminism and Justice: Who We Are, What We Do," in *Faith, Feminism and Scholarship, the Next Generation,* eds. Melanie L. Hayes and Kate M. Ott (New York: Palgrave MacMillan, 2011), 35-51.
43. Ott, "Feminism and Justice," 44
44. Ibid., 43.
45. Ibid., 45.
46. See Jürgen Habermas, *Between Facts and Norms: Contributions to a Discourse Theory of Law and Democracy* (Cambridge, MA: MIT Press, 1998).
47. O4, interview
48. O5, interview, 39:00
49. V1, interview, 55:00.
50. V2, interview, 26:01.
51. See Ott, "Feminism and Justice," 42–43.
52. Doehring, *The Practice of Pastoral Care*, 34.
53. Jacqueline Kelley, "Womanist Pastoral Care Using Narrative Therapy," in *Women Out of Order*, 139.
54. O3, interview, 13:30.
55. Bonnie J. Miller-McLemore and Brita L. Gill-Austern, eds., *Feminist and Womanist Pastoral Theology* (Nashville, TN: Abingdon, 1999), 13.
56. See Pattison, *Pastoral Care and Liberation Theology*, 97–101.
57. West reveals that the characterization of those who have been battered as "masochistic" or suffering from borderline personality disorder "implies an emotionally sick collusion in their own abuse." See *Wounds of the Spirit*, 42.
58. West asserts that when anguish becomes collapsed with psychotic behavior, it becomes "a scientifically validated method of community dismissal." See *Wounds of the Spirit*, 124.
59. V2, interview.
60. Goffman, *Asylums*, 4–12.
61. Neuger, *Counseling Women*, 15.
62. Ibid., 115.
63. See Townes, who draws on Pouissant to note that while black women experience depression, the symptoms are frequently manifested differently. Black women, for example, may experience increased activity as opposed to lethargy, lack of interest in activities, and trouble eating or sleeping. For more see Townes, *Breaking the Fine Rain of Death*, 155.
64. See West, *Wounds of the Spirit*, 134–35.
65. See Townes, *Breaking the Fine Rain of Death*, 155.
66. See Snorton, "What About All Those Angry Black Women?" in *Women Out of Order*, 207-218
67. See Wallace, "A Womanist Legacy of Trauma, Grief and Loss," in *Women Out of Order*, 43-56.
68. West, *Wounds of the Spirit*, 177.
69. Ibid., 153.
70. V5, interview.
71. Lartey, *In Living Color*, 34, quoting Augsburger, *Pastoral Counseling Across Cultures,* 26.
72. Cozad Neuger, *Counseling Women*, 89.
73. Michael Garrett, "Introduction: Psychotherapy for Psychosis," *American Journal of Psychotherapy* 70.1 (2016), 1.
74. For more see the series on psychotherapy for psychosis in the *American Journal of Psychotherapy* 70.1 (2016). The series reveals that therapists practicing a number of different psychological approaches have had positive outcomes with those suffering from psychosis, including (but not limited to) CBT, object-relations approaches, Method of Levels, and general psychological theories that view psychotic symptoms as intrusion of primitive psychological processes, brought into adult life by adverse life events.
75. Garrett, "Introduction: Psychotherapy for Psychosis," 3.

76. Eleanor Longden and John Read, "Social Adversity in the Etiology of Psychosis: A Review of the Evidence," *American Journal of Psychotherapy* 70.1 (2016), 5–35.
77. Richard P. McBrien, *Catholicism* (New York: HarperCollins, 1994), 826–27.
78. O4, interview.
79. Cooper-White, *Shared Wisdom*, 55, quoting Martin Buber, *I and Thou* (New York: Charles Scribner's Sons, 1937), 114.
80. V2, O4, interviews
81. Cooper-White, *Shared Wisdom*, 58.
82. Doehring, *The Practice of Pastoral Care*, 43.
83. Ibid., 44–49.
84. Ibid., 45.
85. Ibid., 47.
86. For more on the development of a contract of care, see chapter 4 entitled "Establishing Caregiving Relationships" in Doehring, *The Practice of Pastoral Care*, 73–83.
87. Doehring, *The Practice of Pastoral Care*, 48.
88. Ibid., 48.
89. O3, interview, 18:00.
90. Townes, *Breaking the Fine Rain of Death*, 2.
91. For more see Doehring, *The Practice of Pastoral Care*, 10.
92. V2, interview, 21:27.
93. Pattison, *Pastoral Care*, 179–82.
94. Ibid., 177–79.
95. While this chaplain was a white man, it is also important that he self-identified as disabled, due to him being classified as "legally blind." F2, interview.
96. While reporting that the team was aware that the woman had a history of abuse, the chaplain did not provide any racial or cultural information about this woman. F2, interview.
97. O3, interview, 14:00.
98. Ulanov, *Spiritual Aspects of Clinical Work*, 45.
99. See John Swinton, *Spirituality and Mental Health Care: Rediscovering a Forgotten Dimension* (Philadelphia: Kingsley, 2001), 11–39.
100. Lartey, *In Living Color*, 140–41.
101. Swinton, *Sp irituality and Mental Health Care*, 18.
102. Ibid., 171.
103. To assess whether aspects of one's lived theology are life-giving or life-limiting Doehring turns to Pargament to speak about engagement with spiritual-orienting systems. For more on this, see Doehring, *The Practice of Pastoral Care*, particularly 89–92. Oates, Pruyser, and Swinton all speak of characterizations of "healthy" versus "non-healthy" religion. See Wayne Oates, *When Religion Gets Sick* (Philadelphia: Westminster: 1970), 15–24; Paul Pruyser, *Religion in Psychodynamic Perspective*, eds. H. Newton Malony and Bernard Spilka (New York: Oxford University Press, 1991), 47–65; Swinton, *Spirituality and Mental Health Care*, 11–39.
104. Swinton, *Spirituality and Mental Health Care*, 172.
105. See Oates, *When Religion Gets Sick*, 15–25; Pruyser, *Religion in Psychodynamic Perspective*, 47–65.
106. Oates, *When Religion Gets Sick*, 30.
107. MS, Interview
108. Doehring, *The Practice of Pastoral Care: A Postmodern Approach,* First Edition (Louisville, KY: John Knox Press, 2006), 8.
109. Doehring, *The Practice of Pastoral Care* (2006), 8.
110. She terms this approach the "critical correlational method." Doehring, *The Practice of Pastoral Care* (2006), 9.
111. Townsend, *Introduction to Pastoral Counseling*, 86-90.
112. Neuger, *Counseling Women*, 153.
113. Ibid.
114. Townsend, *Introduction to Pastoral Counseling*, 75-99.
115. See Part One of Gerkin's *Living Human Document* for his development of these concepts.

116. Neuger, *Counseling Women*, 54.
117. Doehring, *The Practice of Pastoral Care*, 16.
118. See Snorton, "What About All Those Angry Black Women?" in *Women Out of Order*, 214.
119. Ibid., 217.
120. For more see Edwina Ward, "Similarities and Differences in Cross-Cultural Pastoral Supervision," *Journal of Theology for Southern Africa* 116 (2003), 51–64; Homer L. Jernigan, "Clinical Pastoral Education with Students from Other Cultures: The Role of the Supervisor," *Journal of Pastoral Care* 54.2 (2000), 135–45.
121. Jernigan, "Clinical Pastoral Education," 135–45.
122. V3, interview.
123. O5, interview.
124. For example, how are those with mental illness portrayed in the Bible, and what passages are relied upon for communal worship? How are these passages preached about, and what connections (or lack thereof) are made to modern mental illness? What do references to "the voice of God' in liturgy mean to someone who struggles with hearing voices? How might a woman who struggles with PTSD be triggered by the weekly or monthly reenactment of the words of the Eucharist, specifically "this is my body, this is my blood"? How do members name the blessings of "health" or the scourges of "illness" in petitionary prayers (and in other forums), and what does this reveal about the operative historical social, cultural and racial dynamics that have contributed to this construction of the term "health" and "illness"? Who is deemed "worthy" of visits by outreach ministries to the "sick" and homebound, and who is forgotten? How does the denial of white privilege and the entitlement experienced by whites intersect with a church's commitment and/or embrace of those with mental illness?
125. Among these are faith-based organizations such as Mental Health Ministries and Interfaith Network on Mental Illness' Caring Clergy Project. Yet, connections should also be forged between churches and secular organizations, such as the National Alliance on Mental Health (NAMI), the Depression Bipolar Support Alliance (DBSA), Mental Health America (MHA), and the Substance Abuse and Mental Health Services Administration (SAMHSA).

Bibliography

Adler, Alfred. *The Neurotic Constitution: Basic Principles of Comparative Individual Psychology and Psychotherapy Commentary Text-Critical Edition.* Edited by K.H. Witte. Goettingen, Germany: Vandenhoeck and Ruprecht, 1997.

Airhihenbuwa, Collins O. *Health and Culture, Beyond the Western Paradigm*. Thousand Oaks, CA: Sage, 1995.

Albers, Robert H., William Meller, and Steven Thurber, eds. *Ministry with Persons with Mental Illness and Their Families*. Minneapolis, MN: Fortress Press, 2012.

Ali, Caroll Watkins. *Survival and Liberation: Pastoral Theology in African American Context.* Duluth: Chalice, 1999.

Andrews, Jonathan, and Anne Digby, eds. *Sex and Seclusion, Class and Custody: Perspectives on Gender and Class in the History of British and Irish Psychiatry*. New York: Rodopi, 2004.

Asquith, Glenn H. *The Concise Dictionary of Pastoral Care and Counseling*. Nashville, TN: Abingdon, 2010.

Augsburger, David W. *Pastoral Counseling Across Cultures*. Philadelphia: Westminster Press, 1986.

Barnard, David. "Paul Pruyser's Psychoanalytic Psychology of Religion." *Religious Studies Review* 16.2 (1990): 125–26.

Belle, Deborah. "Poverty and Women's Mental Health." *American Psychologist* 45.3 (1990): 385–89.

Boisen, Anton. "A Challenge to our Seminaries." *Journal of Pastoral Care* 5.1 (1951): 8–12.

———. *The Exploration of the Inner World.* New York: Harper and Bros, 1952.

———. *Out of the Depths: An Autobiographical Study of Mental Disorder and Religious Experience*. New York: Harper, 1960.

———. "The Problem of Values in the Light of Psychopathology." *Journal of Clinical Pastoral Work* 2.4 (1949): 187–98.

———. "Religious Experience and Psychological Conflict." *Journal of Pastoral Care* 15.1 (1961): 1–6.

Bonilla-Silva, Eduardo. "The Linguistics of Color Blind Racism: How to Talk Nasty about Blacks Without Sounding 'Racist.'" *Critical Sociology* 28 (2002): 41–62.

———. *Racism Without Racists, Color Blind Racism and Racial Inequality in Contemporary America*. Lanham: Rowman & Littlefield, 2010.

Browning, Don. *Fundamental Practical Theology.* Minneapolis, MN: Augsburg, 1991.

———. *Religious and Ethical Factors in Psychiatric Practice.* Chicago: Nelson-Hall, 1990.

Buber, Martin. *I and Thou.* New York: Charles Scribner's Sons, 1937.

Busfield, Joan. *Managing Madness, Changing Ideas and Practice*. New York: Routledge, 1986.

Bye, Lynn, and Jamie Partridge. "Factors Affecting Mental Illness Hospitalization Rates: Analysis of State-Level Panel Data," *The Social Science Journal* 40.1 (2003): 33–47.

Cabot, Richard, and Russell Dicks. *The Art of Ministering to the Sick*. New York: Macmillan, 1936.

Cahill, Lisa Sowle. *Theological Bioethics: Participation, Justice and Change*. Washington, DC: Georgetown University, 2005.

Cahill, Lisa Sowle, and Margaret Farley, eds. *Embodiment, Morality and Medicine*. Boston: Kluwer Academic, 1995.

Capps, Donald. *The Depleted Self: Sin in a Narcissistic Age*. Minneapolis, MN: Fortress, 1993.

———. *Fragile Connections: Memoirs of Mental Illness for Pastoral Care Professionals*. St. Louis: Chalice Press, 2005.

———. "The Minister and Mental Illness" Pastoral Psychology 63 no 1 (2014): 13–222.

———. *Social Phobia: Alleviating Anxiety in an Age of Self Promotion*. Atlanta: Chalice, 1999.

Capps, Donald, and Nathan Steven Carlin. "Mental Illness Publications in Major Pastoral Care Journals from 1950 to 2003." *Pastoral Psychology* 55.5 (2007): 593–99.

Carlin, Nathan. "The Hospital Room as Uncanny: Psychoanalytic Observations and Recommendations for Pastors and Chaplains." *Pastoral Psychology* 58 (2009): 27–42.

Carmen, Eliane Hilberman. "Inner-City Community Mental Health: The Interplay of Abuse and Race in Chronic Mentally Ill Women." In *Mental Health, Racism and Sexism*, edited by Charles V. Willie, Patricia Perri Rieker, Bernard M. Kramer, and Bertram S. Brown, 217–37. Pittsburgh: University of Pittsburgh Press, 1995.

Chapman, Thomas W., ed. *A Practical Handbook for Ministry from the Writings of Wayne E. Oates*. Louisville, KY: Westminster John Knox, 1992.

Charmaz, Kathy, and Richard G. Mitchell. "The Myth of Silent Authorship: Self, Substance and Style of Ethnographic Writing." In *Reflexivity and Voice*, edited by Rosanna Hertz, 193–215. Thousand Oaks, CA: Sage, 1997.

Charry, Dana. *Mental Health Skills for Clergy: Evaluation, Intervention, Referral*. Valley Forge, PA: Judson, 1981.

Chow, Winnie S., and Stefan Priebe. "Understanding Psychiatric Institutionalization: A Conceptual Review," in BMC Psychiatry (2013). Accessed in January, 2017. https://bmcpsychiatry.biomedcentral.com/articles/10.1186/1471-244X-13-169.

Ciarrocchi, Joseph W. *A Minister's Handbook of Mental Disorders*. New York: Paulist, 1993.

Clebsch, William A., and Charles R. Jaekle. *Pastoral Care in Historical Perspective*. New York: Jason Aronson, 1975.

Clinebell, Howard. *Basic Types of Pastoral Counseling: Resources for the Ministry of Healing and Growth*. New York: Abingdon, 2011.

Collins, Gregory B., and Thomas Culbertson. *Mental Illness and Psychiatric Treatment: A Guide for Pastoral Counselors*. New York: Haworth Pastoral Press, 2003.

Cooper-White, Pamela. *Shared Wisdom: Use of the Self in Pastoral Counseling*. Minneapolis, MN: Augsburg, 2004.

Corrigan, Patrick W., and Amy C. Watson. "Understanding the Impact of Stigma on People with Mental Illness," *World Psychiatry* 1.1 (2002): 16–20.

Cox, John L., Alastair V. Campbell, and K.W.M. Fulford, eds. *Medicine of the Person: Faith Science and Values in Health Care Provision*. Philadelphia: Jessica Kingsley, 2007.

Cozad Neuger, Christie. *Counseling Women: A Narrative Pastoral Approach*. Minneapolis, MN: Augsburg/Fortress Press, 2001.

Coyte, Mary Ellen, Peter Gilbert, and Vicky Nicholls. *Spirituality, Values and Mental Health: Jewels for the Journey*. Philadelphia: Jessica Kingsley Publishers, 2007.

Crenshaw, Kimberle. "Intersectionality and Identity Politics: Learning from Violence against Women of Color." In *Feminist Theory: A Reader*, Third Edition, edited by Wendy Kolmar and Frances Bartkowski, 482–90. Boston: McGraw, 2010.

Dain, Norman. "Madness and the Stigma of Sin in American Christianity." *Stigma and Mental Illness*, edited by Paul Jay Fink and Allan Tasman. Arlington, VA: American Psychiatric Association, 1992.

Davila, Maria Teresa. "A Latina Methodology for Christian Ethics: The Role of the Social Sciences in the Study and Praxis of the Option for the Poor in the United States." In *Faith, Feminism and Scholarship,* edited by Melanie Harris and Kate M. Ott, 89–106. New York: Palgrave MacMillan, 2011.

Dekker, Hannah. *The Making of the DSM III: A Diagnostic Manual's Conquest of American Psychiatry.* New York: Oxford University Press, 2013.

DeMarinis, Valerie. *Critical Caring: A Feminist Model for Pastoral Psychology.* Louisville, KY: Westminster/John Knox, 1993.

DeMoss, Dustin. "The Nightmare of Prison for Individuals with Mental Illness." *Huffington Post,* March 25, 2015 (updated May 25, 2015). Accessed in February 2017, http://www.huffingtonpost.com/dustin-demoss/prison-mental-illness_b_6867988.html.

Digby, Anne. "Women's Biological Straightjacket." In *Sexuality and Subordination: Interdisciplinary Studies of Gender in the Nineteenth Century*, edited by Susan Mendus and Jane Rendall, 192–220. New York: Routledge, 1989.

Dittes, James. *Turning Points in Pastoral Care: The Legacy of Anton Boisen and Seward Hiltner.* Grand Rapids, MI: Baker Book House, 1990.

Doane, Janice. *From Klein to Kristeva: Psychoanalytic Feminism and the Search for the "Good Enough Mother."* Ann Arbor: University of Michigan, 1992.

Doehring, Carrie. *The Practice of Pastoral Care, A Postmodern Approach,* First Edition. Louisville, KY: John Knox Press, 2006.

———. *The Practice of Pastoral Care: A Postmodern Approach*, Revised and Expanded Edition. Louisville, KY: John Knox Press, 2014.

Draper, Edgar. *Psychiatry and Pastoral Care*. Englewood Cliffs, NJ: Prentice Hall, 1965.

Evans, Gillian R, ed. *A History of Pastoral Care*. London, New York: Cassell, 2000.

Fabrega, Horatio, Jr. "Psychiatric Stigma in Non-Western Societies." *Comprehensive Psychiatry* 32.6 (1991): 534–51.

Farley, Margaret. *Compassionate Respect: A Feminist Approach to Medical Ethics.* New York: Paulist Press, 2002.

———. "A Feminist Vision of Respect for Persons." *Journal of Feminist Studies in Religion* 9.1–2 (1993): 183–98.

Farnham, C.R., A. M. Zipple, W. Tyrrell, and P. Chittinanda. "Health status risk factors of people with severe and persistent mental illness." *Journal of Psychosocial Nursing Mental Health Service* 37.6 (1999): 16–21.

Fernando, Suman. *Mental Health, Race and Culture. Third Edition*. New York: Palgrave MacMillan. 2010.

Foucault, Michel. *History of Madness.* Edited by Jean Khalfa and translated by Jonathan Murphy and Jean Khalfa. New York: Routledge, 2006.

———. *Mental Illness and Psychology*. Translated by A. Sheridan. Berkeley: University of California Press, 1987.

Frances, Allen. "DSM 5 is a Guide Not a Bible, Ignore its Ten Worst Changes," Dec 2, 2012. *Psychology Today* website, Accessed Feb 2017 https://www.psychologytoday.com/blog/dsm5-in-distress/201212/dsm-5-is-guide-not-bible-ignore-its-ten-worst-changes.

———. *Saving Normal: An Insider's Revolt and Out-of-control Psychiatric Diagnosis, DSM-5, Big Pharma and the Medicalization of Normal Life*. New York: HarperCollins, 2013.

———. "A Warning Sign on the Road to DSM-5: Beware of its Unintended Consequences," *Psychiatric Times*, June 26, 2009.

Garrett, Michael. "Introduction: Psychotherapy for Psychosis." *American Journal of Psychotherapy* 70.1 (2016): 1–4.

Gerkin, Charles V. *Crisis Experience in Modern Life: Theory and Theology in Pastoral Care*. Nashville, TN: Abingdon, 1979.

———. *The Living Human Document.* Nashville, TN: Abingdon Press, 1984.

Gerson, Gal. "Winnicott, Participation and Gender." *Feminism and Psychology* 14.4 (2004): 561–81.

Giesen, Bernhard. "The Trauma of Perpetrators: The Holocaust as the Traumatic Reference of German National Identity." In *Collective Trauma and Collective Identity*, edited by Jeffrey C. Alexander, Roy Eyerman, Bernhard Giesen, Neil J. Smelser, and Piotr Sztompka, 112–54. Berkeley: University of California Press, 2004.

Gilbin, Marie J. "The Prophetic Role of Feminist Bioethics." *Horizons* 24.1 (1997): 37–49.

Goffman, Erving. *Asylums: Essays on the Social Situation of Mental Patients and Other Inmates*. New York: Anchor Books, 1961.

Gold, Joel, and Ian Gold. *Suspicious Minds: How Culture Shapes Madness*. New York: Free Press, 2014.

Gorsuch, N. *Introduction to Feminist Pastoral Care and Counseling.* St. Louis: Pilgrim Press, 2001.

Govig, Stewart D. "Chronic Mental Illness and the Family: Contexts for Pastoral Care." *Journal of Pastoral Care* 47.4 (1993): 405–18.

———. *In the Shadow of our Steeples, Pastoral Presence for Families Coping with Mental Illness*. Hoboken: Taylor and Francis, 2013.

Graham, Larry Kent. *Care of Persons, Care of Worlds: A Psychosystems Approach*. Nashville, TN: Abingdon, 1992.

Graves, Joseph L., Jr. *The Emperor's New Clothes: Biological Theories of Race at the Millennium*. New Brunswick: Rutgers University, 2002.

Green, Amy Elise. "Critical Components in the Formation of Clinical Pastoral Education Supervisors." DMin diss., Ecumenical Theological Seminary, 2011.

Greider, Kathleen, Gloria Johnson, and Kristen Leslie. "Three Decades of Women Writing for their Lives." In *Feminist and Womanist Pastoral Theology*, edited by Bonnie J. Miller-McLemore and Brita L. Gill-Austin, 21–50. Nashville, TN: Abingdon Press, 1999.

Grote, Nancy, Allan Zuckoff, Holly Swartz, Sarah E. Bledsoe, and Sharon Geibel, "Engaging Women who are Depressed and Economically Disadvantaged in Mental Health Treatment." *Social Work* 52.4 (2007): 295–308.

Habermas, Jürgen. *Between Facts and Norms: Contributions to a Discourse Theory of Law and Democracy.* Cambridge, MA: MIT Press, 1998.

Harding, Sandra. *Feminism and Methodology*. Bloomington: Indiana University Press, 1987.

Harding, Sandra and Merill B. Hintikka, eds., *Discovering Reality: Feminist Perspectives on Epistemology, Metaphysics, Methodology and Philosophy of Science*. Boston: D. Reidel, 1983.

Hiltner, Seward. *Pastoral Counseling*. New York: Abingdon-Cokesbury, 1949.

———. *Preface to Pastoral Theology*. New York: Abingdon, 1958.

Harrison, Beverly. *Justice in the Making: Feminist Social Ethics*. Louisville, KY: Westminster John Knox, 2004.

Harvey, Jennifer. *Dear White Christians: For Those Still Longing for Racial Reconciliation.* Grand Rapids, MI: Eerdmans, 2014.

Hobfoll, Stevan E., Christian Ritter, Justin Lavin, Michael R. Hulsizer, and Rebecca P. Cameron. "Depression Prevalence and Incidence among Inner-city Pregnant and Postpartum Women." *Journal of Consulting and Clinical Psychology* 63 (1995): 445–53.

Holifield, E. Brooks. *A History of Pastoral Care in America: From Salvation to Self Realization*. Nashville, TN: Abingdon, 1983.

Hunt, Mary. *Fierce Tenderness: a Feminist Theology of Friendship*. New York: Crossroad, 1991.

Interlandi, Jeneen. "A Madman in Our Midst," *The New York Times,* June 24, 2012. Accessed in February 2017. http://query.nytimes.com/gst/fullpage.html?res=9402E0DE-1138F937A15755C0A9649D8B63&pagewanted=all.

Ivey, Asha. "Attitudes toward Suicide and Mental Illness in African American Churches." PhD Diss., University of Michigan, 2007.

Jackson, Vanessa. "In Our Own Voices: African American Stories of Oppression, Survival and Recovery in the Mental Health System." *Race, Health Care and the Law*, edited by Vernellia R. Randall. Accessed 2 Feb. 2017. http://academic.udayton.edu/health/01status/mental01.htm.

Jaggar, Alison M, ed. *Just Methods: An Interdisciplinary Feminist Reader*. Boulder, CO: Paradigm, 2008.

Jernigan, Homer L. "Clinical Pastoral Education with Students from Other Cultures: The Role of the Supervisor." *Journal of Pastoral Care* 54.2 (2000): 135–45.

Jordan, Merle. *Taking on the Gods*. Eugene, OR: Wipf and Stock, 2001.

Kelley, Jacqueline. "Womanist Pastoral Care Using Narrative Therapy in Addressing Multicultural Issues." *Women Out of Order*. Minneapolis, MN: Fortress, 2010: 128–48.

Kessler, Ronald C., and Harold W. Neighbors."A New Perspective on the Relationships among Race, Social Class, and Psychological Distress." *Journal of Health and Social Behavior* 27.2 (1986): 107–15.

Kim, Mikyong. "Korean-American Clergymen's Views on Mental Health and Treatment." PhD Diss., University of California, Berkeley, 1990.

Kinzie, David. *Psychiatry and Religion: The Convergence of Mind and Spirit*. Washington DC: American Psychiatric Association, 2000.

Koenig, Harold G. *Faith and Mental Health: Religious Resources for Healing*. Philadelphia: Templeton Foundation Press, 2005.

Kristula, Coleen. "Dispelling the Last Taboo: Helping Clergy and Congregations to Care for Persons and Families Who are Living with Mental Illness." D. Min thesis, Drew University, 2008.

Kujawa-Holbrook, Sheryl, ed. *Injustice and the Care of Sounds: Taking Oppression Seriously in Pastoral Care*. Minneapolis, MN: Fortress, 2009.

Lake, Frank. *Clinical theology: A Theological and Psychiatric Basis to Clinical Pastoral Care*. London: Darton Longman and Todd, 1965.

Lartey, Emmauel. *In Living Color: An Intercultural Approach to Pastoral Care and Counseling*, 2nd edition. New York: Jessica Kingsley Publishers Ltd., 2003.

Leavy, Gerard, Kate Loewenthal, and Michael King. "Challenges to Sanctuary: The Clergy As a Resource for Mental Health Care in the Community." *Social Science and Medicine* 65.3 (2007): 548–59.

Lieberman, Jeffrey A., and Ogi Ogas. *Shrinks: the Untold Story of Psychiatry*. New York: Little, Brown and Company, 2015.

Lindsey, Kenneth P., and Gordon L. Paul. "Involuntary Commitments to Public Mental Institutions: Issues Involving the Overrepresentation of Blacks and Assessment of Relative Functioning." *Psychological Bulletin* 106.2 (1989): 171–83.

Link, Bruce C. "Understanding Labeling Effects in the Area of Mental Disorders: An Assessment of the Effects of Expectations of Rejection." *American Sociological Review* 52.1(1987): 96–112.

Longden, Eleanor and John Read. "Social Adversity in the Etiology of Psychosis: A Review of the Evidence." *American Journal of Psychotherapy* 70.1 (2016): 5–35.

Lynch, J., G. Kaplan, and S. Shema. "Cumulative Impact of Sustained Economic Hardship on Physical Cognitive Psychological and Social Functioning." *New England Journal of Medicine* 337.26 (1997): 1889–895.

MacMillan, Harriet. "Trauma-related and Stressor-related Disorders," in *DSM 5: A Collection of Psychiatrist Views on the Changes, Controversies and Future Directions*. BMC Medicine 2013. Accessed in September 2016. https://bmcmedicine.biomedcentral.com/articles/10.1186/1741-7015-11-202.

Malony, H. Newton, and Bernard Spilka, eds. *Religion in the Psychodynamic Perspective: The Contributions of Paul W. Pruyser*. New York: Oxford University, 1991.

Marshall, Catherine, and Gretchen B. Rossman, *Designing Qualitative Research*. Thousand Oaks, CA: Sage, 2014.

Marshall, Joretta, and Duane Bidwell, eds. *The Formation of Pastoral Counselors: Challenges and Opportunities*. New York: Haworth, 2006.

Mason, Robert L., Carol B. Currier, and John Russell Curtis. *The Clergyman and the Psychiatrist: When to Refer*. Chicago: Nelson-Hall, 1978.

McBrien, Richard P. *Catholicism*. New York: HarperCollins, 1994.

McCrary, Carolyn. "Interdependence as a Normative Value in Pastoral Counseling with African Americans." *Journal of Interdenominational Theological Center* 18, (Fall-Spring 1990–1991): 1–2.

McNeill, John T. *A History of the Cure of Souls*. New York: Harper Collins, 1977.

Meigs, Thomas J. "Pastoral Care Methods and Demonology." *Journal of Psychology and Theology* 5.3 (1977): 234–46.

Miller-McLemore, Bonnie J., and Brita L. Gill-Austern, eds. *Feminist and Womanist Pastoral Theology*. Nashville, TN: Abingdon, 1999.

Miller-McLemore, Bonnie J. "Also a Pastoral Theologian: In Pursuit of Dynamic Theology (or Meditations from a Recalcitrant Heart)." *Pastoral Psychol* (2010) 59: 813–28.

Millon, Theodore. *Masters of the Mind: Exploring the Story of Mental Illness from Ancient Time to the New Millennium*. Hoboken: John Wiley & Sons, 2004.

Moessner, Jeanne Stevenson. *In Her Own Time: Women and Developmental Issues in Pastoral Care*. Minneapolis, MN: Augsburg Fortress, 2000.

Moss, D. "The Circle of the Soul, The Role of Spirituality in Healthcare." *Appl Psychophysiol Biofeedback* 27.4 (2002): 283–97.

Moss, Kary L. *Man-Made Medicine: Women's Health, Public Policy and Reform*. Durham, NC: Duke University Press, 1996.

Myers-Shrink, Susan. *Helping the Good Shepherd: Pastoral Counseling in a Psychotherapeutic Culture (1925–1975)*. Baltimore: John Hopkins University Press, 2009.

Nechas, Eileen, and Denise Foley. *Unequal Treatment: What You Don't know about How Women Are Mistreated by the Medical Community*. New York: Simon and Schuster, 1994.

Nemeroff, Charles B., and Daniel Weinberger. "The DSM Controversy. Tablet from Mt. Sinai: A Step Backward or the Natural Progression of Advances in Medicine?" in *DSM 5: A Collection of Psychiatrist Views on the Changes, Controversies and Future Directions.* BMC Medicine 2013. https://bmcmedicine.biomedcentral.com/articles/10.1186/1741-7015-11-202.

Neuger, Christie Cozad. *Counseling Women, a Narrative, Pastoral Approach.* Minneapolis, MN: Augsburg Fortress, 2001.

———. *In Her Own Time: Women and Developmental Issues in Pastoral Care*, eited by Jeanne Herenson-Moessner, 65–86. Minneapolis, MN: Augsburg, 2000.

Novella, Enric J. "Mental Health Care and the Politics of Inclusion: A Social Systems Account of Psychiatric Deinstitutionalization." *Theoretical Medicine and Bioethics* 31.6 (2010): 411–27.

Nyengele, Mpyana Fulgence. *African Women's Theology, Gender Relations and Family Systems Theory, Pastoral Theological Considerations and Guidelines for Care and Counseling.* New York: Peter Lang, 2004.

Oates, Wayne. *Behind the Masks.* Louisville, Westminster, 1987.

———. "Finding Hope Again: A Pastor's Guide to Counseling Depressed Persons." *Pastoral Psychology* 29.3 (1981): 224–25.

———. *The Religious Care of the Psychiatric Patient*. Philadelphia: Westminster, 1978.

———. *Religious Factors in Mental Illness*. New York: Association, 1955.

———. *When Religion Gets Sick.* Philadelphia: Westminster, 1970.

Ochberg, Frank M., Vincent P. Zarcone, and David Hamburg. "Symposium on Institutionalism." *Comprehensive Psychiatry* 13.2 (1972): 91–104.

Oden, Thomas C. *Pastoral Theology: Essentials of Ministry*. New York: HarperOne, 1983.

Oglesby, William. *Biblical Themes for Pastoral Care.* Nashville, TN: Abingdon, 1980.

Ott, Kate. "Feminism and Justice: Who We Are, What We Do." In *Faith Feminism and Scholarship, The Next Generation*, edited by Melanie Harris and Kate Ott, 35–51. New York: Palgrave, 2011.

Paget, Marriane A. "Experience and Knowledge." *Human Studies* 6.1 (1983): 67–90.

Pattison, Stephen. *Pastoral Care and Liberation Theology*. Cambridge: Cambridge University Press, 1994.

Patton, John. *Pastoral Counseling: A Ministry of the Church.* Eugene, OR: Wipf and Stock, 1983.

Phelan, Jo C., Bruce G. Link, Ann Stueve, and Bernice A. Pescosolido. "Public Conceptions of Mental Illness in 1950 and 1996: What is Mental Illness and Is It To Be Feared?" *Journal of Health and Social Behavior* 41.2 (2000): 188–207.

Pleck, Elizabeth. *Domestic Tyranny*. Urbana: University of Illinois Press, 2004.

Porter, Roy. *Madness: A Brief History*. New York: Oxford University Press, 2002.

Pressley, Arthur. "Liberation Theology, Pastoral Care and the Spirituality of Violence." In *Faith and the Intifada: Palestinian Christian Voices*, edited by Naim S Ateek, Marc H. Ellis and Rosemary Radford Ruether, 170–80. New York: Orbis, 1992.

Prins, Seth J. "Does Transinstitutionalization Explain the Overrepresentation of People with Serious Mental Illnesses in the Criminal Justice System?" *Community Mental Health Journal* 47.6 (2011): 716–22.

Pruyser, Paul W. *The Minister as a Diagnostician*. Philadelphia: Westminster, 1976.

———. *Religion in Psychodynamic Perspective*. Edited by H. Newton Malony and Bernard Spilka. New York: Oxford University Press, 1991.

Puchalski, Christina M. and Betty Ferrel. *Making Healthcare Whole: Integrating Spirituality into Healthcare*. West Conshohocken: Templeton, 2010.

———. "The Role of Spirituality in Health Care." *Proc Baylor Univ Med Cent* 14.4 (2001): 352–57.

Ramakrishan, P. "You are Here: Locating 'Spirituality' on the Map of the Current Medical World." *Curr Opin Psychiatry* 28.5 (2015): 393–401.

Ramsay, Nancy. *Pastoral Diagnosis: A Resource for Ministries of Care and Counseling*. Minneapolis, MN: Fortress, 1998.

"Religion and Ethics." ABC's website. Accessed February 2017. http://www.abc.net.au/religion/articles/2015/10/09/4328908.htm.

Richardson, Ron. *Creating a Healthier Church: Family Systems Theory, Leadership and Congregational Life*. Minneapolis, MN: Augsburg, 1996.

Riessman, Catherine K. *Narrative Analysis*. Thousand Oaks, CA: Sage, 1993.

Rosenblatt, Paul and Beverly R. Wallace. *African American Grief*. New York: Brunner Routledge, 2005.

Rosenhan, David L. "On Being Sane in Insane Places." *Science* 179.4070 (1973): 250–58.

Roman, P.M., and H.H. Floyd, "Social Acceptance of Psychiatric Illness and Psychiatric Treatment." *Social Psychiatry* 16.1 (1981): 21–29.

Schatzberg, Alan F, James H. Scully Jr., David J. Kupfer, and Darrel A. Regier. "Setting the Record Straight: A Response to Frances Commentary on DSM-V." *Psychiatric Times*, July 1, 2009 http://www.psychiatrictimes.com/dsm-5-0/setting-record-straight-response-frances-commentary-dsm-v.

Severino, Sally, and Richard Liew. *Pastoral Care of the Mentally Disabled: Advancing Care of the Whole Person*. New York: Haworth, 1994.

Sheppard, Phillis Isabella. *Fleshing the Theory: A Critical Analysis of Select Theories of the Body in Light of African American Women's Experience*. Dissertation, Chicago Theological Seminary, 1997.

———. *Self, Culture and Others in Womanist Practical Theology*. New York: Palgrave MacMillan, 2011.

Shorter, Edward. *A History of Psychiatry: From the Era of the Asylum to the Age of Prozac*. New York: John Wiley & Sons, 1997.

Showalter, Elaine. *The Female Malady: Women, Madness and English Culture, 1830–1980*. London: Virago, 1987.

Slochower, Joyce Ann. *Holding and Psychoanalysis: A Relational Perspective*. Hillsdale, MI: Analytic Press, 1996.

Smith, Peter Joseph. "Holy Ground, Common Ground: Perspectives of Christian Clergy on Their Mental Health Role." PhD diss., University of Maryland, 1999.

Smith, Archi Jr. *The Relational Self: Ethics and Therapy from a Black Church Perspective*. Nashville, TN: Abingdon Press, 1982.

Snorton, Teresa E. "What about All Those Angry Black Women?" In *Women Out of Order: Risking Change and Creating Care in a Multicultural World*, edited by Jeanne Stevenson-Moessner and Teresa Snorton, 207–17. Minneapolis, MN: Fortress, 2010.

Spitzer, Robert, and Allen Frances. "Spitzer/Frances Letter to APA Trustees:" *Psychology Today*. Accessed February 2017. https://www.psychologytoday.com/blog/dsm5-in-distress/201012/spitzerfrances-letter-apa-trustees.

Sprague, Joey. *Feminist Methodologies for Critical Researchers*. Lanham, MD: Rowman & Littlefield, 2005.

Stevenson Moessner, Jeanne, ed. *In Her Own Time: Women and Developmental Issues in Pastoral Care*. Minneapolis, MN: Fortress, 2000.

———. *Through the Eyes of Women: Insights for Pastoral Care*. Minneapolis, MN: Fortress, 1996.

Stone, Howard W. *Depression and Hope: New Insights for Pastoral Counseling*. Minneapolis, MN: Fortress, 1998.

Stone, Michael H. *Healing the Mind: A History of Psychiatry from Antiquity to the Present*. New York: W.W. Norton, 1997.

Sue, Derald Wing. "The Challenge of White Dialectics: Making the 'Invisible' Visible." *The Counseling Psychologist* 39.3 (2011): 415–22.

Swinton, John. *Spirituality and Mental Health Care: Rediscovering a Forgotten Dimension*. Philadelphia: Kingsley, 2001.

Taylor, Robert Joseph, and Linda M. Chatters. "Importance of Religion and Spirituality in the Lives of African Americans, Caribbean Blacks and Non-Hispanic Whites." *The Journal of Negro Education* 79.3 (2010): 280–94.

Taylor, Robert, Linda M. Chatters, and J.S. Levin. *Religion in the Lives of African Americans: Social, Psychological and Health Perspectives*. Thousand Oaks, CA: Sage, 2004.

Todd, Nathan, and Elizabeth Abrams. "White Dialectics: A New Framework for Theory, Research and Practice with White Students." *The Counseling Psychologist* 39.3 (2011): 353–95.

Townes, Emilie M. *Breaking the Fine Rain of Death: African American Health Issues and a Womanist Ethic of Care*. New York: Continuum, 1998.

———. "Living in the New Jerusalem: The Rhetoric and Movement of Liberation in the House of Evil." In *A Troubling in My Soul: Womanist Perspectives on Evil and Suffering*, edited by Emilie M. Townes, 78–91. New York: Orbis, 2001.

———. "To be Called Beloved: Womanist Ontology in Postmodern Refraction." *Annual Society of Christian Ethics* (1993): 93–115.

Townsend, John. "Racial, Ethnic and Mental Illness Stereotypes." In *Mental Health, Racism and Sexism,* edited by Charles V. Willie, Patricia Perri Rieker, Bernard M. Kramer, and Bertram S. Brown, 119–47. Pittsburgh: University of Pittsburgh Press, 1995.

Townsend, Loren. "Best Practices, Rethinking Pastoral Diagnosis." *Sacred Spaces: The E-Journal of the American Association of Pastoral Counselors*, vol. 5 (2013): 66–101.

———. *Introduction to Pastoral Counseling*. Nashville, TN: Abingdon, 2009.

———. *Suicide: Pastoral Responses*. Nashville, TN: Abingdon Press, 2006.

———. *Pastoral Care With Stepfamilies: Mapping the Wilderness*. St. Louis: Chalice Press, 2000.

Trainor, Mary. *Lighting a Candle: Shedding Some Light on the Pastoral Needs of People with Mental Illness and Intellectual Disability*. Bathurst, New South Wales, Australia: Sister of Mercy Australia Bathurst Congregation, 2000.

Turner, Castellano, and Bernard M. Kramer. "Connections Between Racism and Mental Health." In *Mental Health, Racism and Sexism,* edited by Charles V. Willie, Patricia Perri Rieker, Bernard M. Kramer, and Bertram S. Brown, 3–27. Pittsburgh: University of Pittsburgh Press, 1995.

Ulanov, Ann. *Finding Space: God, Winnicott, and Psychic Reality*. Louisville, KY: Westminster John Knox Press, 2005.

———. *Spiritual Aspects of Clinical Work*. Einsiedeln, Switzerland: Diamon Verlag, 2004.

Ussher, Jane M. *Women's Madness: Misogyny or Mental Illness?* New York: Harvester Wheatsheaf, 1991.

Utsey, Shawn, Carol A. Gernat, and Lawrence Hammar. "Examining White Counselor Trainees' Reactions to Racial Issues in Counseling and Supervision Dyads." *The Counseling Psychologist* 33.4 (2005): 449–78.

Van Ryn, Michelle. “Research on the Provider Contribution to Race/Ethnicity Disparities in Medical Care.” *Medical Care* 40.1 (2002): I-140-I-151.

Vanden Bos, Gary R., ed. *American Psychological Association Dictionary of Psychology*. Washington DC: American Psychological Association, 2007.

Vigen, Aana Marie. *Women, Ethics and Inequality in U.S. Healthcare: To Count Among the Living*. New York: Palgrave Macmillan, 2006.

Walker, Elizabeth Johnson."Counseling Grace: A Pastoral Theology.” *Women out of Order*, Minneapolis, MN: Fortress, 2010: 243-54

Walker, Joyce Lehr. *Creating a Community of Care and Healing for Individuals Who are Victims of Mental Illness*. (school), Thesis/book, 1995.

Wallace, Beverly R. “A Black Widows’ Journey Toward Living Life Anew.” In *Widowed but Not Wounded—The Hustle and Flow of 13 Resilient Black Widowed Women*, edited by Sabra Robinson. Nehemiah Publishing, 2017.

———. “A Womanist Legacy of Trauma, Grief and Loss: Reframing the Notion of the Strong Black Woman Icon.” In *Women Out of Order: Risking Change and Creating Care in a Multicultural World*, edited by Jeanne Stevenson-Moessner and Teresa Snorton, 43–56. Minneapolis, MN: Fortress, 2010.

Ward, Edwina. “Similarities and Differences in Cross-Cultural Pastoral Supervision.” *Journal of Theology for Southern Africa* 116 (2003): 51–64.

Washington, Harriet A. *Medical Apartheid: The Dark History of Medical Experimentation on Black Americans from Colonial Times to the Present*. New York: Doubleday, 2006.

Wattis J. and S Curran, “The Importance of Spirituality in Caring for Patients.” *Br J Hosp Med (Lond)* 77.9 (2016): 500–01.

Weaver, Andrew. J. “Has there been a Failure to Prepare and Support Parish-Based Clergy in their Role as Frontline Community Mental Health Workers: A Review.” *Journal of Pastoral Care and Counseling* 49.2 (1995): 129–47.

West, Traci. *Disruptive Christian Ethics: When Racism and Women’s Lives Matter*. Louisville: Westminster, 2006.

———. *Wounds of the Spirit: Black Women, Violence and Resistance Ethics*. New York: New York University Press, 1999.

Whaley, Arthur L., and Brittany N. Hall. “Cultural Themes in the Psychotic Symptoms of African American Psychiatric Patients.” *Professional Psychology: Research and Practice* 40.1 (2009): 75–80.

Wilson, Michael. *The Hospital: A Place of Truth*. Birmingham, UK: University of Birmingham Press, 1971.

Wimberly, Edward. *Using Scripture in Pastoral Counseling*. Nashville, TN: Abingdon, 1994.

Wise, Carol. *Pastoral Psychotherapy: Theory and Practice*. New York: J. Aronson, 1980.

Website for the Association for Clinical Pastoral Education. Accessed February 2017. https://www.acpe.edu/ACPE/_Students/FAQ_S.aspx.

Wither, Kathleen. “We Heal One Another: How the Parish Community Supports Persons with Mental Illness and Their Families.” D. Min. thesis, St. Mary Seminary and Graduate School of Theology, 2011.

Yarhouse, Mark A. *The Modern Psychopathologies: A Comprehensive Christian Appraisal*. Downer’s Grove: InterVarsity Press, 2005.

Index

About the Author

Leah R. Thomas received her BA (1999) and MDiv (2003) from the University of Notre Dame, and a PhD in Religion and Society (2017) from Drew University. Her areas of study include the intersection of Pastoral Care and Christian social ethics, particularly as this prompts an integration of systemic realities of race, ethnicity, gender, class, and sexual orientation into the practice of pastoral care. Leah is the Visiting Professor of Pastoral Theology at Lancaster Theological Seminary, teaching classes in the areas of pastoral care and religious education. Leah is also the Associate Pastor of Congregational Care at Wisdom's Table at St. Peter's UCC, and a 200-hour certified yoga instructor. Leah resides in Lancaster, PA and enjoys hiking, yoga, and experimenting with new smoothies.

www.ingramcontent.com/pod-product-compliance
Lightning Source LLC
LaVergne TN
LVHW101447200926
848483LV00001B/75
* 9 7 8 1 9 7 8 7 0 1 7 7 9 *